**Gender Violence, th**

# Emerald Interdisciplinary Connexions

Progressive Connexions
*Interdisciplinary Life*

Published in partnership with Progressive Connexions: https://www.progressive connexions.net/

## Series Editors

## About the Series

*Emerald Interdisciplinary Connexions* promotes innovative research and encourages exemplary interdisciplinary practice, thinking and living. Books in the series focus on developing dialogues between disciplines and among disciplines, professions, practices and vocations in which the interaction of chapters and authors is of paramount importance. They bring cognate topics and ideas into orbit with each other whilst simultaneously alerting readers to new questions, issues and problems. The series encourages interdisciplinary interaction and knowledge sharing and, to this end, promotes imaginative collaborative projects which foster inclusive pathways to global understandings.

# Gender Violence, the Law, and Society: Interdisciplinary Perspectives from India, Japan and South Africa

EDITED BY

**M. SUSANNE SCHOTANUS**

*Progressive Connexions, Netherlands*

United Kingdom – North America – Japan – India – Malaysia – China

Emerald Publishing Limited
Howard House, Wagon Lane, Bingley BD16 1WA, UK

First edition 2022

 Open Access

The ebook edition of this title is Open Access and is freely available to read online.

**British Library Cataloguing in Publication Data**
A catalogue record for this book is available from the British Library

ISBN: 978-1-80117-130-4 (Print)
ISBN: 978-1-80117-127-4 (Online)
ISBN: 978-1-80117-129-8 (Epub)

An electronic version of this book is freely available, thanks to the support of
libraries working with Knowledge Unlatched. KU is a collaborative initiative
designed to make high quality books Open Access for the public good. More
information about the initiative and links to the Open Access version can be
found at www.knowledgeunlatched.org

Printed and bound by CPI Group (UK) Ltd, Croydon, CR0 4YY

ISOQAR certified
Management System,
awarded to Emerald
for adherence to
Environmental
standard
ISO 14001:2004.

Certificate Number 1985
ISO 14001

INVESTOR IN PEOPLE

# Table of Contents

## Gender-Based Violence and the Law

## Gender-Based Violence and Society

# About the Editor

**M. Susanne Schotanus** is the Director of Publications for Progressive Connexions and in that position is currently involved in the production of a range of books for the Emerald Interdisciplinary Connexions series. She's one of the co-founders of the Inter/Connexions publishing house as well as a freelance editor for both fictional and academic text. Her work is marked by a passion for inter-disciplinarity and knowledge production, especially on those topics that have traditionally been considered taboo.

# About the Contributors

**Deepesh Nirmaldas Dayal** is a Master of Arts in Counselling Psychology graduate from the University of Johannesburg, in Johannesburg, South Africa. He works as a Counselling Psychologist and Career Counsellor at the Counselling and Careers Development Unit (CCDU) at the University of the Witwatersrand, in Johannesburg. Deepesh's work has been interdisciplinary, with him taking up roles in the education and mental health sector as a trainer, teacher and therapist. His research interests have focused on inclusive education, gender and psychology. Recently, Deepesh completed a study titled 'Microaggressions Against South African Gay Indian Men', which focuses on the intersectional microaggression experiences of South African Indian gay men.

**Gavan Patrick Gray** is a Professor at Tsuda University's College of Policy Studies in Tokyo and holds a PhD in Politics and International Relations from Leicester University. His research interests include the fields of language and communication, national security and propaganda, and gender violence. He is currently engaged in a multi-year research project comparing the social and political responses to gender violence in Japan, Thailand and Ireland.

**Dr Nidhi Shrivastava** completed her PhD in the department of English and Writing Studies at the University of Western Ontario (now Western University) in London, Ontario, Canada and works as part-time faculty in the Department of Languages and Literature at Sacred Heart University. Her research focuses on the #MeToo movement, Hindi film cinema, censorship, the figure of the abducted and raped women, Indian rape culture, and the 1947 partition. She co-edited the volume of *Bridging the Gaps Between Celebrity and Media* with Jackie Raphael and Basuli Deb and her academic research has also been published in *South Asian Review*. She has also contributed to the edited volume, *#Metoo and Literary Studies: Reading, Teaching, and Writing About Sexual Culture*. She is currently co-editing with her colleagues an edited volume on *Reimagining #MeToo in South Asia and the Diaspora* and working on her book proposal to turn her dissertation into a monograph.

# Acknowledgements

In this book, we often talk about communities. And it really did take a community of brave and open-minded people to bring this book into existence. The lengthy process of creation has brought home the conviction that there really is something resembling an international, interdisciplinary academic community. And despite popular belief, this community is rather welcoming of new ways of 'doing publishing'. Though this edited volume has some unique qualities – containing essays by only three authors, and incorporating discussions between the authors into the structure of the book itself – from its first conception, the project has seen a unique level of enthusiasm from a wide variety of people. And without this enthusiasm, it would have been impossible to realise our ambitions in the current format.

First, of course, there is the Progressive Connexions team, led by Rob Fisher. The authors met at a conference on Sexual and Gender-based Violence organised on the brink of the pandemic by the marvellous ProCon team consisting of Teresa Cutler-Broyles, Lorraine Rumson and Elif Çakmak. In this same context, special thanks should go to Kristine Seitz, the leader of this event, who, with her warm and thoughtful attitude, managed to create a safe space where deeply impressive conversations about these painful topics could be had. She also served as an advisor to this book, making suggestions related to inclusive terminology that have proven to be extremely valuable.

Second, there is our publisher: Emerald. Not only did they create the gorgeous book cover that makes this volume a work of art; our Emerald team – Katy Mathers, Lydia Cutmore, Sumitha Selvamani and Ramya Murali – were kind, generous and knowledgeable supporters throughout the entire process. They were generous with their time, but also generous in putting this book forward for selection in the Knowledge Unlatched programme, which is an amazing organisation that has ended up allowing us to publish the book Open Access. For that, Knowledge Unlatched and all the libraries that have pledged funds deserve not only our acknowledgement but also our sincerest thanks.

# Introduction: Gender-Based Violence, the Law, and Society

*M. Susanne Schotanus*

This is not an easy book. It's not an easy book to read, and – for both similar and diverging reasons – not an easy book to write an introduction to. The reason why it is not easy to read is the oftentimes heart-wrenching stories that are at the heart of these authors' well-researched, theoretical arguments. From the personal abuse experienced by women on the Post-Partition Indian Subcontinent, through to the continuing failings of the national legal systems in dealing with cases of rape; from the way the COVID-19 pandemic exacerbated the already precarious positions experienced by sex workers in Japan, to the microaggressions suffered by gay man of Indian descent in South Africa – the topic of gender-based violence is rich in narratives of life-destroying (mental) health-affecting and heart-breaking everyday realities. Though it is essential we talk about and seek solutions to these realities, something the authors in this volume do to an admirable degree, the levels of pain captured in this volume do not make for light reading.

As you'll no doubt understand, the writing of an introduction to such a volume comes with its own specific set of challenges. The first of these challenges is geographical in nature. When we first conceived of this volume, it was the combination of narratives from countries that aren't usually represented in volumes produced by British and American publishing houses that got us excited. What I did not sufficiently reflect on at that point was the fact that I, a white, European woman, would be writing this introduction, which puts me in a rather awkward position. I'm very much aware of the privilege my place of birth has afforded me. To have my name on this book, then, and to present these chapters to you, the reader, opens me up to a wide range of potential critiques – from orientalism (in my holding up stories from these countries as quaint, different conceptions of familiar experiences) to playing the role of white saviour (in my presenting this volume as seeking solutions to the heart-breaking realities analysed in the chapters). I have no defence against these critiques, other than to say: I am aware of the dangers and pitfalls and have aimed to remain vigilant against

Gender Violence, the Law, and Society, 1–9
doi:10.1108/978-1-80117-127-420221001

them with every word I wrote and edited. What's more: I do not seek to speak on behalf of groups that have traditionally been silenced, nor do I see that as my task in this introduction. Rather, I mean to introduce the analyses presented by these commendable authors into the larger, global debates on the topic of gender-based violence. Though in the grand scheme of things good intentions do not account for much, I hope that here they will be enough so you will allow me to introduce the amazing work done by the three authors who've composed the following chapters.

A second challenge is the breadth of both the topic and experiences of gender-based violence, as the table of contents for this volume will already make clear. As a conceptual researcher, I am used to selecting a concept with both the flexibility and strength to – like an elastic band – bundle together the phenomena I want to touch on, and to then trace the historical meaning and usage of this concept through different traditions to come to a comprehensive, interdisciplinary theoretical framework that I can present as the context in which to read the work. For this book, however, I've struggled to find those concepts that could tie the wildly diverging topics together into one logical, cohesive whole. Though they are all relevant, neither my own holy trinity of 'power, agency and consent', nor the concepts offered in this book's title, appeared to do justice to the wide variety of pressing issues touched on by the authors. We're currently seeing an intensity of discussion on sexual assault that we have not seen since the feminist sex wars in the early 1980s, due to the brave people who, inspired by the #MeToo movement, have broken the previously imposed silence to share their personal experiences. Their testimonies of personal abuse and assault are as varied as they are, they are important and need to be heard. However, as the chapters in this book show, sexual abuse is only one way in which gender-based violence is experienced on a daily basis. I finally came to realise that this variety and plurality – the impossibility of capturing the context in a single concept – might actually be exactly the value of this book. Consequently, rather than presenting you with the history of the concept of gender-based violence, and the academic scholarship done on the topic, I'd like to use this introduction to actually introduce this book, rather than it's context. For the theoretical frameworks, I'd like to refer to you to the comprehensive contextualising sections of each individual chapter.

Each chapter in this volume explores the ways in which systems of power, individual gender identities, and cultural norms and practices work together to create and sustain the damaging experiences covered. But what makes this a comprehensive volume, rather than a collection of essays, is not the limited scope that characterises most edited volumes. Instead, what the authors have managed to do is to make the case for a pluralistic understanding of gender-based violence. The issues they discuss are explored on different (institutional) levels such as politics, law, economic status, (former) class and caste systems, media, subculture and the family. Though books could be, and have been, dedicated to gender-based violence on each of these levels, in this book they are not considered separately but rather in their interweaving and dynamic relationships.

The same is true for the methodologies employed and therefore the disciplines with which this book would be associated. Each chapter in this book can stand on its own, due to the exemplary rigour of the authors' work. Nidhi Shrivastava expertly blends her analysis of Hindi film and TV shows with the historical realities that their scenes reflect. Gavan Patrick Gray has managed to make Japanese academic, political and activist discourses not only available to the wider audience that this book aims to cater to but also to do this in a particularly rich, informed, critical and sensitive way. Deepesh Dayal's analysis of (online) magazines and interviews with gay men in South Africa make, to paraphrase a popular feminist slogan, the personal political and the political personal. However, it is where the insights derived from the different disciplines come together – in the transcripts of the authors' discussions, which form the introductions to each of the three sections of this book – that it becomes clear how only an international, interdisciplinary, intersectional and diverse understanding of gender-based violence is equipped to accurately explore and reflect the multifaceted lived realities of those affected.

It's hard to come up with a satisfying definition of gender-based violence that can bring all these different strands together. Therefore, in this book, gender-based violence is understood in its broadest interpretation: any type of violence, whether physical, economical, social or psychological, that is perpetrated against a person because of their gender. Which, of course, brings us to the question how to understand gender. Again, any simple definition will necessarily fall short. However, despite the recent development of alternate ways of thinking about gender, in this book, only cases of violence directed at people who identify as either male or female are explored. Gender, here, pertains to those ideas, assumptions and expectations that relate to the male and female identities. Please note that the exclusions of violence inflicted upon people who don't identify as either male or female is not the result of any political or ideological decision. Rather, it is the unintended result of our decision to emphasise and explore the different forms of violence that are inflicted upon people, instead of exploring the different ways in which people of different genders become victim-survivors of such violence.

## Gender-Based Violence

The first section delves into the concept of gendered violence in more detail. In their introduction to this section, the authors discuss the increasingly common understanding that societies are becoming less violent. Though they acknowledge that progress has been made on many fronts, an understanding of violence beyond the physical dimension shows that utopia has not yet been achieved. The authors discuss overt violence mostly in terms of precarity: the precarious circumstances in which many women, sex workers and homosexuals find themselves. These people's positions in society are accompanied by feelings of learned shame as well as limited access to power, which makes them particularly vulnerable to various types of abuse. However, it is these systems themselves, the structures that produce this lack of power and induce shame, which the authors identify as themselves violent. Commodified violence, microaggressions and shaming into suicide may be less graphic than sexual and physical abuse, but are no less violent – as is further explored in the individual chapters of this section.

Nidhi Shrivastava's first chapter is entitled 'Genocidal Violence, Biopolitics, and Treatment of Abducted and Raped Women in the Aftermath of 1947 Partition'. In it, she discusses what she calls a 'dark chapter' in India's past. When in 1947 the Indian Subcontinent was divided into India, West Pakistan and East Pakistan (current Bangladesh), it was decided that this Partition would take place based on religion: Pakistan would house people of Muslim faiths, whereas India would be the home to non-Muslims. As a result, mass migrations and violent clashes took place, costing an estimated 1 million people their lives. However, only in the past decade have scholars come to realise that in the midst of this chaos and unacknowledged genocide, an estimated 75.000 women were abducted, forced to marry their abductors and bear children. In their attempts to redress these traumatic events, the Pakistani and Indian governments spent the years between 1948 and 1957 tracking down these abducted women and returning them to their 'native communities'. However, these women were not consulted. Rather, if a woman was married to a man of a different faith, it was assumed she had been abducted and she was transported to underfunded camps where she could be housed in terrible conditions before being returned to her original family. Her family members, however, often perceived her as a dishonour on the family name and had responses ranging from turning her away to asking or forcing her to commit suicide. In her impressive, bold chapter, Shrivastava explores the different layers of violence and trauma that these women experienced at different hands, as well as the relationships of these various types of violence to biopolitics, genocide and traditional gender roles.

Whereas the most familiar attitudes towards sex work fall into one of two camps – either as inherently violent or a legitimate form of enterprise – in the second chapter, 'The Commodification of Sex in Modern Japan: Outdated Attitudes and Overdue Reforms', Gavan Patrick Gray shows that in Japan the debate on legalising the sex industry is quite different. Here, the negative view of the industry also contains the idea that the existence of the industry is proof of a failure to adhere to Western (modern) norms, while positive attitudes contain the idea that the industry contributes to social harmony and sexual health. Still, though both views make their arguments on collective, societal levels, the political status of the sex industry in Japan is precarious. Prostitution is not legal, though the sex industry is condoned. In these dynamics, Gray identifies 'symbolic violence': a form of domination embedded in everyday actions that prevents its victims from expressing grievance, due to acceptance that the system that harms them is regarded as natural, unchangeable, or in some ways beneficial. After discussing in detail the public, legal and political attitudes towards the sex industry, Gray shows that the failure of current systems in offering support to sex workers became especially clear at the start of the COVID-19 pandemic. In a section entitled 'Double Standards and Inadequate Support Systems', he notes that sex workers were excluded from a system established to support parents who were forced to leave their work due to school closures, and shows how this is only a symptom of the larger failing of the system. He argues that commodified violence and symbolic violence are engrained in this system, and need to be properly addressed on political, legal and societal levels.

A third form of often-overlooked violence based on gender is discussed by Deepesh Nirmaldas Dayal in the third chapter: 'Sexual Orientation Microaggressions in South Africa'. Though people with LGBT+ identities have held constitutional protection from discrimination in South Africa since 2006, Dayal identifies a plethora of covert forms of violence, called microaggressions, that are still very prevalent within this country. Sexual orientation microaggressions occur in several forms, and are used to mock, demean and negate the lived experiences of LGBTQ+ people. In this chapter, the author looks at microaggressions specifically in the context of LGBTQ+ people of Indian descent who live in South Africa. Due to stigmatisation within Indian communities, as well as their status as ethnic minorities in a society that is working to overcome the effects of Apartheid, these people experience additional layers of microaggressions, adding up to a volatile mix of psychological challenges. The microaggressions they experience lead to internalised homophobia, shame and highly compartmentalised and isolating ways of living. By analysing three types of microaggressions – microassaults, microinsults and microinvalidations – through excerpts from interviews with South African Indian gay men and magazines that cater to them, Dayal shows the violent nature of these covert forms of discrimination, and argues that they have the potential of harming their recipients just like physical/overt violence. Therefore, they should be included in any discussion of violence, whether in an academic, legal, therapeutic or cultural context.

## Gender-Based Violence and the Law

In the second section, the authors focus on the way gender-based violence is addressed within each country's legal systems. The discussion that introduces this section explores how – even though rape and sexual assault are illegal in each country discussed – both the nature and cultural perceptions of the systems that should execute this legal protection fail to live up to their promises. Factors such as access to financial resources; class, caste and racial backgrounds; and adherence to gender expectations are shown to still play a large role in the legal trajectories following official reports of sexual assault – and to determine to a large extent whether the perpetrator will be convicted and punished for their crime. However, the authors also discuss factors that prevent victim-survivors from reporting these experience in the first place: a lack of trust in the system, and the fear that the legal process will be as violent as the initial crime. Finally, the authors touch on the importance of finding an appropriate terminology when speaking about gender, sexual orientation and the violent crimes committed in response to them. These discussions all serve to introduce the three individual chapters which deal with issues of gender-based violence in relation to the legal system.

In Chapter 4, 'The Insidious Culture of Fear in Indian Courts', Nidhi Shrivastava explores cases of rape, both real and fictional, to show the problems inherent in India's current legal system when it comes to rape and sexual violence. Shrivastava argues that the current system does not support the rape victim-survivor, rendering her helpless and re-traumatising her in the process. The Hindi movies she analyses criticise and problematise the current systems, exposing the widespread and harmful practice of judging the victim based on her previous sexual history and reputation, as well as the role access to financial resources plays in a victim-survivor's ability to seek justice. What's more, even where the systems themselves are reformed, there's a lack of commitment to and enforcement of these systems due to socio-political and cultural structures that serve to induce fear, humiliation and shame in the would-be accuser. A 1980s cult classic the author analyses appears to suggest that the only way a victim-survivor of rape can gain justice is by seeking it on her own terms, even if that means breaking the law. Other films Shrivastava explores show the different ways in which women are silenced throughout the process, as well as highlighting the role that class and caste still play in determining the victim-survivors' chances of success. By drawing links to the 2013 Amendments to rape laws in India, as well as real-world rape cases, she takes her conclusions out of the realm of fiction to make a strong case for more significant reforms, to allow rape victim-survivors to finally get the justice they deserve.

In Chapter 5, Gavan Patrick Gray discusses 'Legal Responses to Sexual Violence in Japan: First Steps in a Lengthy Process of Rehabilitation'. Though Japan has a strict judicial system that has resulted in low crime rates, when it comes to sexual violence the picture is quite different. Gray locates the problem in the slow changes Japanese culture has seen in its change of perceptions of gender identities. Though in 2017 Japan made the first major changes to its penal code on sex crimes in more than 110 years, this has by no means eradicated the weaknesses in the legal system when it comes to punishing perpetrators of rape. Between the statute of limitations on rape and sexual assault, and gaps in legal definitions of terms such as voyeurism, some issues can be addressed with changes to the laws themselves. However, as Gray points out, there are other changes necessary that are related less to the laws themselves, and more to how they are interpreted and executed. Though the Japanese system generates circumstances similar to those described in the case of India – meaning that only an estimated 10% of instances of sexual violence are reported – Gray shows that the major hurdles preventing perpetrators from conviction, even if they are identified, are victim hesitancy and the strongly developed 'settlement industry'. By presenting the current situation, highlighting barriers and issues within both the current legal system and culture, and drawing from activist discourses to make suggestions for reform, this chapter presents a nuanced picture of the gaps and possibilities of Japan's justice system on its own terms.

In 1994, South Africa was reborn as a democracy, promising freedom and equality for all citizens. However, Deepesh Dayal shows in this sixth chapter, 'The Paradox of Constitutional Protection and Prejudice Experienced by LGBTQ+ People' that though constitutionally the freedoms of people with LGBTQ+ identities are protected, this does not mean they experience the freedom and equality promised. He looks specifically at the category of violence called 'hate crimes', showing that about 7% of the South African population fears being the recipient of hate crimes, and that simultaneously peoples' faith in the justice system is in sharp decline. People believe there's a lot of corruption in the courts, sentences passed are too lenient, and the system is too slow to be efficient. What's more, similar to what was reported in the preceding two chapters, people who are the victims of hate crimes fear that they will receive secondary victimisation by the system itself if they choose to file a report. It is here that the concept of intersectionality is first introduced: though these figures are harrowing when related to the South African population, LGBTQ+ people of Indian descent experience particularly high rates of verbal abuse, threats of physical violence, sexual assault and abuse by family members. By exploring all these intersecting factors, Deepesh Dayal explores and brings to light the particular challenges that still exist, in a country that was one of the first to constitutionally protect the rights of its LGBTQ+ citizens.

## Gender-Based Violence and Culture

In their introduction to the third section, the authors explain the social and cultural factors that shape the form of, and attitudes to, gender-based and sexual violence. They point out that though in the EU and US discussions on, and analyses of, these types of violence are becoming more commonplace and easy to examine, in many areas of the world there are regional or national perspectives that problematize these practices. Factors like shame, family honour and collective identity perceptions place additional burdens and stress on victim-survivors that are not taken into account in standard Western approaches to these issues. The cases analysed by all three authors in their individual chapters in this section specifically look at factors that silence victim-survivors, and pressure them to not speak up. As the lack of reporting of crimes is one of the main barriers in any statistical analysis on the topic, the deeper understandings of these processes of silencing form a major contribution to scholarship on gender-based and sexual violence. What's more, the authors discuss different ways in which these cultural barriers might be removed: through media, education or a combination of both. Finally, the authors end on a discussion of their own role within these processes.

In Chapter 7, 'Rape and the Prevalent Culture of Silence in India', Nidhi Shrivastava discusses the factors that determine whose rape will be discussed and debated, and which will be forgotten. Because of caste, class, gender, honour and shame, only certain narratives are privileged in mainstream media and popular culture. The culture of silence Shrivastava discusses, however, pertains to more than just media: as she already indicated in her previous chapters, factors such as honour and shame often cause the victim-survivors' own families to pressure them into silence – especially when the perpetrator of violence is one of their family members. After outlining these issues, Shrivastava goes on to analyse two media representations that aim to break the culturally imposed silence. These media texts show that child sexual abuse and gender-based violence are not only committed by the poor, lower classes but take place in both the public and private spheres of the elite and upper middle classes as well. Shrivastava teases out those threads in the texts that relate to the culture of silence that protects the upper-class perpetrators and allows them to repeatedly commit their crimes unpunished.

Though in preceding chapters on sexual assault the roles of female gender norms have been discussed, in Chapter 8, 'Japanese Gender Norms and their Impact on Male Attitudes Towards Women', Gavan Patrick Gray dives into the male gender norms that to a large extent determine gender relations in Japan. Gray shows how the male gender stereotype of the industrious, productive and distant breadwinner has created an emotional crisis among many Japanese men. The gender expectations dissuade these men from forming meaningful intimate relationships with their families and cause a range of sometimes psychologically harmful responses: from fixating upon unthreatening juvenile women to rejecting romantic entanglement of any kind. In his chapter, Gray gives a brief overview of the history of gender relations in Japan, before diving into these two different responses to the lack of companionship experienced by these men due to the gender stereotypes. Then, he explores in more detail the *ikumen* concept – which is used to refer to men who are attractive to women because they take an active role in raising children – and has become part of an ongoing project by the Ministry of Health, Labour and Welfare to promote gender equality in the home. Though many Japanese men are emotionally mature and do not suffer from the issues first explored, the outlier cases are so harmful and widespread that they help illuminate some of the deeper problems with Japan's gender norms. As gender norms are often analysed in the context of harm to women, this chapter will prove essential for both the debates on gender and on gender-based violence, as these male gender stereotypes have the ability to harm everyone involved.

Deepesh Dayal's Chapter 9, 'Intersectional Influences on Sexual Orientation Microaggressions', similarly explores the gender stereotypes that contribute to violence – in this chapter in the specific form of microaggressions – but does so in an intersectional framework. He builds this framework out of the seemingly disparate layers of class, gender, ethnicity and minority cultures which were all addressed to some extent in preceding chapters, to explore the specific experiences testified to by homosexual men of Indian descent in South Africa. Where on a national level LGBT identities are often seen as un-South African and a Western import, within the Indian communities, in particular, there's an added layer of hegemonic male gender expectations – often emphasised and exacerbated by Bollywood movies – which are perceived to preclude gay male identities. Effeminate male behaviour is conflated with gay sexual orientation, meaning that often boys are punished and bullied for 'being gay' even before they themselves are aware of their sexual identity. What's more, as a result of Apartheid, Indian communities in South Africa are particularly tight-knit and collectivist, meaning there is a strong level of social control. Add to this the influence of religion in the country, and what you find is a volatile, intersectional mix of factors that support and sustain the use of microaggressions as a response to LGBT identities.

Combined, these chapters show the many forms gender-based violence can take, specifically in the collectivist communities that are often overlooked in scholarship on the subject. Whether violence is committed through rape or harmful gender stereotypes; by individuals or supposedly protective systems; the effects of this violence can traumatise generations. By analysing their case studies in their respective national and cultural contexts, the authors manage to outline the field of issues related to gendered violence on a previously unimagined scale while remaining cognizant of the complicated networks of influences that problematise any simple (Western) solution to these issues. Combining an unprecedented scope with great depth and specificity, this volume shows through practice the value and potential of an international, interdisciplinary and intersectional approach to the topic of gendered violence.

# Gender-Based Violence

# Section I: Gender-Based Violence

*Gavan Patrick Gray, Nidhi Shrivastava*
*and Deepesh Nirmaldas Dayal*

## Abstract

This chapter is a transcript of an open-ended discussion that occurred between the authors when they met to discuss the subject matter of the first section of the book, which focuses on areas where serious ongoing problems of gender violence are receiving insufficient attention. The discussion took place after preliminary drafts had been completed and the authors share their thoughts on the subjects they will each discuss in more detail in the following chapters – including the cultural representation of historical gender violence in India, the treatment of women in Japan's sex industry and attitudes towards LGBTQ+ groups in South Africa.

*Keywords*: Gender violence; Japan; India; South Africa; gender equality; precarity

**Gray:** I think we can agree that this is a very broad topic and we are only likely to touch on some specific and quite focused areas of it in the following chapters. In this space though, we have a little more freedom to explore elements of the encompassing theme. If I can begin, I would like to ask if either of you have read Steven Pinker's *Better Angels of our Nature*? He argues that human civilisation has been steadily growing less violent and that we are becoming, and will continue to become, more civilised, including an increase in empathy and protection of various rights. I wonder if you feel that gender violence is in decline?

Personally, I think it's clear that there are significant improvements over past social norms. However, I have a deep thread of cynicism about political systems that always makes me fear the dystopian potential of civilisational change, the

Gender Violence, the Law, and Society, 13–21
doi:10.1108/978-1-80117-127-420221002

1984s and Brave New Worlds, the 'darkest timelines'. A decrease in overall violence that doesn't safeguard the fundamental rights of all people could be portrayed as a utopia for the significant majority that it benefits. However, in terms of gender violence, I have concerns that satisfaction with an overall improvement in well-being for the majority might make it easier for some minority groups to be consigned to potential abuse in the shadows of society. This is why I think it is so important to examine the marginalised and minority groups as they are the ones that are most in danger of being overlooked by people who might think that gender violence is decreasing and not realise that there are those who have been passed by and remain trapped in institutionalised systems of oppression, violence or exploitation.

**Dayal:** I agree Gavan, this section is quite broad and there are many different avenues that can be debated. Looking at South Africa, the 1994 elections saw citizens from all racial groups help to give birth to a new democracy that represented freedom, equality, social justice and opportunities for all. However, two decades later a paradox exists where, despite numerous new policies and legislation guaranteeing civil and political rights, significant levels of crime, corruption and human rights violations still plague the country. Despite the strong evidence for this, some people are in denial and claim that these high levels of crime and inequality are normal and on par with other countries. The fear of crime that exists is persistent and debilitating and hate crimes are a particular problem, including those that focus on race, nationality and sexuality. In 2016, a survey found that more than seven percent of South Africans have a fear of being targeted by hate crimes. There have been some recent victories though, where perpetrators faced legal punishments and in 2018 new hate crimes legislation focusing on the crimes against LGBTQ+ people was presented for passage. These new laws have resulted in a change in the type of hate crimes being committed. Where previously there were more overt hate crimes now you see more covert forms of discrimination. As you mentioned, Gavan, there seems to be a narrative expressing relief that gender violence is on the decline, but there are new and equally painful ways in which violence is being inflicted.

**Shrivastava:** Do you feel there is a particular way that sexual and gender-based violence is seen in Japan?

**Gray:** Of course, though it has changed a lot, especially in the past decade. Women had significantly lower status in Japan throughout most of its history. Similar to many societies, women had a much stronger role within the private family structure but publicly and officially they were almost invisible. It was only after the Meiji Restoration in the late 1800s that things began to change as a result of Western influence. My own university was founded by a woman, Umeko Tsuda, who travelled to the United States at just 6 years of age and on her return to Japan set up one of the first institutes of higher learning open to women. It was only after World War II, however, that women's rights became firmly entrenched in Japanese law. Ironically, the new constitution, thanks to the efforts of a woman called Beate Sirota Gordon, gave Japanese women even more rights than American women of the time; however, because they had not fought for these rights in the same manner as American women, actual deep societal change was much slower to occur, which is one of the reasons why Japan still ranks very poor in terms of gender equality. To answer your question, there is a split between modern Japan, which views gender violence in much the same way as the West, and older attitudes whereby domestic violence can be considered a private matter, and where the wearing of improper clothing can still be viewed as being partially responsible for crimes that affect women. From my own experience, this is not a generational issue though, as much as it is one of lack of education on these matters. Well-educated older people are unlikely to hold the latter views and poorly educated young people are more so.

**Shrivastava:** How would you define 'commodified violence'?

**Gray:** I think it relates to the concept of 'precarity' that you speak about in your chapters so if perhaps you could define precarity first, I can build off that.

**Shrivastava:** Well, for me, precarity is the ontological state of being of an individual who is rendered powerless and vulnerable due to the circumstances they face and who may be left feeling helpless against the actors that are responsible for their situation.

**Gray:** Thank you. A common danger for women in the sex industry is that they can be viewed by many, both their customers and wider society, not as the workers of an industry but as its products. In this view, they are things and as such devoid of human rights. This is the nature of what I consider commodified violence: it depersonalises the subject and strips them of rights, dignity, agency and their voice. It is not so much about the action of 'sale' but the action of making them into a 'commodity' that can be traded without regard for how this act affects them on a human level. It certainly includes the elements of power-lessness and vulnerability that you mentioned. Of course, it doesn't apply to all women in the sex industry and some can take stronger personal control of their roles within it, but a great many are left in far more precarious states. Even where they can achieve economic stability, as long as they remain within the industry, their place in society remains fragile and open to abuse, whether by public discrimination or political exploitation.

**Shrivastava:** Are there any social or political barriers when it comes to reforming the sex industry in Japan? In India, for example, sex work is a controversial subject and NGOs or social workers are putting their lives at risk to try to break the chain of sexual trafficking. Also, the system in India is riddled with corruption which also makes the process difficult.

**Gray:** There is definitely not as much direct threat to life as might exist in India. From what I know from speaking to activists and people working in the industry, physical violence of any kind, while a constant threat, is not among the top concerns that sex workers have and it certainly isn't a significant problem for those working to support them. Generally, the problem is far more economic in nature. For the workers in the industry, avoiding becoming trapped in a spiral of debt and achieving economic stability and independence are key goals. For the majority of workers, alleviating economic pressure is the entire reason for their entry into the industry. However, those who are not in debt when they enter it are often forced into debt by unscrupulous business practices or by falling into the unhealthy lifestyle that surrounds much of the industry.

The average sex worker has little knowledge of how to handle money or deal with contracts that are often used to tie workers to specific shops or pressure them into work they would rather not do. Another key aim for many is to preserve their anonymity. Again, while they have chosen the industry as a means of addressing economic problems they may have, they typically wish to do this anonymously, to the extent possible. In other words, they want to keep their working life and personal life separate. The contracts they sign can be used, again by the worst companies, to pressure workers – by saying that if they break contracts, quit their job or fail to repay debts, the company will contact their families or they will sue them publicly, exposing their career choice to the world. For similar reasons, workers are often hesitant to file tax returns listing their employment as sex work, not because they want to cheat the system but because they are worried about loss of privacy. They are left with a choice of sacrificing their anonymity or risking falling foul of the law. This is a key element of the precarious state they exist in; their industry is legal in name but in practice lacks the support systems and access to official systems that other industries typically have. Because of the bias against sex work, there is a widespread image of those involved in it as shiftless, greedy or parasitical. As a result, the public, police and politicians often view them as a group that is breaking social or legal rules and which needs to be punished rather than a group that are pursuing legal work and who are in need of support to address the hazards associated with their industry. Beyond debt and privacy concerns, these extend to things like STDs, mental health, addiction, child-rearing, stalkers and more.

**Shrivastava:** Do they have an avenue to speak/protest against the violence they face?

**Gray:** Although the sex industry has a centuries old history in Japan, in the past there was never any strong, centralised organisation through which its workers could find a voice. This doesn't mean that the industry was unsupervised. On the contrary, the Japanese government, for the purposes of disease prevention and simple efficiency, if not necessarily an interest in women's rights, has long had bureaucratic systems to regulate the rules governing the industry. In terms of safeguarding the workers' own interests, however, there has been little beyond loose collectives and affiliated publications that were small in size and wielded little political influence. In 1956 the government passed a law that would end legal prostitution and one of the groups, the Shin Yoshiwara Joshi Hoken Kumiai, criticised it by saying, 'We do not want to do this work but before you end it please tell us how we will feed our parents'. There are a lot of sex workers in Japan who still engage in their work to support parents who are poor, ill or in debt, to support their own single-parent families, or to pay for expensive college fees. Yet there are still negative stereotype of sex workers as people who are chasing easy money. There are groups that try to represent their collective voice, like the SWASH workers alliance, but there needs to be much greater support from outside the industry if the tired misconceptions, bias and lack of understanding are going to alter in any meaningful way.

**Gray:** Nidhi, in your chapter you focus on the violence women experienced during the Post-Partition period. I'm curious to what extent the events of this period have been explored by female writers and directors? Have there been any? Were there any barriers to female voices arising in the artistic world?

**Shrivastava:** That is an excellent question, Gavan. Yes, there are novels and films by female writers, including Amrita Pritam who wrote the novel, *Pinjar*, which was made into a film in 2003. It was about a strong, female lead who is abducted and later forced to marry. However, she has conflicting feelings as her abductor is someone who has good values and who abducted her due to ancestral traditions. There are other authors such as Pakistani-American writer, Bapsi Sidhwa, who writes about her experience as a young Parsi girl witnessing the events of the Partition in Lahore in the novel *Cracking India*. Deepa Mehta's *Earth* dealt with similar themes, and then there is another writer, Anita Rau Badami, who has written a novel about the Canadian diaspora's experience of the aftermath of the Partition in *Can You Hear the Nightingale Singh*? Therefore, yes, there are numerous contributions of women writers and filmmakers who have worked on this topic and they have typically placed a strong focus on subjects such as rape, the abduction of women, the tattooing of their names on their wrists and so on.

I don't think there are any specific barriers against women's artistic voices. However, there was a popular Urdu writer, Ismat Chugtai, who explored themes of female sexuality and femininity. In 1942, her story *Lihaaf* caused an uproar because it dealt with themes of female homosexuality. She was, in fact, called to trial at the Lahore High Court for it. So, there are indeed female writers who have produced important works covering the treatment of women during that period.

**Gray:** As I mentioned in regard to sex work in Japan, the public view of the issue is often oversimplified and inaccurate. Is this the same case regarding the people's understanding of the gender element of genocide in India, or regarding the experience of minority gay men and women in South Africa? One concern I have with public attitudes to this issue in Japan is not that they are bad but, apart from within small, directly involved groups, that they have not really evolved in any significant way over recent decades. For those that are not directly connected, such issues are often presented to broader audiences by focusing on the most dramatic and titillating elements, reducing the subject to oversimplified tropes rather than really trying to educate people or generate a shift in perceptions. Do you experience anything similar in your own studies?

**Shrivastava:** Yes, you are right Gavan. In India, the Partition is seen as a dark chapter in India's history and it is often eclipsed by the topic of India's independence. It is also only in the last decade that there has been a felt urgency to memorialise the cataclysmic event. For example, the first museum on the Partition was established in 2017 in Amritsar, Punjab. There are also two new archives that have been established in Berkley, California in the United States and in Pakistan. However, the issue for the public is that it is still somewhat taboo. In fact, I have spoken with another Indian academic who said that only now, in 2021, was she comfortable sharing stories of the Partition with her family. Earlier, they had felt that the wound was too raw and painful to talk about. Thus, it is not shown in mainstream discourse, even in an oversimplified way. Rather, it was rendered invisible to the public until the last decade or so. I did not hear about the Partition myself within my family. It was only as I pursued my academic career and began my graduate studies that I began to realise its importance, especially in regard to India's contemporary rape culture.

**Gray:** Nidhi, you mentioned that 'there is an inexorable link between genocidal and sexual or gender-based violence', and from what I know about the Partition this seems to be quite evident. I have read that the attacks on women are often for the purpose of humiliation and that, perhaps because of this, other women would often be involved in the attacks. Setting aside the inherent violent and sexual element of such crimes, do you feel that this element of humiliation is a significant part of why women are targeted? Perhaps, that they are seen as a symbol of cultural or ethnic purity and that by attempting denigrate them, the perpetrators can indirectly attack that which they are perceived to represent?

**Shrivastava:** Thank you for highlighting this point, Gavan. I do think a better word that speaks further of the idea that you are calling attention to is that of *shame*, rather than humiliation. Even though humiliation was definitely part of the violence the women experienced, I don't think it fully captures the reasons why the women in the South Asian subcontinent faced the treatment they did from not just their own kin but also their communities, as well as the newly formed India and Pakistan. Yes, indeed, there were multiple reasons why the women were seen as the ultimate target for violence. For one, the loss of their sexual honour would bring shame to the respective ethnic community. Second, rape is arguably a weapon of war – a method by which the female population can be controlled. However, during the Partition, these concepts were intertwined and complex in their own way, in that the fear of rape and abduction drove relatives, especially male members of a family, to encourage female victims to commit suicide, or to kill them themselves, in order to protect the honour of their family.

In my research, I came across the story of Bir Bahadur Singh and his mother, Basant Kaur. Kaur was among the women who had survived in spite of trying numerous times to jump to her death into a well. During an interview with Singh, he makes mention of women who jumped into the well survived multiple times, but he never informs the interviewer that Kaur was *his* mother. Later, the interviewee realises that that Singh 'had not mentioned that she was his mother because in having escaped death, she could not be classed with the women who had, in fact, died. Much easier, then, to speak of his sister who died an 'honourable' death than the mother who survived'.

This is part of the way that the ultimate goal of this genocidal violence was broader than the crime itself and sought to bring shame and dishonour to the other community. So, yes, I think you are right in stating that women's bodies, especially their sexual purity, are treated as what Menon and Bhasin have called, 'territories to be conquered, claimed or marked by the assailant'. But, the violence as you can see was multifaceted and the assailants were not just men from other communities, but sometimes men who were from the same family. This is one of the reasons why it is such an uncomfortable and uneasy issue that has been silenced over the years. Because it is something that touches on family honour and shame, it is something which can have generational impact.

**Gray:** Do either of you think that the forms of gender-based violence have changed from what existed in the past? Deepesh, I think you are looking at one form that has only recently been recognised, though, of course, that does not mean it has not always been a problem.

**Dayal:** Yes Gavan, whilst the forms of violence you mention are quite overt in nature, I have been researching the covert forms of violence called micro-aggressions. When these microaggressions are directed towards a person's sexual orientation they are referred to as sexual orientation microaggressions. Examples of these are when gay men are told that they are confused about their sexual orientation. Perpetrators also use derogatory words when referring to LGBTQ+ people. In my research, I have found that such microaggressions decrease social cohesion and adversely impact the mental well-being of gay men. In particular, I have been looking at their prevalence within the South African Indian community, microaggression perpetrated by South African Indian people against South African gay Indian men. This is something that has been written about in newspaper articles but it has not yet been properly studied through actual research.

**Shrivastava:** Gavan, you mention the impact of the COVID-19 pandemic and how it has affected the sex industry in Japan. I was wondering if you could speak more about suicide within the sex industry. Would you consider it as a form of violence as well? I'm wondering because mass suicides were common and part of the national narrative in India during the Partition.

**Gray:** Japan has a serious issue with suicide and has one of the highest rates for highly developed economies. I think the number is over 20,000 per year, which is actually a decline from past levels. However, in Japan it tends to affect significantly more men than women and the primary demographic groups it affects are company workers and the elderly. Of course, to say that women make up a smaller proportion of overall victims, should not be taken to mean that the impact on individual women is any less severe, or that specific groups of women might not suffer far higher rates. The increase in female suicide rates in 2020 is a strong sign that women have been disproportionally impacted by the pandemic when compared to men. Yet, the sex industry is simply one area of work in which women are especially vulnerable and trapped in an economically precarious position: these economic pressures also affect other women in temporary or unstable employment, or single-parent mothers. I don't think I would classify these broader economic forces as violence though, unless you think of them in the same way as the violence of a storm. Though generated by the economic system they do not have a direct source of agency, in effect, they are system-wide forces rather than targeted effects and I think in terms of harm done to women (and sex workers) it is the failure to protect them from the effects of this economic violence that is a charge that can reasonably be laid against the government. In other words, the government is not directly committing the violence that would cause suicide rates to increase, instead it is showing a high level of apathy towards those factors when it has the capability and responsibility to do something to offset them.

**Shrivastava:** You also mentioned something called 'father industries' in your article. I know that there is also a commodification of the Lolita girl culture and I was wondering if you could speak further to this point?

**Gray:** In Japan this is something now most commonly referred to as 'Papa Katsu', which means father activities, and it is similar to what would be called Sugar Daddies or 'sugaring' in the West. However, the cultural forces at play are quite different and this is something I will be looking at in my later chapter focusing on gender norms in Japan. Suffice to say, that it is an area with some serious unaddressed problems but also one that tends to be very poorly understood by the West, which tends to judge it through its own particular cultural lens. I think this is a good example of the problems that we face, though. Many issues, like the Lolita issue in Japan, can seem quite clear-cut to Western viewers. In this case, they equate it to paedophilia and wonder why Japan allows it to persist so openly. However, the nature of the problem, as well as the way in which it connects to society, traditions and norms, is very different in Japan and external perspectives are, generally and predictably, quite superficial in their analysis.

**Shrivastava:** Do either of you feel that governmental responses to these forms of violence are sufficient or effective?

**Gray:** I think one issue in this regard is the false choice between an immediate, shallow response or a gradual, deeper, long-term response. In Japan, with regard to the sex industry, some activists favour the Nordic model – which criminalises the purchase of sex – and this is typically seen as a step towards abolition of the sex trade. Others would prefer to see complete legalisation of the industry. In either case, these are both long-term goals and with Japan being an especially risk averse country, these would take years, if not decades to achieve. Regardless of which option you would prefer, the danger is that a lot of political effort can be focused on achieving only the long-term goals and that meaningful, immediate, short-term assistance can be neglected.

In Japan's case at least, I think these kinds of issues should always be approached in a two-track fashion, one that researches and considers long-term changes and others that look at current and on-going harm and how that can be alleviated in the interim. With the Japanese sex industry we can see very slow, long-term change occurring but more needs to be done to offset the persisting harm – such as by providing greater funding to NGOs that actually work to support the women who are affected. This is why, when you study issues like this, I think an interdisciplinary approach is an excellent basis to start from but it needs to evolve into an inter-institutional approach, where the various parties involved – those working on long-term aims and those dealing with short-term solutions – need to be sharing data and toolsets, learning from one another and supporting one another's goals.

**Dayal:** I think these types of flaws in government response, the apathy you mentioned, are quite common. Although the South African Constitution sets everyone on a nominally equal level, LGBTQ+ people still experience high levels of hate crimes which extends to violence, assault, bullying and cyberbullying. Although they have achieved certain rights, such as the rights to marry a partner of the same sex, adopt a child together and automatically inherit their partner's estate, there are still many areas in which they are vulnerable and unprotected. As such, South African LGBTQ+ persons can be said to straddle two worlds, one that offers intricate legal protections and another, in which continuing and violent persecution is commonplace and where there is no abatement of these socially ingrained problems in sight.

**Shrivastava:** In my case, Partition has been seen as a dark chapter of India's national history and it is only in the last decade that we are seeing an increasing interest in its impact and the Diaspora community. Alongside the Partition archives that were created in the United States, there are also events happening in India itself to memorialise the event. In Kolkata, they have set up the first virtual Partition museum, which focuses on the collective trauma in Bengal during the Partition. But, with that said, the wounds are still continuing to heal as people slowly begin to confront the realities that their ancestors would have experienced during this time. While there is an increasing interest in the Partition, it's still not a primary focus in mainstream culture and I think it will take some time for both the government and public to come to terms with its full legacy. Of course, the first step in such patterns of change is to raise awareness of and become able to talk openly about these issues.

# Chapter 1

# Genocidal Violence, Biopolitics, and Treatment of Abducted and Raped Women in the Aftermath of 1947 Partition in India

*Nidhi Shrivastava*

## Abstract

As we reckon with the #MeToo movement, the gender-based violence that occurred during the 1947 Partition continues to remain forgotten in mainstream discourses and is an emotive and polarising issue within both India and its diaspora. Just like mainstream news in the United States covered the Gabby Petito case, causing a controversy as it led to the realisation that the rape and gender-based violence of missing indigenous women were not covered, it can be suggested that mainstream news channels both within India and in the diaspora construct narratives that privilege the stories of some over others – with issues of shame, *izzat* ('honour') and policing of women's bodies compounding the silence in South Asian communities. In this chapter, I argue that we need to rethink the Partition as a genocide to recognise the gender-based violence that occurred on women's bodies as the cataclysmic event occurred. I discuss the feminist historiographical research led by Urvashi Butalia, Kamla Bhasin and Ritu Menon who interviewed survivors in the aftermath of the 1984 anti-Sikh riots that triggered their research and reminded them of the Partition violence. It is only recently when the 1947 Partition Archives (in 2010) and the Partition Museum (in 2017) that the conversations of Partition are also taking place in academic spaces.

*Keywords*: 1947 partition; the #MeToo movement; genocide studies; partition studies; central recovery operation; 1947 partition archives

Gender Violence, the Law, and Society, 23–33
doi:10.1108/978-1-80117-127-420221003

In August 1947, the Indian subcontinent was partitioned into Hindu-majoritarian India and Muslim-majoritarian Pakistan. The Partition displaced an estimated 10 million to 20 million people in its aftermath, which led to an outbreak of sectarian violence as Hindu-Muslim communities that had co-existed for centuries were enveloped in carnage – looting, massacres, forced religious conversions, mass abductions, and heinous sexual and gender-based violence. Unlike the Holocaust, which was the state-led, the Partition is more akin to brutal, ethnic violence that has been observed in genocides like Rwanda – a by-product of decolonisation.[1]

During the years leading up to Indian independence, the Partition became imminent after Mohammad Ali Jinnah (the leader of Muslim league) believed that there would not be enough Muslim representation in India, and demanded a separate country – Pakistan. The borders that divided India and Pakistan were hastily drawn by British civil servant, Cyril Radcliffe, and were not known to citizens even on the eve of India and Pakistan's Independence Day (Pollack, 2007). As a result, brutal ethnic and sectarian violence took place. Political scientist Paul R. Brass (2003) describes the violence that occurred at this time as 'retributive genocide' (p. 72). Unlike most genocides, it was neither sanctioned by the state nor spontaneous. Rather, Brass points out, '...there were also local acts of violence carried out for a multiplicity of reasons and motives that were not genocidal in intent: loot, capture of property, abduction of women. Moreover, much of the larger-scale violence was mutual' (p. 72). Historian William Dalrymple calls it a 'mutual genocide' (2015) and describes the violence in the following terms: 'the carnage was especially intense, with massacres, arson, forced conversions, mass abductions, and savage sexual violence. Some 75,000 women were raped, and many of them were then disfigured or dismembered'. American photojournalist Margaret Bourke-White (1963), who had witnessed the liberation of Nazi camps and later found herself in India as the Partition became imminent, describes the violence that took place during the Direct Action Day in 1946 Calcutta as follows:

---

[1]Paul Rusesabagina's *An Ordinary Man* (2006) speaks at length about the history of Rwanda, which was colonised by the Belgians who considered Tutsis more superior than Hutus. They were responsible for creating identity cards, which were later used during the Rwandan genocide. In *Midnight's Furies: The Deadly Legacy of India's Partition* (2016), Journalist Nisid Hajri has also drawn a similar comparison between the Partition and Rwandan genocide. He writes, 'The conflagration stands as one of the deadliest and most brutal civil conflicts of the twentieth century, unrivaled in scale until the 1994 massacres in Rwanda. Yet like Rwanda, the riots were relatively confined in time and space. The worst killings lasted only about six weeks. While the chaos spread throughout most of western Pakistan and great swathes of northern India, much of the rest of the subcontinent was not directly affected. Today Partition is a horrific memory for millions – but it is just that, a memory' (Hajari, 2015, Chapter 1, paragraph 12). Though rape was declared a war crime in 1919, this status was not finalised until 1997 during the trial of Jean-Paul Akayesu in the International Criminal Tribunal for Rwanda (ICTR).

On the heels of this announcement [Jinnah's declaration of Direct Action Day], violence broke out in Calcutta. I flew there from Bombay and found a scene that looked like Buchenwald. The street were literally strewn with dead bodies, an officially estimated six thousand, but I myself saw many more...In Calcutta, a city larger than Detroit, vast areas were dark with ruins and black with the wings of culture that hovered over impartially dead Hindus and Muslims. Like Germany's concentration camps, this was the ultimate result of racial and religious prejudice.

(p. 283)

Indeed, Dalrymple notes that 'the comparison with the death camps is not so far-fetched as it may seem. Partition is central to modern identity in the Indian subcontinent, as the Holocaust is to identity among Jews, branded painfully onto the regional consciousness by memories of almost unimaginable violence'.

Partition remains an emotive and polarising issue within India and in the diaspora communities. Just like mainstream news in the United States covered the Gabby Petito case, which inspired controversy as it led to the realisation that the rape and gender-based violence of missing indigenous women were not previously covered, it can be suggested that mainstream news channels both within India and in the diaspora construct narratives that privilege the stories of some over others – with issues of shame, *izzat* ('honour') and policing of women's bodies compounding the silence in South Asian communities (Shrivastava & Bibi, 2021).[2] At the peak of the #MeToo movement in 2018, Rochelle G. Saidel and Batya Brutin held an exhibition entitled *Violated: Women in Holocaust and Genocide* at the Ronald Feldman Gallery in New York. Although the exhibition brought up pivotal questions on genocidal sexual violence from countries such as Bosnia, Rwanda, Darfur, Yazidi and Guatemala, the 1947 Partition was *not* highlighted at the exhibition. Only in the last decade, academics and activists have started the work to preserve and research the Partition, leading to the establishment of the Partition Archive (in 2010), the citizenship archive of Pakistan and India's first museum dedicated to the Partition which was founded in 2017 in Amritsar.

While sexual and gender-based violence received worldwide recognition during the #MeToo movement in 2017,[3] the turning point in India was the 2012 Delhi

---

[2] Recently, sociology scholar Somia R. Bibi and I published a conversation on the silencing of Partition narratives within the context of the #MeToo movement in the South Asia diaspora in the United Kingdom and United States, that was published in the following article. To learn further about this issue, please see the following link: https://bloomsburyliterarystudiesblog.com/continuum-literary-studie/2021/12/metoo-in-south-asia-subcontinent-and-diaspora.html.

[3] Found by Tarana Burke in 2006, the #MeToo movement gained popularity after actress Alyssa Milano tweeted the hashtag #MeToo to encourage victims of sexual violence to publicise allegations of sex crime against their preparators in 2017.

gang-rape case, when a young woman was heinously gang-raped in a bus while she and her friend were returning home after seeing a movie together. During this time, the news coverage called attention to rape cases that dated back to the 1970s (*BBC* 2013, *Newsable* 2018), but they did not cover the brutal sexual violence that occurred during the Partition.

In this chapter, I argue that we *need* to recognise the Partition as a genocide, not only on a global level but on a national level as well. The Partition is rarely acknowledged in private spheres, and if it is brought up in popular culture, the representations do not acknowledge or recognise the gender-based violence that occurred during this tumultuous period. Recent trends in Genocide studies, as represented in the works of Barta (1985), Rashed and Short (2012), Totten, Theriault, and Joeden-Forgey (2017), have shown that the field is recasting jurist Raphael Lamkin's original definition of the term – genocide – to make it more inclusive and include countries that have been undergoing the process of decolonisation. In his article, 'After the Holocaust: Consciousness of Genocide in Australia', Tony Barta (1985) contends that the word genocide has been associated globally with the Holocaust but he suggests that it should be also thought of within the context of the massacre of Australian aborigines (p. 157) and that the 'prospect of genocide – "the most certain getting rid of the race"' also applies to countries that had been colonised in the past. As Hitchcock, Flowerday, and Babchuk (2017) point out in their study, the definition of genocide initially established by the UNCHR that says that a genocide is 'a set of acts committed with the intent to destroy groups whole or in part' (p. 10), other scholars have also included 'actions as intentional prevention of ethnic groups from practicing their traditional customs; forced resettlement; denial of access to food relief, health assistance and development funds; and/or purposeful destruction of the habitats utilised by indigenous populations' (p. 10). Interestingly, in their edited volume about the controversies in genocide studies, Theriault and Joeden-Forgey only focus on trends of genocides within Rwanda, Darfur and Armenia, but the Indian Partition is still not recognised in these conversations.

Haifa Rashed and Damien Short (2012)'s article, however, sheds light on recent conversations in which scholars are locating a 'nexus between colonial processes and genocidal practices' (p. 1144). Rashed and Short contend that Lamkin's conceptualisation of genocide is 'intrinsically colonial' (p. 1144). Thus, their new perspective sheds light to the ways in which genocide studies and the definition of genocide itself is evolving. As has been shown in the opening paragraphs with figures and quotes from the historians and photographers who have studied the Partition and witnessed its violence, the genocidal violence that occurred was not due to one state actor that was determined to destroy a race/ethnicity. Rather, the violence was similar to Rwanda and Cambodia, in that the act of partitioning India left many displaced. People were unaware where the boundaries of their own new countries were and they feared that their ethnic majority village would go to the country they did not belong to. Hence, the brutal and heinous ethnic and sectarian violence that occurred since 1946. Therefore, the Partition does not enter into the national consciousness or raise awareness among younger generations who may be unfamiliar with the genocidal violence that occurred during this time.[4] In the next section, I discuss how rape was used as a weapon of genocide. Furthermore, I'll show that the violence that women experienced was not only perpetrated by members of other communities but also by their own family members, who reiterated the problematic idea that women should embrace death over being abducted or raped by men from other communities. If the women escaped and did not experience violence from their own family members, then they faced ostracisation and rejection from their family after they were often forcibly recovered by the Central Recovery Operation (1948–1957).

## Rape as a Weapon of Genocide: The Story of Women's Experiences During the Partition

There is a powerful link between genocides and sexual/gender-based violence. In fact, after a decades-long silence that followed both the Holocaust (1941–1945) and the Rwandan genocide (1994), only recently have scholars started to explore and acknowledge the testimonies of women who either witnessed or suffered sexual assault, rape and brutal accounts of violence during these genocides.[5] The discourse of Partition has been absent from India's national imagination. As film historian Bhaskar Sarkar (2009) notes, in post-independence India the Partition was seen as a 'one-time aberration in an otherwise continuous tradition of secular unity' (p. 34). According to Sarkar, the 'post-Partition Indian ego' was constructed by 'the experience of loss' (p. 35) which the individual was never able to face, thus never able to recognise the pain and trauma of that loss. Undeniably, Sarkar also suggests that the goal of Indian politicians was to find ways to erase the Partition – as if the sectarian violence, mass rape and abductions had never occurred. This mentality shaped the arduous and complex work of nation-building. Because of this, we have not developed the language needed to address the pain and trauma that many families experienced. Also, until recently, there were no monuments to mourn the aftermath of the violence within India. Therefore, families, including my own, have never discussed the Partition, nor its impact on our lives.

The various types of violence that took place on women's bodies have been largely neglected and are missing from the discourse surrounding India's

---

[4]During my online writing sessions, one of the academics from Calcutta realised that in her family, the Partition is not discussed because the memories are too painful. She also shared this with me after she learned more about my research.

[5]Research on sexual violence during the Holocaust began in the 1980s. For example, in 1983, Esther Katz and Joan Ringelheim planned the first ever *Conference on Women Surviving the Holocaust* in New York, NY (Hedgepeth & Saidel, 2010). But it wasn't until Saidel & Hedgepeth's 2010 anthology that the academic conversation among feminist scholars gained traction and wider visibility, perhaps not unlike Menon and Bhasin (1993) research in relation to the genocide in India.

contemporary rape culture.[6] While the actual numbers are unknown, Urvashi Butalia (2000) notes that at least 75,000 women were kidnapped (p. 3). However, this history has only recently been recognised in India. It was largely disregarded until 1984 when the anti-Sikh violence took place that motivated scholars such as Butalia (1993, 1995, 1997, 2000), Ritu Menon and Kamla Bhasin (1993, 1996, 1998), and Veena Das (2006) to raise concern over the State's treatment of women. During the Post-Partition violence, often, these women experienced multi-layered traumatic experiences. Not only were they forcefully kidnapped during the mass migrations and forced to marry their abductors, they also experienced a second separation from their newly formed families and children and faced rejection from their society and families if they returned to their 'original nation' (which was determined based on their religion), experienced forced abortions and feelings of helplessness as they experienced abandonment.

Numerous women were subject to state, communal and intra-violence. The degrees of their trauma, however, varied in each individual case. Menon and Bhasin (1998) use the expression 'honourably dead' to demonstrate the sexual violence that women experienced during this time. The authors mention that the forms of gender-based violence included 'stripping; parading naked; mutilating and disfiguring; tattooing or branding the breasts and genitalia with triumphant slogans; amputating breasts; knifing open the womb; raping; killing foetuses...' (p. 43). This is not different from the narratives of gender-based violence that we have seen in the Rwandan genocide, as an example. On 2 September 1998, the International Criminal Tribunal of Rwanda (ICTR) convicted Jean Paul Akayesu for rape and inhumane treatment of women. As Bijleveld, Morssinkhof, and Smeulers (2009) note 'this was a landmark decision because for the first time ever rape was being prosecuted as a crime against humanity and as a war crime for an international tribunal' (p. 213). They further discuss instances of sexual violence that occurred during the Rwandan genocide upon the bodies of Tutsi women – 'many of whom were subjected to the worst public humiliation, mutilated and raped several times in public, in the Bureau communal premises, and often by more than one assailant' (qtd. in Bijleveld, Morssinkhof, and Smeulers, p. 213).

---

[6]Here, when I discuss the term – contemporary Indian rape culture – I am specifically referring to the actions of toxic masculinity and GBV that have been widespread in the South Asian subcontinent. In fact, a recent article by Rudabeh Shahid, Kaveri Sarkar, and Azeem Khan (2021) also addresses the following: 'The weaponizing of women's bodies *has always been part of the fabric of South Asia, with mass rapes in 1947 and 1971* being integral to the birth of the three most populous countries in the region. Women's bodies became a battlefield for national honor, and the shame continues to be laid on the door of the victim while perpetrators face no repercussions' (emphasis added). Although the term 'rape culture' was originally coined by the second-wave feminists in 1970s, I use it as a way to talk about the complexities and nuances regarding the culture of gender-based violence as it has existed within India, specifically. But, as can be seen in the work of Shahid, Sarkar and Khan, the issue of GBV is widespread within the South Asian subcontinent. My work also does not address the GBV that occurs within the LGBTQ+ community in India, because their sexualities themselves are often criminalised.

The quote belongs to *the Prosecutor v. Jean Paul Akayesu* case and, yet, the similarities in the practices that occurred in the Partition and the Rwandan genocide are striking.

During their research, Menon and Bhasin were unprepared to listen to narratives of women who were 'forced to die – at the hands of men in their *own* families, or by their own hands' (1998, p. 45; emphasis added). To prevent rape and abduction, women were either 'poisoned, strangled, or burned to death, put to the sword or drowned' (1998, p. 45). The authors further argue that 'it was made abundantly clear to them that death was preferred to "dishonour", that in the absence of their men the *only* choice available to them was to take their own lives' (1998, p. 45; emphasis added). Urvashi Butalia (2000) concurs with Menon and Bhasin's observations, sharing with her readers that during her research she met Prakashvanti, a Partition victim-survivor, who was living in the Gandhi Vanita Ashram at Jalandar, Punjab. During an interview with Butalia, Prakashvanti mentioned that 'her husband came to her and suggested he kill her. "Else", he told her, "they will dishonour you"' (p. 170). She ultimately notes that she recalls very little of the aftermath because she had lost consciousness after her husband violently struck her (p. 170). Butalia notes that according to cultural perceptions 'women could not, therefore, be *named* as violent beings. Therefore, their actions are narrated and sanctified by the tones of heroic, even otherworldly, valour. Such narratives are meant to keep women within their *aukat* [Hindi: status], their ordained boundary, which is one that defines them as non-violent' (p. 171; author's emphasis). In other words, the men, for the most part, problematically assumed that women were not capable of defending their honour and sexual purity, and thus, were vulnerable to gender-based violence by men from the othered ethnic communities. If they chose to defy their family members, especially their fathers and brothers, the women were seen as pariahs and as bringing shame and dishonour to their respective families. Thus, even after they had been recovered, Hindu and Sikh families rejected them. Examples of such rejection can be seen in films such as *Pinjar* (Hindi: Cage, 2003) and *Khamosh Pani* (Hindi: Silent Waters, 2003), which explore the psychological, social and emotional experiences that women experienced after they met their families years after their traumatic abduction. Indeed, this national narrative, which privileges and celebrates women who died to protect their own and their respective communities' honour, supersedes the stories of women who were raped and abducted during the chaotic violence of the Partition.

The nation-building project in India located the women who had been exposed to gendered Partition violence in a site of precarity in the aftermath of the Partition.[7] Feminist philosopher Judith Butler's (2004) theoretical concept of precarity allows us to understand how biopolitics functions when a country faces

---

[7]Precarity is defined as an ontological state of being when an individual who is left vulnerable due to conditions they face and who may be left to feel helpless against the actors that are responsible for their situation. In this case, I'll take it to mean that the person faces either social, economic, political, religious or gender persecution or a combination of all the aforementioned.

a political crisis. Biopolitics, in this context, can be defined as the Indian government's responsibility towards its citizens. Although it was not responsible for the initial displacement of these women, the role of the Indian government in the violence the women experienced contains two prime examples of biopolitics directed at women, which created precarious identities and circumstances.

In the aftermath of the Partition, both India and Pakistan decided to restore the abducted women to their 'original countries' based on their religion, often without their agreement. The precarious circumstances that these abducted women experienced on the outset were products of communal violence rather than the Indian State. In fact, with the creation of the Central Recovery Operation (1948–1957), the State worked to reinstate them within the newly formed India. The programme began with an agreement – the Inter-Dominion Treaty of 6 December 1947 – between the Indian and Pakistani governments, which had the goal to restore as many abducted women as possible. Mridula Sarabai, a politically influential chief social worker, and Rameshwari Nehru oversaw the programme. At this time, Sarabai received a team which mostly composed of male policemen, who were to aid her in the recovery and restoration process. According to Menon and Bhasin, the recoveries were carried out between 1947 and 1952, but women were still being recovered until at least 1956. During this period, about 30,000 women were recovered (Menon and Bhasin, 'Abducted Women', 16).

In a state of emergency, the government created laws that defiled the rights that abducted women had in the process of their re-integration into modern India. It problematically assumed that if a woman was found cohabiting with a man of a different religion after a certain date in 1947, she had been forcefully abducted (and potentially converted). While some women were happy to be recovered, the Indian state was unprepared for women who resisted the actions of the social workers (Menon & Bhasin, 1996, p. 16). Menon and Bhasin note that their identities 'were in a continual state of reconstruction and construction, making them, as one woman said to us, "permanent refugees"' (Menon & Bhasin, 1996, p. 16).

The term *permanent refugee* underscores the precariousness that was related with the Central Recovery Operation because it was ineffective in its cause to restore the recovered women. In theory, Butalia observes, every 'citizen had a choice in the nation s/he wished to belong to. If a woman had the misfortune of being abducted, however, she did not have such a choice' (p. 111). The social worker and tribunal's decisions often left the women who were recovered meaningless often by forcibly removing them from their newfound relationships, their children, and families and sometimes encouraging them to live in ashrams (Hindi: 'a secluded dwelling') for the remainder of their lives if they did not want to live away from their children from mixed unions. Their families perceived these children as illegitimate and did not want to see the women bringing dishonour and shame to them, and thus would ostracise them. The 1960 Hindi film, *Chhalia*, represents this moment when Shanti (Nutan) introduces her husband Kewal (Rehman) to their son, Anwar. Kewal immediately rejects them, believing that Rehman is the product of her rape and abduction, while, in actuality, he was conceived at a time before Kewal and his family abandoned Shanti in the chaos of the Partition violence.

A second way in which the government played a pivotal role in Post-Partition violence against women was revealed in a conversation that occurred in 1996 between Aparna Basu and Kamla Patel, a social worker who worked with Mridula Sarabai in the Central Recovery Operation. During the interview, Patel mentions that the refugee camps where the women were living after their recovery were worse than cattle sheds (p. 127). She notes that the camps were 'overcrowded' due to a 'lack of sanitary facilities – there were frequent outbreaks of epidemics and deaths. Within the limited budget, it was not possible to provide for more than two meals a day and a pair of clothes' (p. 127). We only see rare representations of the camps in film depictions, especially in the early depictions of Partition films. In *Chhalia* (1960), for example, the camps are represented as being clean but are not the focal point of the film. The recovery camps can also be seen in films such as Govind Nihalani's *Tamas* (1989), Deepa Mehta's *Earth* (1998), Chandra Prakash Dwivedi's *Pinjar* (2003), Rahat Kazmi's *Mantostaan* (2017) and Nandita Das's *Manto* (2018). With that said, these filmmakers do not depict the camps as being unsanitary or unkempt but rather as sanitised versions of crowded areas that can be found in refugee camps worldwide. It is evident that filmmakers are staying away from depicting the government's role in the Partition, and especially the recovery of women in its aftermath.

## Conclusion

In my experience, the Partition was not brought to light in conversations with elders in my family who may have witnessed it. Rather, the stories that I hear are of my family's treating other ethnicities with respect and helping them. But we rarely speak of the Partition, by stating that since our family belongs to central India (and not Punjab and Bengal, where most of the atrocities took place) we were not directly affected by it. As post-colonial theorist Nandi Bhatia (2013) notes, the 'Partition has been subjected to a haunting silence marked by survivors too traumatized or faced with "collective guilt" to talk about it publicly'. (p. 89) The Partition has always been viewed as a dark chapter in modern Indian history – as a rupture that took place. Although there have been initiatives such as the 1947 Partition Archive and the Partition Museum, it is only in the last decade that the Partition has become a focus for academics, cultural critics, historians and archivists. Nonetheless, I argue that the Partition was and is in fact a genocide that was shaped by interethnic, communal violence as well as rape and sexual violence, and the subsequent silencing of events as if they never happened. Yet, events such as the 1984 anti-Sikh riots, 1992–1993 Bombay riots, the 2000 Gujarat riots and, more recently, the anti-CAA protests, all serve as reminders that the spectre of the Partition continues to haunt the subcontinent and the wounds from the cataclysmic event are yet to heal.

Because there remains a silence in India and the diaspora, these women's traumatic experiences of gender-based violence are not acknowledged, especially as we continue to make sense of the #MeToo movement. Similar to how the narratives of gender-based violence experienced by indigenous women continue to remain obscured in Western mainstream culture, the narratives of these women also do not enter into the conversations of gender-based violence in South Asia and in the diaspora. Therefore, we need to *urgently* recognise the narratives of raped and abducted women to acknowledge the heinous gender and sexual violence that occurred during the genocidal violence that took place during the Partition.

## References

Barta, T. (1985). After the Holocaust: Consciousness of genocide in Australia. *Australian Journal of Politics & History*, *31*(1), 154–161. doi:10.1111/j.1467-8497.1985.tb01330.x

Bhatia, N. (2013). "I know the difference between what I see and what I only want to see": Remembering India's partition through children in cracking India. In J. Haslam & J. Faflak (Eds.), *The public intellectual and culture of hope*. Toronto, ON: University of Toronto Press.

Bijleveld, C. C. H. J., Morssinkhof, A., & Smeulers, A. (2009). Counting the countless – Rape victimisation during the Rwandan genocide. *International Criminal Justice Review*, *19*(2), 208–224. doi:10.1177/1057567709335391

Bourke-White, M. (1963). *Portraits of myself*. New York, NY: Simon & Schuster.

Brass, P. R. (2003). The partition of India and retributive genocide in the Punjab, 1946–1947: Means, methods, and purposes 1. *Journal of Genocide Research*, *5*(1), 71–101. doi:10.1080/14623520305657

Butalia, U. (1993). Community, state and gender: On women's agency during partition. *Economic and Political Weekly*, *28*(17), WS12–WS24.

Butalia, U. (1995). Muslims and Hindus, men and women: Communal stereotypes and the partition of India. In T. Sarkar & U. Butalia (Eds.), *Women and the Hindu right: A collection of essays*. New Delhi: Kali For Women.

Butalia, U. (1997). Abducted and widowed women: Questions of sexuality and citizenship during partition. In M. Thapan (Ed.), *Embodiment: Essays on gender and identity*. Oxford: Oxford University Press.

Butalia, U. (2000). *The other side of silence: Voices from the partition of India*. Durham, NC: Duke University Press.

Butler, J. (2004). *Precarious life: The powers of mourning and violence*. New York, NY: Verso.

Darymple, W. (2015, June 19). The great divide: The violent legacy of India's partition. *The New Yorker*. Retrieved from https://www.newyorker.com/magazine/2015/06/29/the-great-divide-books-dalrymple

Das, V. (2006). *Life and words: Violence and the descent into the ordinary*. Berkeley, CA: University of California Press.

Hajari, N. (2015). *Midnight's Furies: The deadly legacy of India's partition*. Boston, MA: Houghton Mifflin Harcourt.

Hedgepeth, S. M., & Saidel, R. G. (2010). *Sexual violence against Jewish women during the Holocaust*. Waltham, MA: Brandeis University Press.

Hitchcock, R. K., Floweday, C., & Babchuk, W. A. (2017). The case of aché: The genocide debate continues unabated. In S. Totten, H. Theriault, & E. Von Joeden-Forgey (Eds.), *Controversies in the field of genocide studies* (1st ed.). Milton Park: Taylor & Francis.

Menon, R., & Bhasin, K. (1993). Recovery, rupture, resistance: Indian state and abduction of women during partition. *Economic and Political Weekly*, *28*(17) WS2–WS11. *JSTOR*. Retrieved from www.jstor.org/stable/4399640

Menon, R., & Bhasin, K., & American Council of Learned Societies. (1996). Abducted women, the state, and questions of honour: Three perspectives on the recovery operation in post-partition India. In K. Jayawardena & M. d. Alwis (Eds.), *Embodied violence: Communalising women's sexuality in South Asia*. London: Zed Books.

Menon, R., & Bhasin, K. (1998). *Borders and boundaries: Women in India's partition*. New Delhi: Women Unlimited.

Pollack, R. (Director). (2007). The day India burned [film]. *British Broadcasting Company (BBC)*.

Rashed, H., & Short, D. (2012). Genocide and settler colonialism: Can a Lemkin-inspired genocide perspective aid our understanding of the Palestinian situation? *The International Journal of Human Rights*, *16*(8), 1142–1169. doi:10.1080/13642987.2012.735494

Saidel, R. G., & Batya, B. (2018). *Violated! Women in Holocaust and genocide*. New York, NY: Remember the Women Institute.

Sarkar, B. (2009). *Mourning the nation: Indian cinema in the wake of partition*. Durham, NC: Duke University Press.

Shahid, R., Sarkar, K., & Khan, A. (2021). Understanding "rape culture" in Bangladesh, India, & Pakistan. *Atlantic Council*. Retrieved from https://www.atlanticcouncil.org/blogs/southasiasource/understanding-rape-culture-in-bangladesh-india-pakistan/

Shrivastava, N., & Bibi, S. (2021). Why are we silent? #MeToo in South Asia sub-continent and diaspora: A conversation. *Bloomsbury Literary Studies Blog*. Retrieved from https://bloomsburyliterarystudiesblog.com/continuum-literary-studie/2021/12/metoo-in-south-asia-subcontinent-and-diaspora.html

Ten Rape Cases that India Will Never Forget. (2018, March 21). *Newsable*. Retrieved from https://newsable.asianetnews.com/india/ten-rapes-cases-that-india-will-never-forget

The Rapes that India Forgot. (2013, January 5). *BBC News*. Retrieved from https://www.bbc.com/news/world-asia-india-20907755

Totten, S., Theriault, H., & Von Joeden-Forgey, E. (2017). *Controversies in the field of genocide studies* (1st ed.). Milton Park: Taylor & Francis.

Chapter 2

# The Commodification of Sex in Modern Japan: Outdated Attitudes and Overdue Reforms

*Gavan Patrick Gray*

## Abstract

This chapter looks at the sex trade in Japanese society and the manner in which it has been accepted for decades, both socially and legally, as a 'necessary evil'. This passive and disinterested tolerance of the industry's quasi-legal state, neither banning prostitution completely nor ensuring that it follows the transparent rules and regulations expected of other industries, means that it fails to satisfy either of the primary views on transactional sex: prohibition or legalisation. The result is that the women involved in the industry are subject to various forms of exploitation and abuse that the Japanese government, by failing to take active steps to reform the industry in either direction, becomes complicit to. Shaped by personal interviews with members of the industry and the NGOs that provide them with support, the chapter provides an examination of the industry's historical development, its portrayal in popular media and the prevailing social norms regarding the industry. It then assesses the political and legal responses to the industry and the glaring oversights that exist in their failure to provide adequate support. Finally, it considers, based upon the self-expressed interests of the women working in the industry, in what areas meaningful reform might occur.

*Keywords*: Japan; prostitution; sexual violence; women's rights; sexuality; sexual norms

Gender Violence, the Law, and Society, 35–50
doi:10.1108/978-1-80117-127-420221004

The relationship between prostitution and violence is complex, nuanced and contested and in Japan this is especially true.[1] Perhaps as a result of never succumbing to the sexual stigmatisation that is common in cultures shaped by more puritanical, monotheistic religions, Japan has generally taken a pragmatic view of the commercial elements of sexual relationships. This gives it a distinct variation on what Mulvihill (2018, p. 223) sees as the two primary views of prostitution: one which considers transactional sex as inherently violent and a result of deep-rooted patriarchal structures of gender inequality, and another which considers it a legitimate form of enterprise which should be regulated to guarantee the well-being and rights of those involved. In the Japanese view, negative attitudes also contain an element of the sex industry representing a failure to adhere to the aforementioned Western norms, while positive attitudes consider it a necessity that contributes to broader issues of social harmony and sexual health (Koch, 2016). In this way, Japanese perspectives are not as solely focused on the effects of the industry on individual women but also on how it relates to society at a broader level.

Mulvihill (2018, p. 230) also refers to what she calls 'symbolic violence' as a form of domination embedded in everyday actions that prevents its victims from expressing grievance, due to acceptance that the system that harms them is regarded as natural, unchangeable or in some way beneficial. This is something that applies very strongly to Japan's particular form of commercialised sex, where long-standing social perception of the industry as a natural, inevitable and even essential element of society both normalises women's participation in the industry and weakens their ability to critique or reform it. This chapter considers the Japanese sex industry as existing in a specific limbo-state, between illegality and acceptance, that means it satisfies the desires of neither of the two main perspectives on prostitution and cannot claim to be safeguarding the welfare of the women involved.[2] For those who would seek to protect women by prohibiting prostitution entirely (or at least aspire to implement the Nordic Model),[3] its open acceptance can be seen as a disregard for the sexual oppression of women. For those who would rather see those women protected by having the sex industry treated as a legitimate form of employment, its nebulous legality leaves those working in the industry in a tenuous and vulnerable state.

The current, poorly regulated and monitored nature of the industry can be considered to constitute a form of commercial sexual exploitation, which many governments recognise as a form of gender-based violence.[4] The United Nations

---

[1] This work was supported by a Kaken grant (18K13005) from the Japan Society for the Promotion of Science.
[2] Although women make up the overwhelming majority of Japan's sex workers the industry also contains male and LGBTQ+ members and the points raised in this chapter should be considered to apply equally to these groups.
[3] The Nordic Model aims at decreasing the overall demand for transactional sex by making the purchase, but not the sale, of sex illegal.
[4] For example, the United States in the Abolish Human Trafficking Act of 2017, S. 1311 (115th): Section 8.3.

also considers gender-based violence to include the imposition of mental and economic harm,[5] and the failure of the Japanese government to proactively support the mental and economic welfare of those involved in the industry should be viewed as passive and apathetic participation in an ongoing system of systemic exploitation. It has frequently been shown that those involved in prostitution and transactional sexual activities are especially vulnerable to various forms of harm, including suicide, mental and emotional health problems, sexually transmitted diseases, addiction issues, physical violence and economic coercion (Henriksen, 2020). Japan is no different in this regard and those working in the industry are often living in situations of significant precarity, whether as a result of poverty, exposure to danger, or the impact of mental and emotional harm.

Yet, even as the industry has grown in size and financial value, its workers continue to remain in such precarious economic and social states. The events of the COVID-19 pandemic beginning in 2019, in particular the Japanese government's response to the difficulties faced by sex workers, only served to highlight the extent to which their work is treated in a contradictory manner, open and semi-legal, yet held to separate standards of social acceptance. While the government itself does not list prostitution as an element of its campaign to end violence against women, its highlighting of the role of exploitation, sexual violence and stalking within both the AV (adult video) industry and the JK industry[6] show that it has begun to examine the problems faced by sex workers.[7] However, as yet, it has taken few steps to generate meaningful reform and it remains to be seen whether its purported support for sex workers will result in more than mere lip service. Regardless of whether such work is seen as inherently harmful to women or the legitimate independent enterprise of people expressing their economic agency, the industry as it exists now cannot be said to properly protect those involved from various forms of exploitation and abuse and those who have the power to intervene to prevent this, yet fail to do so, should be considered culpable or actively enabling any harm done.

## Public Attitudes Towards Sex Work

Commodification refers to the process of treating an object purely in terms of its market value, in other words, judging it purely on the basis of what it can be sold for. Other elements of intrinsic worth, such as cultural heritage, aesthetic beauty or, in the case of people, their individual identity and fundamental rights, become relevant only insofar as they influence the potential price of the commodity in

---

[5]Something clear stated on the website of the UN High Commissioner for Refugees, https://www.unhcr.org/gender-based-violence.html.

[6]JK is short for Jyoshi Kousei (high-school girl) and refers to various enterprises related to the sexualisation of high-school girls. Although some prefectures have laws prohibiting those under 18 from such employment, even in these areas younger girls are often exploited by businesses that skirt the law.

[7]As shown on the Japanese Cabinet Office's Gender Equality Bureau page on Violence Against Women, https://www.gender.go.jp/policy/no_violence/.

question. In relation to sex, commodification means that it is stripped of other elements, whether romance, procreation or an element of marital fidelity, and is instead made purely transactional. The formal commodification of sex has a long history in Japan, stretching back to the government-sanctioned *yūkaku* (red-light districts) that included Edo's (modern Tokyo) Yoshiwara area. The sex industry grew from these initial roots to a more dispersed, varied and nebulous modern form that includes both the *mizu-shōbai* (Water Trade), consisting of night-time entertainment via clubs, bars and cabarets featuring, nominally non-sexual, female companionship, and *sei-fūzoku* (Sexual Customs), incorporating the variegated forms of direct sexual exchange. It represents a significant industry, employing hundreds of thousands of women and men, and generating billions of dollars of annual revenue (Ogiue & Iida, 2013)[8]. From love hotels and hostess clubs to soaplands[9] and delivery health[10] stores, the Japanese sex industry incorporates numerous distinct elements that exist outside of legally prohibited prostitution in a manner significantly different from more clearly delineated understandings of 'sex work' that may exist in the West.

The industry also exists in a quasi-shadow realm, cordoned off but gaudily lit. Red-light districts, such as Kabuki-chō, are clearly demarcated from the surrounding business areas but there is no effort to hide what they sell. Instead, large, colourful posters and neon signs loudly proclaim what is on offer to passers-by and potential customers. Despite its open nature, the sex industry is considered, by most, to be a disreputable career choice and associated with the criminal underworld, though government crackdowns on Japan's organised crime have made their direct influence far less than it was in the past. The sex industry is tolerated, rather than being openly accepted, and those who work in it suffer stigmatisation stemming from these social mores that only compounds the economic and physical hardships they already face (Kamise, 2013).

Public awareness of, and attitudes towards, the industry are often shaped by its representation in popular culture. Over the past century, many directors have examined the issue of sex work through film, such as Kenji Mizoguchi's *Akasen Chitai* (1956) and Shohei Imamura's *Nippon Konchūki* (1963). Imamura also examined the issue in documentary form with *Karayuki-san* (1975) through the recollection of one woman's experiences working as a sex worker in Japanese holdings throughout the Pacific during the early 1900s. Other films framed the changing nature of the sex trade in relation to Japan's shifting economic welfare, with Masato Harada's *Baunsu Ko-garusu* (1997) highlighting the rise in teenage 'compensated dating' that followed the collapse of Japan's economic bubble in the 1990s.

---

[8]Kindle Edition, Chapter 1, Page 1, Paragraph 2.
[9]A soapland is a sex business that uses the façade of paying to be bathed by another person as a means of evading the prohibitions against explicitly selling sexual intercourse. Any sexual acts that occur are presented as being coincidental and unrelated to the transfer of money for other services.
[10]Similarly, delivery health services offer out-call massage services that are presented as being physical therapy rather than the blatantly sexual exchange that they are in reality.

Movies such as these helped show changes in public understanding of the sex industry as it moved from an attitude prevalent in the 1960s which saw it almost as an extension of the male-dominated business world (Norma, 2011) to the post-bubble participation of young women as a form of sexual self-determination or even resistance against patriarchal structures (Ueno, 2003). In the interim, greater nuance has been added by works such as Penelope Buitenhuis' *Tokyo Girls* (2000), which looked at the experiences of foreign women in the industry, Itako's *Baibai Bōizu* (2017) and its examination of *'urisen'*, the male prostitution industry, and most recently Kana Yamada's *Taitoru, Kyozetsu* (2019), which provided a dramatic and realistic view of women working in contemporary conditions.

The aforementioned works appeal, however, to a relatively limited audience and popular television dramas, such as *Kiken'na Aneki* (2005), *Joutei* (2007), *Hitsudan Hosutesu* (2010), have a broader reach and a larger impact in shaping public conceptions. In their examination of the reasons why the hostess industry was an attractive career option for many young women, Miura and Yanagiuchi (2008) highlighted the impact of the positive portrayals found in such dramas which frequently showed the industry to be one in which girls from poor backgrounds could find financial success and social status.

The hostess industry portrayed in these programmes is only on the periphery of the broader sex industry and comprises clubs and bars where men, and frequently women, pay to have their more social and emotional desires catered to by attractive members of the opposite sex. Although, as Allison stated, it exists 'primarily at the level of conversation' (1994, pp. 7–8), there is considerable overlap with the more explicit sex industry and workers frequently engage in sexual activity with clients (Takeyama, 2005). As such, the tendency of popular dramas to portray only the glamorous and successful elements of the hostess industry, both undersells the darker elements of the reality of sex work and promotes a distorted understanding of the industry that is only likely to reinforce the public viewpoints that were dominant during the 1980s 'Bubble' era, wherein the primary reason women engaged in sex work was considered to be as a means of acquiring pocket-money and to have fun (JCO, 1985).

It is unclear whether public perceptions have altered significantly in the interim. Thankfully, however, academics and professionals have developed a much clearer and more nuanced view of the industry and of the backgrounds of many of those involved. There is a growing awareness of the precarious existence faced by many sex workers, whether runaway teens, women in debt, single mothers, women with psychological and emotional problems, or older women lacking support networks (Nakamura & Suzuki, 2016). Many are women who have chosen to leave more superficially 'respectable' careers such as kindergarten teaching and nursing due to the low salaries and lack of economic freedom these paths offered, sacrificing stability and security for opportunities to reinvent themselves and potentially achieve a greater degree of long-term economic independence (Nakamura, 2016). The agency of these, and other, workers must be respected. While some have chosen sex work as a response to debt or to support dependents, for many, it is a deliberate rejection of alternative, minimum-salary labour in poor conditions, in favour of an industry they see as a means of advancement, either because they see a path to success within the industry or because they seek to use it as a stepping-stone to financial independence and the ability to pursue a different, long-term career path (SWASH, 2018)[11]. In all cases, the key factor must remain that the rights and welfare of the workers themselves remain preeminent.

There is a tendency for studies of sex work to incorporate secondary themes, which can be either negative (portraying the women purely as victims of a social ill) or positive (portraying the industry as an economic boon or as providing a necessary social function) (SWASH, 2018)[12]. While these views are all elements of developing a holistic understanding, this examination considers them secondary to providing support for the well-being, whether economic, physical, emotional or professional, of the workers involved in the industry. It is also important to resist instilling the sex industry as a whole with a motive force that would present it as exerting a causative effect on wider society. We must remember that it is wider society that gives rise to the sex industry and which provides the demand for which supply will be generated. Koch (2020, p. 24) quotes a young Japanese woman who sees her work in the industry as providing 'essential elements', without which, 'lots of people would be negatively affected', and certainly in Japanese society there are clear socio-cultural factors that are deeply connected to the role the industry plays.

It seems to be true at least that there is an increasing trend towards sexless relationships in Japanese society. The Japanese Family Planning Association reported that almost half of all couples are in sexless marriages (Kitamura, 2015), with one of the key reasons given being the pressures of work (Hosokawa, 2017). Suzuki (2013, p. 330) speaks of a traditional viewpoint in Japanese society wherein men view their own wives in an almost asexual manner, while wives considered extramarital sex as being tolerable, especially where it did not threaten the family structure. While such views have no doubt altered considerably in the present day, studies have found that at least 14.6% of Japanese men admit to having used prostitutes, with higher rates among those who reported poor family connections or a lack of intimacy (Ui et al., 2008). The success and broad appeal of the, again nominally, non-sexual elements of the sex industry – such as hostess clubs or the even more mainstream maid cafes – show that this need for intimacy is, if not as strong a factor as the desire for sexual gratification, a significant element of Japan's sex industry. Therefore, examination of it cannot be done with the narrow focus on penetrative sexual intercourse that is common in many Western studies.

Lest the sex industry be viewed in purely gendered terms, it should be made clear that Japanese women are also perfectly capable of participating as customers of both the Mizu-Shoubai and Fuzoku worlds, if to a lesser extent. Takeyama (2020) examined middle-aged Japanese women's pursuit of commercialised intimacy as a means of re-establishing their own sexual subjectivity, while

---

[11]Kindle edition, Chapter 1, page 4–5.
[12]Kindle edition, Chapter 1, page 8.

Ho (2019, p. 26) described how some young, married women would form groups to visit strip clubs, host clubs or enjoy 'erotic massages'.

The sex industry in Japan, whether considered in positive or negative terms, is clearly a significant element of Japan's social fabric and one with considerable economic heft. The pertinent questions, therefore, are why, legally, it continues to be so poorly defined and, ethically, why is continues to be so poorly regulated in regard to safeguarding the physical and psychological health of its workers.

## Legal and Political Views of the Industry

The initial *yūkaku*, the Edo-era pleasure districts of the 1600s, were very tightly regulated and the movement of the workers strictly controlled. This system, whereby prostitution was open and fully legal though restricted to specific areas, continued up to and through the Second World War with the state taking a direct role in the legal management of the sex trade (Lie, 1997). However, in the wake of the post-war Americanised systems of control, calls for criminalisation of the sex industry became stronger. During this period the former *yūkaku* were reclassified as 'red line' areas within which legal prostitution could occur. There were also other 'blue line' areas that were designated as night entertainment areas (including present-day Kabukichō) that were nominally 'sex free'. However, a blurring of the lines between the two soon occurred (Kato, 2009).

In 1956, after hundreds of years of tacit legal acceptance, prostitution was finally criminalised in the Prostitution Prevention Law on the grounds that it 'harms the dignity of the individual, is against sexual virtue and disrupts the proper morals of society' (GoJ, 1956). However, two key factors of the law have continued to have a major impact on the status and nature of the sex industry in intervening years. The first is that prostitution was defined as being, 'sexual intercourse with a non-specified person in exchange for compensation or the promise of such'. This meant that by taking a narrow definition of 'sexual intercourse' to be heterosexual, genital penetration, numerous other sex acts could remain legal. Additionally, the definition of 'stranger' and 'compensation' were vague enough that other ways to bypass these restrictions were quickly found that made determining whether prostitution had indeed taken place a very difficult task. The second factor was that even where prostitution was identified, there was no proscribed punishment. As a result, although prostitution in Japan is technically illegal, a wide variety of perfectly legal stores and services exist that cater to more narrowly defined sexual acts and any legal problems they incur will typically be in relation to breaches of other laws (e.g. the Customs Business Law, The Employment Security Law, or the Worker Dispatch Law). In such cases, they are prosecuted for crimes such as solicitation or brothel-keeping. Although specific prostitution arrests do occur, they dropped from a rate of 24,000 in the year following the establishment of the law, to 447 in 2016 (Maeda, 2018).

Evidence of the decline in efforts to strictly enforce criminalisation can be seen in the role played by the 'Women's Guidance Centres'. Originally introduced in 1958, it was intended that these reform centres would be established throughout

Japan to provide re-education and re-training of women convicted of prostitution. In practice, only one centre was created, in Akishima Tokyo, where the number of 'residents' declined from 400 per year in the 1960s to just 4 during the 2010s, with the expectation that it will soon be shut down permanently (Kihara, 2020). In his analysis of the industry, Yokohama (1995) considers the passive attitude of those in law enforcement as having effectively decriminalised the industry, due to their unwillingness to proactively enforce the laws to their fullest extent. The result is that Japan is a country where prostitution is illegal, yet the government has other laws (GoJ, 1952) that carefully regulate the ways in which sexual services are offered and organised on an industrial basis.

This apparent dichotomy has created a situation where the definition of prostitution, its legal standing, and the status and treatment of those working in the sex industry remain incredibly nebulous. The question of whether sex workers should be treated like other forms of labour under the law, with equal rights and protections, was already being raised in the mid-1990s (Kataiki, 1996). Yet, in the intervening years, not only has little been done to clarify the issue, the precarious conditions of these workers have only been exacerbated.

As previously mentioned, Japan's sex industry is a significant employer. A 2006 government study estimated more than 140,000 people whose sole profession was sex work (Kadokura, 2006). For many, however, sex work is a side job and representatives of the SWASH sex workers support group estimate at least 300,000 workers with almost one third of these having children (Chiba, 2020). With Japan having roughly 70 million working age adults, this would represent 0.4% of this total. The number of these who are considered 'mature', over 26 in the Japanese context, has been steadily increasing and now makes up half of the total number (Nakamura & Suzuki, 2016). For these women in particular, the profession can be highly unstable. As is common in sex work, the older you become, the fewer opportunities will be available to you. Consequently, Nakamura (2016) has collected numerous accounts of such mature women living on the edge of destitution. These include single mothers, women who have been left homeless, and those who had previously worked in the adult video industry but found it increasingly difficult to acquire such work as they grew older. One of his interviewees, a woman he calls Yuko, recounts how her extreme poverty drove her more than once to attempted suicide. She then lists all her friends in the industry who have died from different forms of suicide: hanging, overdose, asphyxiation, jumping in front of trains, drowning and more (Takahashi, 2018)[13]. During the COVID-19 pandemic, these dangers have only become more pronounced with suicide rates among women reaching 1.8 times more than those of the previous year (Konno, 2020).

The increasing popularity of Social Networking Services (SNS) and their growing use as a means of facilitating sexual services has also seen a shift away from the traditional 'shop' system through which sex workers were typically afforded a level of management and oversight that reduced worker's

---

[13]Kindle Edition, Chapter 1, Section 8, page 3.

independence but provided a safety net of sorts (Shibui, 2019). The unregulated nature of the sites that are used to facilitate meetings means that they are prone to exploitation by men seeking, or actively, grooming underage girls. They also remove any opportunity to vet unstable or violent customers, with the result that girls are frequently assaulted, drugged, or secretly filmed and blackmailed with threats to release the illicit videos (Takahashi, 2018).

The industry had already been experiencing a decline in its customer base due to Japan's ageing population and there had been hopes that foreign tourism, especially surrounding the Olympics, would counterbalance these demographic changes, at least temporarily (Maruyama, 2014). Instead, in 2020 the opposite occurred, with the COVID-19 crisis seeing custom as a whole dropping dramatically and foreign tourism drying up completely. This was, of course, a common pattern internationally as sex workers across the globe were affected economically, physically and psychologically by the negative pressures of both the pandemic and the ensuing lockdowns (Platt et al., 2020).

In Japan, the pandemic has especially impacted women who, compared to men, are significantly more likely to work in part-time, contract or temporary employment. The rate of job loss for women in non-regular employment was 1.8 times more than that of men (Zhou, 2020) and an estimated 900,000 women have been left substantially unemployed as a result of the crisis (Takeda, 2021). Loss of employment and increased levels of borrowing and resulting debt are pushing more and more of the most vulnerable women to turn to sex work as a means of economic survival at the same time as the downturn in the industry makes such work even more precarious and open to exploitation.

In April 2020, comments by a famous Japanese comedian highlighted the callous attitude held by many to such women when he said that the pandemic could be seen as a good thing because it would push more pretty, young women into the sex industry (Shioda & Kamito, 2020). Thankfully, these comments received considerable backlash. Sadly, they were merely crudely insensitive, not inaccurate, and many women have given direct accounts of how the crisis has forced them to enter the sex industry as the only means they had of providing for themselves, supporting their families or of repaying the debt they held (Nakamura, 2020).

One indirect form of exploitation can be seen in the grey areas surrounding what is known as *Papa Katsu* (father activities), an evolution of the previous 'compensated dating' in which young women match with potential sugar daddies, for what are supposedly non-sexual relationships. Again, it can be hard for Western readers to imagine that such exchange could be non-sexual in nature, but many are indeed based upon non-sexual companionship that offers emotional and social satisfaction. Many, of course, does not mean all, and, in the wake of COVID-19, there is even more leeway for young women to be exploited and pressured to provide physical services through such interactions which, conducted as they are through unmonitored and unregulated apps, make it sadly inevitable that many vulnerable young women will fall victim to predatory older men (NHK, 2020).

Throughout 2020 and 2021 there were several cases of politicians being accused of engaging in such Papa Katsu, or visiting sex shops, and suffering a career-ending backlash, not because of the activities themselves but because they occurred during the COVID-19 pandemic (Sankei, 2021; Yomiuri, 2020). In other words, politicians can expect to be forced to resign positions for breaking a lockdown curfew but it is clear that at any other period in time, simple engagement in Papa Katsu or patronage of elements of the sex industry would have generated negligible outcry on both social and political levels. As such, one might expect such politicians to treat the sex industry and its workers, where they remain within the bounds of the law, along similar standards to any other legal business. Unfortunately for the workers involved, however, that has not been the case; although politicians are happy to make use of the services the sex industry offers, when it comes to the government determining how it should treat those workers, a certain level of hypocrisy soon becomes evident.

## Double Standards and Inadequate Support Systems

Sex workers in Japan have long stated that even though their profession is, usually, within the boundaries of legality, they frequently face social stigmatisation. This became more openly evident when, following the initial wave of COVID-19 infections in Japan, sex workers were excluded from a system established to support parents who were forced to leave their work due to school closures (Fujisawa, 2020). Although this exclusion was soon reversed, it made it abundantly clear that there was social and political prejudice at play that significantly affected not only the working conditions of those employed in the industry but also their wider lives.

Tsunehiko Maeda (2020), a former Chief Prosecutor of the Special Investigations Department of Tokyo Public Prosecutors Office, explains that sex workers face additional problems regarding the nature of their work status as their contracts are often indirect compared to those of standard office or factory workers. The wording of the Customs Business Law, which governs the legal sex industry, leaves significant room for interpretation so that workers are unclear whether they are direct employees of stores they work at or indirect, contracted labour. These grey areas have existed for decades but until the COVID-19 pandemic, there was never any pressure to clarify their precise nature.

Now, however, pressure for a clearer definition is increasing from both representatives of the sex industry and those who oppose it. Despite the reversal on parental support, the government continued to exclude sex shops from another subsidy to support small businesses impacted by the pandemic and, as a result, they are being sued by at least one sex shop manager who claims that their business is being discriminated against (Osaki, 2020). The government has its supporters though, among those who argue that the sex industry, due to perceived ties to organised crime, frequent cases of tax evasion, and, for some, the threat it represents to public morals, does not deserve to benefit from public taxes. Additionally, 'abolitionists' – who perceive the sex industry as being inherently exploitative – hope to use the public fear of direct interaction as an opportunity to call for greater restrictions on the industry.

Prior to the beginning of the pandemic, discussions had already begun to revise the Prostitution Prevention Law, which has remained unchanged for over 60 years. While they are still ongoing, it is unlikely that they will result in a dramatic change to the industry. So far, the focus has been upon abolishing Chapter 4 of the law, which introduced the aforementioned reform centres and provided greater support for women in the industry who are in distress – whether due to age, family status, debt, violence or other problems (GoJ, 2019). While such changes are needed and may do considerable good, it is unlikely that the revisions will adequately address all the problems that exist.

The changes are certainly unlikely to appease the abolitionist groups and activists who might hope to see such revisions lead to the introduction of the Nordic Model of sex laws, wherein the purchase of sex, but not its sale, is criminalised (a format which activists argue protects the agency of sex workers and reduces demand, but which many workers see as making their work less safe and more economically precarious). Such changes are incredibly unlikely to occur in Japan though, as they would upend a multi-billion-dollar industry that has a deeply entrenched position, no matter how vaguely defined, in Japanese society. Reforms to the existing law, and changes in the way in which women in the industry are treated, are far more likely to take place on a slow and incremental basis which only increases the importance of understanding the various factors that might positively impact the lives of the women involved.

One of the most important things for women in the industry is their ano-nymity. Typically, they work far from their own home areas to avoid what some call the danger of 'social suicide' and the work is seen by some as a means of addressing economic problems without exposing their identity to public scrutiny (Sakatsume, 2018)[14]. Shingo Sakatsume, director of the White Hands NGO, which provides various support systems for women in the industry, including the Fu-Terasu counselling service, highlighted the fact that in his own hometown the minimum hourly wage was ¥830, whereas women would expect to earn at least ¥5,000–6,000 at a 'delivery health' store. They also have considerable flexibility over when and for how long they are willing to work, something that appeals to students who might have debt, or single parents who need to provide for children. What these women lack, however, is business knowledge. Much of the advice that Fu-Terasu provides relates to issues of budgeting, contract advice and dealing with debt or bankruptcy (Hojo, 2020).

Despite having hundreds of thousands of workers, Japan's sex industry lacks any formal union for those it employs. Since 2009, the *Kyabakura Yunion* (Cabaret Club Union) has acted as a subcommittee to the *Friitaa Zenpan Rōdō Kumia* (Freeter General Labour Union) to represent the interests of men and women in the subsidiary hostess industry but they appear to have both limited membership and bargaining power. Some NGOs exist to support the wider sex

---

[14]Kindle edition, Chapter 4, page 9, paragraph 2.

work industry, with some such as White Hands offering outreach; and others, such as *Nihon Fūzoku Joshi Sapōto Kyōkai* (Japan Sex Workers Support Association) and SWASH, made up of women involved in the industry themselves. The former focuses more on support for women within their workplace, while the latter looks more at how society can change in order to provide broader support for the difficulties and challenges faced by sex workers. SWASH in particular seeks full decriminalisation of the sex industry, similar to what occurred in New Zealand in 2003, and argues that no policy reform should occur without first gathering broad survey data on the opinions of officials, lawyers, researchers and sex workers (SWASH, 2018)[15].

Among the key targets SWASH have highlighted as being priorities for safeguarding the welfare of the sex workers themselves are the following: (1) Improving Sexual health and prevention of STDs, (2) protection of workers' right to privacy, (3) reducing trouble with and danger from customers, (4) improving work conditions, (5) providing counselling and support for psychological problems, (6) offering assistance with contractual issues and matters of economic exploitation, (7) providing assistance to address debt and other financial problems (SWASH, 2018)[16].

These problems are not, however, matters that require purely legal remedies; for some, a change to the law will make little difference and broader social changes are required in the way that people view the sex industry and the women and men who work in it. Significant adjustments of both attitudes to and the conditions of the sex industry could result in improvements to the health, safety and quality of life of the hundreds of thousands of people in Japan who depend upon it for their economic survival. At present, however, many misconceptions and harmful stereotypes still remain and it is necessary to have a more open, holistic view of the industry, both good and bad, if reforms are to be properly applied. The sex industry is not the glamorous path to riches that it is often portrayed as in television dramas, nor is it a thoroughly criminal system existing only to exploit those in poverty. To differing extents, both of these might at times be true but the industry is made up of many types of people with a very wide and varied set of problems. All of them, however, suffer from some level of stigmatisation associated with the work they are involved in. All-encompassing stereotypes that portray the whole as either victims in need of saving, or immoral, anti-social forces, do a disservice to the complexity and importance of the problem at hand. Far more study is required that will allow policy to be shaped by examination of the working conditions of those in the industry, the full extent of the problems they face and their opinions on which reforms are of most urgency and benefit to the people directly affected by the industry's negative factors.

---

[15]Kindle edition, Chapter 6.
[16]Kindle edition, Chapter 7.

# Conclusion

Like any large institution, Japan's sex industry needs to be examined in a methodical manner, its problems carefully analysed and solutions drafted in a scientific and socially responsible manner. It is without question that the industry is deeply flawed and significant poverty and exploitation does exist within it. It is also self-evident that the economic opportunities that it provides are a vital lifeline for many people who are living in precarious states. While the subject of sex work can have a polarising effect on people, it is vital that extreme positions are set aside and holistic study is carried out in an academically neutral manner, guided by empathetic concern and free from moral judgement.

It is equally important to examine the industry within the context of its national culture and history. Japan's value systems and cultural mores are unique and distinct from those of Western countries, and the modern sex industry is the product of a long and complex history and many waves of social and political influence. There are commonalities to be found. But to think that Western conceptions of 'pimps', 'brothels', 'prostitutes' and 'selling sex' translate directly into Japanese language or thought in the same way they do in other countries, displays a lack of cultural awareness that will hamper effective responses to the issues that exist.

In one way, however, the fact that that the sex industry in Japan is such an open part of the social fabric and that it already enjoys a certain legal status means that the potential exists for reforms to be enacted in a broader and more complete way than in countries where the status of the sex industry is publicly and legally far more opaque. If political will is sufficiently harnessed, and the problems of the industry given the necessary level of study and analysis, the potential exists for Japanese reforms to act as a model for the ethical and effective restructuring of the sex industry in ways that safeguard the welfare, rights and agency of those involved. To do so though, the requisite first step will be to adjust political and public attitudes to prioritise the needs of the industry's workers over the services that they provide.

# References

Allison, A. (1994). *Sexuality, pleasure, and nightwork: Corporate masculinity in a Tokyo hostess club.* Chicago, IL: The University of Chicago Press.

Chiba, Y. (2020, April 2). 子育て世代への新型コロナ支援金、なぜ夜の街で働く人には不支給? [Why is the new corona support fund for the child-rearing generation not paid to those who work in the sex industry?]. *Yahoo Japan.*

Fujisawa, M. (2020, May 22). 性風俗産業はなぜ保護者支援制度から一時除外されたのか [Why the sex industry was temporarily excluded from the parent support system]. *Mainichi Shimbun.*

GoJ. (1952). 風俗営業等の規制及び業務の適正化等に関する法律 [Law concerning regulation of customs business]. Government of Japan, Law No. 122. Retrieved from https://elaws.e-gov.go.jp/document?lawid=323AC0000000122

GoJ. (1956). 売春防止法 [Prostitution Prevent Law]. Government of Japan, Law No. 118. Retrieved from https://elaws.e-gov.go.jp/document?law_unique_id=331AC000 0000118

GoJ. (2019, October 4). 第9回困難な問題を抱える女性への支援のあり方に関する検討会 [9th study group on support for women with difficult problems]. Government of Japan, Ministry of Health Labour and Welfare, Child and Family Affairs Bureau, Family Welfare Division.

Henriksen, T. D. (2020). Do prostitution and social vulnerability go hand in hand? Examining the association between social background and prostitution using register data. *Sociological Research Online, 26*(3), 525–543. Retrieved from https://doi.org/10.1177%2F1360780420965988

Ho, S. L. (2019). 'License to drink': White-collar female workers and Japan's urban night space. *Ethnography, 16*(1), 25–50.

Hojo, K. (2020, April 14). 新型コロナ不況が襲う「風俗業界」をどう救うのか [How to save the "sex industry" hit by the new corona recession]. *Mainichi Shimbun, Weekly Economist, 788*. Wide Interview.

Hosokawa, T. (2017, February 11). 夫婦半数がセックスレス割合最高 [Half of couples have the highest sexless rate]. The survey of Japan Family Planning Association. *Mainichi Shinbun*.

JCO. (1985, September). 性意識世論調査 [Sexual attitudes opinion poll]. Japanese Cabinet Office, Public Relations Office.

Kadokura, T. (2006). 公式統計に現れない隠れた副業の規模と実態 [The scale and reality of hidden side jobs that do not appear in official statistics]. Japan Institute for Labor Policy and Training, 552.

Kamise, Y. (2013). Occupational stigma and coping strategies of women engaged in the commercial sex industry: A study on the perception of "Kyaba-cula hostesses" in Japan. *Sex Roles, 69*, 42–57.

Kataiki, H. (1996). 売春防止法40年の理論的到達点と問題点 [*40years of prostitution prevention law theoretical achievements and problems*]. Welfare Research Institute Annual Report (Vol. 2, pp. 1–7). Retrieved from http://id.nii.ac.jp/1136/00001743/

Kato, M. (2009). 敗戦と赤線~国策売春の時代 [*Defeat and the red line: The era of national prostitution*]. Tokyo: Kobunsha.

Kihara, I. (2020, April 20). 売春防止法違反の女性を「処罰」…婦人補導院に廃止求める声 [Punishment for women who violate the prostitution prevention law … Voices calling for the abolition of the Women's Guidance Center]. *Tokyo Shimbun*.

Kitamura, K. (2015). 性教育の新しい課題について考えるヒントを得る第七回男女の生活と意識に関する調査結果から [Get tips to think about new challenges in sex education: From the results of the 7th survey on men and women's life and consciousness]. *The Japanese Association for Sex Education, 45*, 1–7.

Koch, G. (2016). Producing iyashi: Healing and labor in Tokyo's sex industry. *American Ethnologist, 43*(4), 704–716.

Koch, G. (2020). *Healing labor: Japanese sex work in the gendered economy*. Stanford, CA: Stanford University Press.

Konno, H. (2020, December 7). コロナ禍の女性たちの苦境「絶望」に陥らないために考える [The plight of women in the Corona disaster: Thinking about how not to fall into 'despair']. *Yahoo Japan*.

Lie, J. (1997). The state as pimp: Prostitution and the patriarchal state in Japan in the 1940s. *Sociological Quarterly, 38*(2), 251–263.

Maeda, T. (2018, August 26). 買売春、なぜ違法なのか [Why prostitution is illegal]. *Yahoo Japan*.

Maeda, T. (2020, May 3). コロナ休業で死活問題の風俗業界、持続化給付金は出る? [The sex industry is in a state of 'life and death' due to Corona. Will benefits be issued?]. *Yahoo Japan*.

Maruyama, Y. (2014, June 5). 風俗業界で英語教育過熱?なぜ外国人観光客受け入れ加速? [English education in the adult entertainment industry? Why are we accepting more foreign tourists?]. *Business Journal*.

Miura, T., & Yanagiuchi, K. (2008). 女はなぜキャバクラ嬢になりたいのか? [Why do women want to become hostesses?]. Kobunsha.

Mulvihill, N. (2018). Prostitution and violence. In N. Lombard (Ed.), *The Routledge handbook of gender and violence*. London: Routledge.

Nakamura, A. (2016). 熟年売春 女子の貧困の現実 [*The reality of poverty in middle-aged sex workers*] (Vol. 573, pp. 172–181). Tokyo: Million Publishing loc.

Nakamura, A. (2020). 新型コロナと貧困女子 [New Corona and the poor girls]. Takarajima-sha.

Nakamura, A., & Suzuki, D. (2016). 貧困とセックス [*Poverty and sex*]. East Press.

NHK. (2020, December 1). パパ活の闇:コロナ禍で追い詰められる女性たち [The dark side of Papakatsu: Women who are trapped by Corona]. *NHK Close-up Gendai*.

Norma, C. (2011). Prostitution and the 1960s' origins of corporate entertaining in Japan. *Women's Studies International Forum*, *34*(6), 509–519.

Ogiue, C., & Iida, Y. (2013). 夜の経済学 [Economics of the night]. SPA Books.

Osaki, T. (2020, October 4). 'Shocking discrimination': Japan's sex industry cries foul over exclusion from government aid. *Japan Times*.

Platt, L., Elmes, J., Luca, S., Holt, V., Rolles, S., & Stuart, R. (2020). Sex workers must not be forgotten in the COVID-19 response. *The Lancet*, *396*(10243), 9–11.

Sakatsume, S. (2018). 身体を売る彼女たち」の事情: 自立と依存の性風俗 [The circumstances of those who sell their bodies: Sexual customs of independence and dependence]. Chikuma Shobō. loc pp. 1651–1740.

Sankei. (2021, February 17). 自粛破りの白須賀議員「売り上げの足しにと…」、辞職はせず [Representative Shirasuka loses self-restraint, "I wanted to offer my custom…" But will not resign]. *Sankei Shimbun*.

Shibui, T. (2019, February 26). Dangerous rendezvous: A history of Japan's Hookup industry. Nippon.com.

Shioda, A., & Kamito, A. (2020, April 27). 岡村隆史さん「コロナ明けたら可愛い人が風俗嬢やります」発言に批判 [Criticism of Takeshi Okamura's comments that "After Corona ends cute girls will do sex work"]. *Mainichi Shimbun*.

Suzuki, M. (2013). The husband's chastity: Progress, equality, and difference in 1930s Japan. *The University of Chicago Press Journal*, *38*(2), 327–352.

SWASH. (2018). セックスワーク・スタディーズ: 当事者視点で考える性と労働 [Sexwork Studies: Gender and labor thinking from a participant perspective]. Nihon Hyorosha.

Takahashi, A. (2018, November 18). 「パパ活」を甘く見る女子中高生に迫る超危険 [Dangers lie in wait for high school girls who see Papa Katsu as something sweet]. *Tokyo Keizai Shimbun*.

Takeda, K. (2021, January 18). 労働移動の支援急げ 非正規女性、コロナで実質失業90万人 [Urgent support for labour mobility: 900,000 irregular women and real unemployment in Corona]. *Nikkei.com.*

Takeyama, A. (2005). Commodified romance in a Tokyo host club. In M. McLelland & R. Dasgupta (Eds.), *Genders, transgenders and sexualities in Japan.* London: Routledge.

Takeyama, A. (2020). Marriage, aging, and women's pursuit of commercial sex in Japan. *Sexualities, 24*(4), 592–613.

Ueno, C. (2003). Self-determination on sexuality? Commercialization of sex among teenage girls in Japan. *Inter-Asia Cultural Studies, 4*(2), 317.

Ui, M., Matsui, Y., Fukutomi, M., Narita, K., Kamise, Y., & Yashiro, K. (2008). 成人男性の買春行動及び買春許容意識の規定因の検討 [Examination of the determinants of adult male prostitution behaviour and prostitution tolerance]. *Psychology Research, 79*(3), 215–223.

Yokoyama, M. (1995). Analysis of prostitution in Japan. *International Journal of Comparative & Applied Criminal Justice, 19*(1), 47–60.

Yomiuri. (2020, April 15). 緊急事態宣言後に風俗店、高井議員を立民が除籍処分 [Democratic Party expels Takai after visiting brothel during state of emergency]. *Yomiuri.*

Zhou, Y. (2020, December 7). データで見る：新型コロナ 働く女性への影響は [View from data: New Corona impact on working women]. *NHK.*

# Chapter 3

# Sexual Orientation Microaggressions in South Africa

*Deepesh Nirmaldas Dayal*

## Abstract

Discrimination against LGBTQ+ people in South Africa has shifted from overt hate crimes to covert microaggressions. Microaggression is a term used in psychology to describe casual discrimination against socially marginalised groups, and they occur in three forms: microassaults, microinsults and microinvalidations. Microassaults include verbal and non-verbal discriminatory behaviours. Microinsults include actions or statements which demean a person's identity, and microinvalidations negate the thoughts, feelings or lived experiences of a certain people. Microaggressions have detrimental impacts on lives of people experiencing them and on their interpersonal relationships. The chapter presents a focus on microaggression theory together with microaggression experiences of South African Indian LGBTQ+ people, who have been under-researched. Reference is made to interview extracts from research studies focusing on South African Indian LGBTQ+ people and from e-zine articles focusing on the experiences of South African Indian LGBTQ+ people.

*Keywords*: South African Indian; LGBTQ+; microaggressions; covert discrimination; mental health; homophobia

South African lesbian, gay, bisexual, transgender and queer people as well as people who otherwise identify with minority labels for sexual orientation and gender identities (LGBTQ+) face violence, discrimination and oppression despite the presence of legal protections in South Africa (Marais, Nel, & Govender, 2022). South Africa's history of Apartheid led to racial segregation, and the

Gender Violence, the Law, and Society, 51–65

doi:10.1108/978-1-80117-127-420221005

discrimination of LGBTQ+ people during the Apartheid regime meant that LGBTQ+ people of colour experienced discrimination on many different levels. Research shows that beyond the abolishment of Apartheid, discrimination against LGBTQ+ people continues to be influenced by factors such as race and class, where different population groups experience sexual orientation and gender identity discrimination in different ways (Davis, 2012). The experiences of ethnic and religious minority people in South Africa, such as LGBTQ+ people of Indian descent, also differ greatly from the promise offered by the unwavering Constitutional protection for gender and sexuality minorities (Khan, 2017).

Amongst South Africans of Indian descent, conservative values, patriarchy, religious beliefs and collectivist living are linked to the discrimination experiences of LGBTQ+ people (Khan, 2017; Pillay, 2017). In previous research findings of the author (Dayal, 2021), who conducted a recent study on the sexual orientation discrimination experiences of South African gay Indian men, it is identified that the discrimination against LGBTQ+ people within the South African Indian community is also covert in nature. This covert form of discrimination is known as sexual orientation microaggressions. Microaggressions can occur in several forms, and their intention is to mock, demean and negate the lived experiences of LGBTQ+ people (Nadal, 2013). These microaggressions are written about by many journalists in news articles (Akoob, 2018; Igual, 2018; Jagmohan, 2017; Khan, 2017, 2018; Pillay, 2017). This chapter aims to uncover the foundations of microaggression theory, and how South African Indian LGBTQ+ people are affected by sexual orientation microaggressions. Some quotes and ideas from research studies and opinion pieces will be integrated with microaggression theory in order to make sense of the experiences of South African Indian LGBTQ+ men.

## LGBTQ+ People's Experiences in South Africa

A landmark move in 2006 led to South Africa becoming one of the first countries in the world to introduce legislation that prevents the discrimination of citizens based on their sexual orientation (Bhana, 2012). These legislations allow for same-sex marriages, the ability of same-sex couples to adopt, and legal rights for same-sex couples to inherit from each other (Thoreson, 2008). Despite these advanced laws, LGBTQ+ people in South Africa face relentless discrimination and high rates of violence (OUT, 2016). This discrimination, being either overt or covert, happens across many different settings: schools, healthcare, government offices, workplaces, police stations and higher education institutions (Francis, 2017; Soeker et al., 2015). South African LGBTQ+ people therefore straddle worlds of protection and persecution. There are many factors which contribute to this condemnation, and the chapter on intersectional discrimination later in this volume will allow for a closer inspection of these intersectional influences.

The public views on same-sex relationships in South Africa continue to oscillate between acceptance and rejection. Empirical research conducted by the Human Sciences Research Council in South Africa, titled: *Progressive Prudes: A*

*Survey of South African Attitudes to Homosexuality and Gender Non-Conformity*, revealed that of the 3,000 participants, 72% of people had a firm belief that same-sex relationships were morally wrong (Sutherland, Roberts, Gabriel, Struwig, & Gordon, 2016). Also, 70% of the participants found same-sex sexual interactions to be wrong and disgusting. Two fifths of respondents in another study by Mahomed and Trangoš (2016) found identifying as gay as being against community values. In this study, some 12% of respondents approved of hate crimes as a response to gay men. The 'Love Not Hate' (2016) survey revealed a rise in negative attitudes towards LGBTQ+ people, where 14% of South Africans agreed to violence against LGBTQ+ people; and the percentage of respondents who believed in equal rights for LGBTQ+ people fell from 71% in 2013 to only 56% in 2015. These startling figures paint a bleak picture of the levels of acceptance of LGBTQ+ people in South Africa. Currently, there are organisations in South Africa that cater to the needs of LGBTQ+ people who face the challenges, and new legislation aimed to protect LGBTQ+ people against hate crimes continues to be passed. But these may not be enough to change public perceptions of LGBTQ+ people. The experiences of LGBTQ+ people of Indian descent in South Africa mirrors those of other communities in South Africa; however, there are some unique cultural influences which will be discussed next (Khan, 2017).

## LGBTQ+ People in Indian Communities

Due to the cultural similarities between the people of Indian descent in South Africa and people of Indian descent in other countries, this section will discuss studies of LGBTQ+ people of Indian descent in the United Kingdom, India and lastly South Africa. An attempt will be made to integrate some direct quotations from studies in order to demonstrate the ideas and thoughts surrounding some of the experiences of LGBTQ+ people.

Despite the global presence of the Indian diaspora, most of the research on LGBTQ+ people of Indian descent has been conducted in India and the United Kingdom. These studies show that LGBTQ+ Indians experience prejudice and discrimination based on their gender identity and sexual orientation. This discrimination is perpetrated in many different settings and often by people in personal relationships with the victims, such as family members, employers, friends, and members of the schooling and healthcare sectors who are close to LGBTQ+ people (Bhugra, 1997a, 1997b; Jaspal, 2012, 2014; Kar, Mukherjee, Ventriglio, & Bhugra, 2018; Sharma & Subramanyam, 2020). The following two quotes from two gay men from a large study by Sharma and Subramanyam (2020) in India reveal the difficulties that are present within societies in India. They noted:

> It was suffocating for me to suppress my sexual desires during my childhood because of society. It made me have a distaste for sexual

things. I remained isolated sexually for years and suppressed these
feelings.

(Sharma & Subramanyam, p. 10)

I was extremely uncomfortable, partly because back then it was
not accepted socially and culturally. There was no political
correctness, and homophobia was extreme, which made me more
uncomfortable with my sexuality. I realized that I am gay when I
was in 11th but could not accept it. There was no support system. I
considered it to be socially and politically incorrect.

(Sharma & Subramanyam, p. 9)

These participants share how concealing their identities made them feel isolated and unsupported. Gay men experience internalised homophobia and
emotional challenges due to stigmatisation within Indian communities. Psychological challenges are further alluded to in a study in the United Kingdom (Jaspal,
2012), where a British Indian gay man reveals:

Everyday being gay is like getting harder for me because I can just
see it in my head – mum is crying, dad is crying too and like just
thinking 'he can't be my son' and my brothers would be like
freaking out that I'm queer.

(Jaspal, 2012, p. 773)

According to studies conducted in India and the United Kingdom, discrimination is linked to conservative community values, family honour, cultural
practices, hegemonic masculinity, patriarchy and heterosexism (Bhugra, 1997a,
1997b; McKeown, Nelson, Anderson, Low, & Elford, 2010; Mimiaga et al., 2013;
Sharma & Subramanyam, 2020). There have been many efforts by rights groups
and LGBTQ+ organisations in India and the United Kingdom. However, talk
about LGBTQ+ identities remains taboo and a challenging conversation to have
within Indian communities (Bhugra, 1997a, 1997b; Jain, 2015; Jaspal, 2012).
Discrimination is further perpetuated through Indian media, in particular within
Bollywood movies, where gay men are portrayed in foolish roles involving comic
relief (Kaur, 2017). All these societal restraints have led to some gay men being
subjected to corrective therapy practices, where they are taken to psychiatrists in
order to be 'cured' of same-sex attraction (Bhugra, 1997a; Jain, 2015).

## Difficulties Experienced by LGBTQ+ People of Indian Descent in South Africa

South African Indian people constitute 2.6% of the South African population
(Statistics South Africa, 2020). Although South African Indian people are quite
visible within South Africa, there have been very limited studies which have

focused on the experiences of South African LGBTQ+ people (Pillay, 2017). Even fewer studies have selected the accounts of LGBTQ+ Indian people as a research focus. Most of the research that has been done has been in the form of graduate studies dissertations. The little research that has been conducted focusing on LGBTQ+ people of Indian descent in South Africa, such as that by Bonthuys and Erlank (2012), Dave (2011), Dayal (2021), Moonsammy (2009) and Nair (2020), reveals that LGBTQ+ people in South Africa do experience discrimination related to the expression of sexual orientation within the Indian communities.

Studies focusing on the 'coming out' experiences of lesbian women and gay men emphasised the ideologies related to heterosexism, stereotypical gender roles, community values, religious beliefs and conservative attitudes (Dave, 2011; Nair, 2020). Community beliefs would mostly be centred on concerns about appeasing the community and abiding by the rules and regulations set out by the community (Dayal, 2021; Moonsammy, 2009). As a participant in Dayal's (2021) study confirms:

> So particularly when coming out was things said [people from the community to participant's mother], 'Do you know that your son is doing this, this is not accepted, it's not part of our culture. How're you going to show your face within the community? This is a bad example for our children'. Those kinds of things affect just not only yourself, but your family as well. 'What will people say? What do people say?'
>
> (Dayal, 2021, p. 70)

The gay man in Dayal's (2021) study was made to believe that identifying as gay is wrong and that gay men follow lifestyles that are against cultural norms. The notion of family honour is seen as being deeply negatively affected by having family members who identify with sexual orientations that are not accepted. Family and community members find it difficult to accept LGBTQ+ people and there are often utterances that identifying as LGBTQ+ is a choice or a 'phase' and that it can be changed. These were noted in many studies, as highlighted by these selected quotes:

> Like I brought it up to my mom once that I like chicks and guys, and she was like oh my god you're just going through a phase. The 'you're going through a phase' quote is a thing that is just going to appear on my skin one day, I've heard it so often.
>
> (Nair, 2020, p. 58)

> I told my sisters one by one. The first one I told when I was about 18 and she was actually completely fine with it. I did have a problem with my eldest sister who didn't wanna accept it, she

said it was a phase that I was going through and that I'll grow out of it.

(Dave, 2011, p. 20)

She [participant's mother] actually went very quiet, and she actually said, 'Can you not try to not be gay?' And I told her, 'Can you try to grow an arm?' And she said, 'No!' And then I said, 'Well that's like asking me to not be gay'. And she said, 'No, it's not the same'. I'm like, 'Yes it is the same'.

(Dayal, 2021, p. 66)

What can be concluded is that the family members of the participants in these studies were adamant about the fact that they believed that identifying as LGBTQ+ was a choice and that there was pressure placed on the participants to change. These LGBTQ+ people also feared hostility from family members who did not accept them (Moonsammy, 2009). The reasons behind the non-acceptance of LGBTQ+ people are varied. However, some key ideas revealed from research studies are that conservatism, traditional beliefs and fixed gender roles are often used as anchors to discriminate against anyone who behaves in a way that is in opposition to these fixed ideas (Dayal, 2021; Nair, 2020). This will be discussed in a later chapter.

## Microaggressions

In research findings and opinion articles, it is commonly understood that the discrimination against LGBTQ+ people of Indian descent in South Africa is mainly covert in nature (Akoob, 2018; Dave, 2011; Igual, 2018; Jagmohan, 2017; Khan, 2017, 2018; Pillay, 2017). The fact that the violence is overt, not covert, may be due to the legal protections offered to LGBTQ+ people in South Africa. Still, the people who commit these microaggressions are labelled as 'perpetrators', and they commit verbal and non-verbal homonegative acts of discrimination against LGBTQ+ people (Sue et al., 2007).

Microaggression theory was first presented by Pierce, Carew, Pierce-Gonzalez, and Willis (1978), who defined microaggressions as 'subtle, stunning, generally automatic and nonverbal "put-downs" of Black people by offenders' (p. 66). This definition of microaggressions has been extended to sexual orientation micro-aggressions, which affect people who define themselves by different sexual orientations. These sexual orientation microaggressions often start early in the lives of LGBTQ+ people. Initially, these sexual orientation microaggressions begin with the implementation of traditional gender roles (Francis & Reygan, 2016). Within society, gender usually begins with the identification of biological sex. Sex assigned at birth is defined as a person being born as male, female or intersex based on the appearance of genital organs at birth, whereas gender identity is a person's sense of identifying as male, female, both, or neither, or another gender.

Society, however, commonly defines gender within the binaries of masculinity for males, and femininity for females (Beasley, 2005). This classification based on gender, and the equation of gender and sex, is criticised, as it presents a very narrow view on gender.

Judith Butler has famously offered a critique of this narrow definition, and argues that gender should be understood, rather, as a repetition of certain acts over a period of time (Butler, 1990). These acts are passed down from one generation to the next. Gender can be expressed free of binaries (Butler, 1990); however, within society, pre-existing 'traditional gender roles' legitimise gender binaries, reinforcing beliefs that men are supposed to be strong, dominant and unemotional; and women emotional and submissive. Early microaggression accounts begin when younger children express their gender differently to what society dictates (Eliot, 2009; Francis, 2012, 2017). For example, a young boy who enjoys toys that are usually reserved for young girls will be assumed to be gay and discriminated against. In this way, gender expression becomes linked to sexual orientation, before an individual even decides who they are attracted to romantically.

These sexual orientation microaggressions have been summarised by Sue (2010) and Nadal, Rivera, and Corpus (2010) into a taxonomy which allows us to categorise sexual orientation microaggressions. Some of the categories are quite similar. The first category, 'use of heterosexist or transphobic terminology' makes reference to utterances that demean LGBTQ+ people. The second category, 'endorsement of heteronormative or gender normative culture and behaviours' signifies the pressure that LGBTQ+ people face to behave in ways that endorse cisgenderism. 'Assumption of sexual pathology/abnormality' refers to the portrayal of LGBTQ+ people as being sexually deviant. The category 'denial of reality of heterosexism or transphobia' looks at how people who commit sexual orientation microaggressions may not be aware of the bias associated with their comments. 'Sinfulness' and 'assumption of abnormality' are two other themes which highlight that identifying as LGBTQ+ is associated with committing a sin, and is also seen as being unnatural. Finally, the last two categories of 'denial of heterosexism' and 'endorsement of heteronormativity' involves people that deny LGBTQ+ bias, and those who place an over-importance on heteronormative attitudes and behaviours. An additional category of the taxonomy presented by Nadal et al. (2010) is the category of 'exoticisation', where LGBTQ+ people are objectified. This may be linked to Sue's (2010) theme of 'over-sexualisation', where LGBTQ+ people are identified as being overly sexual beings by heterosexual people. Another theme signalled by Nadal et al. (2010) is that of the 'assumption of universal LGBT experience', where LGBTQ+ people are assumed to all experience their sexual orientation in the same way. Some of these themes will be practically illustrated with excerpts from research studies and e-zine articles.

## Types of Microaggresions and Outcomes of Microaggressions

There are characteristically three types of microaggressions: microassaults, microinsults and microinvalidations (Nadal et al., 2011; Sue et al., 2007). Microassaults occur at interpersonal and environmental levels, and they may be seen to be similar to overt discrimination. They are direct actions that are aimed at demeaning recipients of these microaggressions. They can also be overt acts of non-acceptance, such as a gay man being refused service at a restaurant or signs that are anti-LGBTQ+. The use of derogatory words against South African Indian LGBTQ+ people is identified in some studies. In studies by Dayal (2021) and Nair (2020), the following was revealed by participants:

> They would use words like 'moffie' you know these types of...
> Basically it reflected that the greater part of society made fun of.
> They found gay people to be um a part of society that we
> discourage, that we make fun of, that they're a point of humour
> [nods head]. And that's on the outside of things. At the inside of it,
> gay people weren't [shakes head] accepted or encouraged to be gay
> or encouraged to be themselves or be true to themselves. It was
> very very [sniffs] strongly established and maintained that it's not
> acceptable, and there's no place for people like that.
>
> (Dayal, 2021, p. 60)

> I couldn't really understand this, but there was this attached level
> of shame and guilt from that point to why am I feeling this? And
> attempting to make sense of it because words like 'moffie' and
> 'faggot' were those words that the boys all around me would
> always use ... that if you are not a boy, that's liking girls then
> you are a 'moffie'. If you are a boy taking part in a speech contest
> or in plays in school, then you are a 'moffie' – that was assigned to
> me from primary school.
>
> (Nair, 2020, p. 54)

'Moffie' is a derogatory word that is used to describe men who are seen as effeminate (Malan & Johaardien, 2010). Effeminacy is tied to 'individuals [who] appear to fall short of a more aggressive, masculine ideal' (Holmes & Meyerhoff, 2003, p. 406). These effeminate men are seen to oppose traditional gender roles and are often discriminated against. It was discovered that the word is frequently used in South Africa school settings when younger boys discriminate against their peers (Cilliers, 2017; Msibi, 2011).

'Faggot' is another word used to make derogatory reference to gay men. In an incident of cyber bullying, Naufal Khan (2018), the publisher of Indian Spice e-zine, was told that he is 'A faggot with a mouth' (Khan, 2018). The perpetrator, with the knowledge that Naufal Khan is an openly gay man, called him a 'faggot' in response to an article that he had written. What is alarming is that there is an insinuation that gay men are supposed to be invisible, and should not 'have a mouth'. This further reflects the discrimination faced by gay men and the silence that they suffer within the South African Indian community.

Another type of microaggressions are microinvalidations. These types of microaggressions are typically more difficult to categorise as they are verbal or non-verbal messages that are usually subconscious or subtle in nature (Nadal et al., 2011). Microinvalidations negate the experiences of LGBTQ+ people, and they are deeply rooted in societal biases and social norms. An example of microinvalidations are instances when gay men are told that what they are going through is a phase or when the difficulties of a gay person are not spoken about by family members, and instead are simply ignored. In an article by Igual (2018), a South African movie about members of the South African Indian community is reviewed. In this review, discrimination against gay men is noted, where the uncle of one of the gay characters gives the gay man heterosexual porn in an attempt to assist him in becoming 'straight'. Igual writes: 'He [uncle] also hands him [gay character] a package of heterosexual porn claiming that watching it will turn a gay person straight' (Igual, 2018). The direct link to porn is also a micro-aggression on a second level linked to the over-sexualisation of gay men, where gay men are seen to have an unnatural interest in sex and sexual practices (Sue, 2010).

In an online blog on the experience of coming out by a South African media personality of Indian descent (Vagar, 2020), it is shared that due to strong link-ages to family honour in the South African Indian community, often talks around sexuality are concealed. He reveals:

> Hardwired into the Indian value-system, for example is a social or cultural code known as 'izzat', which can be translated to refer to everything from family honour, reputation and prestige to an individual's personal dignity. Similar to the concept of 'saving face' that is core to a lot of Asian cultures, the notion of izzat sounds like a pretty noble and decorous aspiration on paper, but it has a decidedly dark downside. As an unintended consequence, it also engenders a culture of 'don't ask, don't tell' behaviour that results in people concealing, suppressing or obfuscating the truth – or worse yet, simply denying its existence. As a result, important conversations are seldom had or ever brought up, difficult situations and pressing issues are left unaddressed and therefore, unresolved – and inconvenient truths and problems are just wished away or swept under the rug.
>
> (Vagar, 2020)

Another participant in Nair's (2020) study expressed that during the 'coming out' experience, there was a large amount of avoidance and secrecy surrounding talk around sexuality.

> Big sense of avoidance. Indians don't talk about things. It's swept
> under the carpet and bubbles up and bites …Very toxic, and as
> well it's a big thing they have to adjust to, and every other
> emotional response following that to any emotional issues is
> inevitably informed by that toxicity of not addressing the
> problem at hand … So, it's just like, Indian families in general
> are very invasive and there's no boundaries and I have to
> accommodate that.
>
> (Nair, 2020, p. 67)

A South African Indian gay man in the study by Dayal (2021) also revealed
that his identity as a gay man was negated and denied. During his coming out
experience, his mother 'assumed sexual pathology and abnormality' (Sue, 2010)
and made reference to him seeking a cure to become 'normal'.

> I can remember about my mum is that when I came out to her, she
> was quite compassionate. Almost too compassionate to the point
> of saying, 'Don't worry, we'll take you for healing and find a cure
> for you. We'll make sure you get better'. Kind of you know
> treating me as somebody that's unwell or mentally infirm.
>
> (Dayal, 2021, p. 66)

All these experiences reveal a deeply rooted rejection of LGBTQ+ identities,
where LGBTQ+ people are seen to not receive the necessary support from their
friends, family and community. Their lived realities of identifying as LGBTQ+
and the challenges that arise due to this are not acknowledged. Furthermore, what
they experience when speaking about their experiences makes them feel worse and
discriminated against.

Microinsults are the final type of microaggressions. They include 'statements
or actions that indirectly belittle a person and are often unconscious and unintentional' (Nadal, 2008, p. 22). Microinsults contain 'communications that
convey stereotypes, rudeness and insensitivity and that demean a person's sexual
orientation' (Sue, 2010, p. 31). These are reflected in the following extracts from
Dayal's (2021) study where a gay man is subjected to being given gifts meant for a
woman at a party. And there are also references made at his workplace to him
owning a certain type of car, which is often stereotyped as being a car owned by
gay men:

> At a Christmas party, we had this secret Santa theme, where we
> drew people's names and we didn't know who was going to buy us
> a gift. And the gift I received turned out to be a pair of bras. Which
> was very embarrassing. Because we had to open our gifts in front
> of everybody, and they laughed.
>
> (Dayal, 2021, p. 87)

The other thing was my manager made a comment saying [participant] is a [type of hybrid car] kind of a guy. I knew what he was trying to insinuate. Because it's mostly gay people that drive cars like that.

(Dayal, 2021, p. 87)

These messages display unconscious or possibly unintentional ways in which people commit microaggressions against gay men. These messages may be seen as harmless by the perpetrators of microaggressions but they cause harm and unsettling feelings to those who are recipients of these microaggressions.

Another microinsult is found in the online article by Igual (2018), where he comments on a discriminatory scene in a South African movie relating to a South African Indian community. Within the movie, a dominant male character makes hand gestures relating to sex between two men. His gesture suggests:

Heterosexual sex is compared to a train going into a tunnel while gay sex is depicted as unnatural and compared to a train approaching another train, which will lead to a crash.

(Igual, 2018)

Sex between two men is therefore portrayed as unnatural and is poked fun at. This may be seen as an act of comic relief by the perpetrator; however, the person at the receiving end of the microaggression does not receive it in the same way.

After outlining the different types of microaggressions, what becomes evident is that only one of them, microassaults, is seen as an overt form of micro-aggression, whereas microinvalidations and microinsults are unconscious acts of discrimination that negatively impact the recipients of microaggressions. Unconscious acts are often difficult to identify and to comment on, as they are experienced very differently by different recipients based on their subjective backgrounds. Microaggressions lead to minority stress experiences: LGBTQ+ people experience debilitating responses to distressing events, which may cause them great discomfort in their interpersonal and work lives (Dayal, 2021).

## Conclusion

This chapter provides greater insight into the lives of LGBTQ+ people of Indian descent who reside in South Africa. The discrimination experienced by these LGBTQ+ people is mostly covert in nature, and these acts of discrimination are known as microaggressions. Microaggression theory and the practical catego-risation of the types of microaggressions were carefully unpacked in this chapter. These microaggressions create unpleasant environments and interactions for LGBTQ+ people and measures need to be instated to protect LGBTQ+ people against these discriminatory acts. Though 'violence' is often seen as something physical and overt – and is both constitutionally illegal and actively persecuted in South Africa – microaggressions, as I've shown here, constitute forms of sexual and gendered violence that have the potential to harm their recipients and should therefore not be overlooked in any academic, legal, therapeutic or cultural context.

## References

Akoob, R. (2018, May 18). Toxic masculinity in the South African Indian community. *Daily Maverick*. Retrieved from https://www.dailymaverick.co.za/opinionista/ 2018-05-18-toxic-masculinity-in-the-south-african-indian-community/

Beasley, C. (2005). *Gender and sexuality: Critical theories, critical thinkers.* Thousand Oaks, CA: Sage.

Bhana, D. (2012). Understanding and addressing homophobia in schools: A view from teachers. *South African Journal of Education, 32*(3), 307–318. doi:10.15700/ saje.v32n3a659

Bhugra, D. (1997a). Experiences of being a gay man in urban India: A descriptive study. *Sexual & Marital Therapy, 12*(4), 371–375. doi:10.1080/02674659708408180

Bhugra, D. (1997b). Coming out by South Asian gay men in the United Kingdom. *Archives of Sexual Behavior, 26*(5), 547–557. doi:10.1023/A:1024512023379

Bonthuys, E., & Erlank, N. (2012). Modes of (in)tolerance: South African Muslims and same sex relationships. *Culture, Health and Sexuality, 14*(3), 269–282. doi:10. 1080/13691058.2011.621450

Butler, J. (1990). *Gender trouble: Feminism and the subversion of identity.* London: Routledge.

Cilliers, C. P. (2017). Being a moffie with toxic parents – An autoethnography of bullying and coming out. *South African Review of Sociology, 48*(1), 4–18. doi:10. 1080/21528586.2016.1204246

Dave, P. (2011). *Experiences of Indian gay and lesbian individuals.* Honours thesis, University of Cape Town, Cape Town, South Africa. Retrieved from http://www. psychology.uct.ac.za/sites/default/files/image_tool/images/117/Punam.Dave.pdf

Davis, R. (2012, October 9). Joburg pride: A tale of two cities. *Daily Maverick*. Retrieved from http://www.dailymaverick.co.za

Dayal, D. N. (2021). *Microaggressions against South African gay Indian men.* Master's thesis, University of Johannesburg, Johannesburg, South Africa. Retrieved from https://ujcontent.uj.ac.za/vital/%20access/manager/Repository/uj:43235?view= null&f0=sm_creator%3A%22Dayal%2C+Deepesh+Nirmaldas%22&sort=sort_ ss_title%2F

Eliot, L. (2009). *Pink brain, blue brain: How small differences grow into troublesome gaps and what we can do about it.* Boston, MA: Houghton Mifflin Harcourt.

Francis, D. (2012). Teacher positioning on the teaching of sexual diversity in South African schools. *Culture, Health and Sexuality, 14*(6), 597–611. doi:10.1080/ 13691058.2012.674558

Francis, D. A. (2017). Homophobia and sexuality diversity in South African schools: A review. *Journal of LGBT Youth, 14*(4), 359–379. doi:10.1080/19361653.2017. 1326868

Francis, D., & Reygan, F. (2016). Let's see if it won't go away by itself: LGBT microaggressions among teachers in South Africa. *Education As Change, 20*(3), 180–201. doi:10.17159/1947-9417/2016/1124

Holmes, J., & Meyerhoff, M. (2003). *The handbook of language and gender.* Oxford: Blackwell.

Igual, R. (2018, July 31). Local film Broken Promises accused of insulting gay community. *Mamba Online.* Retrieved from http://www.mambaonline.com/2018-/07/ 31/local-film-broken-promises-4-ever-accused-of-insulting-gay-community/

Jagmohan, K. (2017, November 26). Mother's heartache after gay son's death. IOL. Retrieved from https://www.iol.co.za/sunday-tribune/news/mothers-heartache-after-gay-sons-death-12156567

Jain, R. (2015, June 1). Parents use corrective rape to straighten gays. *Times of India.* Retrieved from http://timesofindia.indiatimes.com/lifestyle/relationships/parenting/ Parents-use-corrective-rape-to-straighten-gays/articleshow/47489949.cms

Jaspal, R. (2012). 'I never faced up to being gay': Sexual, religious and ethnic identities among British South Asian gay men. *Culture, Health and Sexuality, 14*(7), 767–780. doi:10.1080/13691058.2012.693626

Jaspal, R. (2014). Arranged marriage, identity, and well-being among British Asian gay men. *Journal of GLBT Family Studies, 10*(5), 425–448. doi:10.1080/1550428X. 2013.846105

Kar, A., Mukherjee, S., Ventriglio, A., & Bhugra, D. (2018). Attitude of Indian medical students towards homosexuality. *East Asian Archives of Psychiatry, 28*(2), 59–63. doi:10.12809/eaap181728

Kaur, P. (2017). Gender, sexuality and (be) longing: The representation of queer (LGBT) in Hindi cinema. *Amity Journal of Media and Communication Studies, 7*(1), 22–30. Retrieved from https://ajmcs.blogspot.com/

Khan, N. (2017, August 14). What's it like being gay in the South African Indian community? *Indian Spice.* Retrieved from https://www.indianspice.co.za/2017-/07/ whats-it-like-being-gay-in-the-indian-community

Khan, N. (2018, September 12). Calling me a faggot is not ok. *Indian Spice.* Retrieved from https://www.indianspice.co.za/2018/03/calling-me-a-faggot-is-not-okay-says-naufal-khan/

Love Not Hate. (2016). Shocking new stats show that South Africans are becoming more homophobic. *Love Not Hate.* Retrieved from http://www.lovenothate.org.za/ 2016/06/30/shocking-new-stats-show-that-south-africans-arebecoming-more-homophobic/

Mahomed, F., & Trangoš, G. (2016). An exploration of public attitudes toward LGBTI rights in the Gauteng city-region of South Africa. *Journal of Homosexuality, 63*(10), 1400–1421. doi:10.1080/00918369.2016.1157999

Malan, R., & Johaardien, A. (Eds.). (2010). *Yes, I Am!* Cape Town: Junkets.

Marais, A., Nel, J. A., & Govender, R. (2022). Emotional consequences of hate incidents: Experiences of a South African cohort. *South African Journal of Psychology, 52*(1), 122–134. doi:10.1177/0081246320985343

McKeown, E., Nelson, S., Anderson, J., Low, N., & Elford, J. (2010). Disclosure, discrimination and desire: Experiences of black and South Asian gay men in Britain. *Culture, Health and Sexuality, 12*(7), 843–856. doi:10.1080/13691058.2010. 499963

Mimiaga, M., Biello, K., Sivasubramanian, M., Mayer, K., Anand, V., & Safren, S. (2013). Psychosocial risk factors for HIV sexual risk among Indian men who have sex with men. *AIDS Care, 25*(9), 1109–1113. doi:10.1080/09540121.2012.749340

Moonsammy, D. (2009). *What will people say? Three stories of Indian women loving women in Jozi*. Master's thesis, University of the Witwatersrand, Johannesburg, South Africa. Retrieved from http://wiredspace.wits.ac.za/handle/10539/45/browse? value=Moonsammy%2C+Davina&type=author

Msibi, T. (2011). The lies we have been told: On (homo) sexuality in Africa. *Africa Today, 58*(1), 54–77. doi:10.1353/at.2011.0030

Nadal, K. L. (2008). Preventing racial, ethnic, gender, sexual minority, disability, and religious microaggressions: Recommendations for promoting positive mental health. *Prevention in Counseling Psychology: Theory, Research, Practice and Training, 2*(1), 22–27.

Nadal, K. L. (2013). *That's so gay! microaggressions and the lesbian, gay, bisexual, and transgender community*. Washington, DC: American Psychological Association.

Nadal, K. L., Issa, M., Leon, J., Meterko, V., Wideman, M., & Wong, Y. (2011). Sexual orientation microaggressions: "Death by a thousand cuts" for lesbian, gay and bisexual youth. *Journal of LGBT Youth, 8*(3), 1–26. doi:10.1080/19361653.2011.584204

Nadal, K. L., Rivera, D., & Corpus, M. (2010). Sexual orientation and transgender microaggressions in everyday life: Experiences of lesbians, gays, bisexuals, and transgender individuals. In D. W. Sue (Ed.), *Microaggressions and marginality: Manifestation, dynamics and impact* (pp. 217–240). New York, NY: Wiley.

Nair, V. (2020). *Negotiating the coming out process within the South African Indian community*. Master's thesis, University of the Witwatersrand, Johannesburg, South Africa. Retrieved from https://wiredspace.wits.ac.za/handle/10539/30590

OUT. (2016). *Hate crimes against lesbian, gay, bisexual and transgender (LGBT) people in South Africa*. Retrieved from https://out.org.za/index.php/library/reports

Pierce, C., Carew, J., Pierce-Gonzalez, D., & Willis, D. (1978). An experiment in racism: TV commercials. In C. Pierce (Ed.), *Television and education* (pp. 62–88). Beverly Hills, CA: Sage.

Pillay, S. (2017, September 13). Exhibition brings to light LGBT Indians in SA. *Post*. Retrieved from https://www.pressreader.com/south-africa/post-southafrica/20170913/28205050 7228253

Sharma, A. J., & Subramanyam, M. A. (2020). Psychological wellbeing of middle-aged and older queer men in India: A mixed-methods approach. *PLoS One, 15*(3), e0229893. doi:10.1371/journal.pone.0229893

Soeker, S., Bonn, G. L., de Vos, Z., Gobhozi, T., Pape, C., & Ribaudo, S. (2015). Not straight forward for gays: A look at the lived experiences of gay men, living in cape town, with regard to their worker roles. *Work, 51*(2), 175–186. doi:10.3233/WOR-141848

Statistics South Africa. (2020). *Mid-year population estimates*. Retrieved from https://www.statssa.gov.za/publications/P0302/P03022019.pdf

Sue, D. W. (2010). *Microaggressions in everyday life: Race, gender, and sexual orientation*. Hoboken, NJ: Wiley.

Sue, D. W., Capodilupo, C. M., Torino, G. C., Bucceri, J. M., Holder, A. M. B., Nadal, K. L., & Esquilin, M. (2007). Racial microaggressions in everyday life: Implications for clinical practice. *American Psychologist, 62*(4), 271–286. doi:10.1037/0003-066X.62.4.271

Sutherland, C., Roberts, B., Gabriel, N., Struwig, J., & Gordon, S. (2016). Progressive prudes: A survey of attitudes towards homosexuality & gender non-conformity in

South Africa. Retrieved from http://ecommons.hsrc.ac.za/handle/20.500.11910/10161

Thoreson, R. (2008). Somewhere over the rainbow nation: Gay, lesbian and bisexual activism in South Africa. *Journal of Southern African Studies, 34*(3), 679–697. doi: 10.1080/03057070802259969

Vagar, I. (2020). Coming out #2: The calling. An examined life. Retrieved from https://www.anexaminedlife.co.za/coming-out-2-the-calling/

# Gender-Based Violence and the Law

# Section II: Gender-Based Violence and the Law

*Gavan Patrick Gray, Nidhi Shrivastava*
*and Deepesh Nirmaldas Dayal*

## Abstract

This chapter is a transcript of an open-ended discussion that occurred
between the authors when they met to discuss the subject matter of the
second section of the book, which focuses on the effectiveness of legal
responses to gendered violence. As with the previous introductory dialogue,
the discussion takes place after preliminary drafts had been completed, and
the authors share their thoughts on the subjects they will each discuss in
more detail in the following chapters. These include the impact of cultural
and gender bias within the Indian legal system, the insufficient impact of
long-overdue reforms in Japan's sexual violence laws and the weaknesses
that exist in constitutional protections offered to LGBTQ+ people in South
Africa.

*Keywords*: Gender violence; law; legal reform; Japan; India; South Africa

**Gray:** In the World Economic Forum's Global Gender Gap rankings for 2020,
South Africa does quite well in 17th place. India fares far worse at 112th.
However, Japan sits at 120 and there is little reason, on paper, for this to be the
case. I mentioned previously that the United States had a strong role in adding
women's rights to the post-war constitution and this set the framework for a
system where women, in theory, have considerable room for advancement within
social institutions. In practice, the outcomes are far different and while some of
the reasons for this can be explained by the male dominance of these institutions,

Gender Violence, the Law, and Society, 69–77

doi:10.1108/978-1-80117-127-420221006

an entrenched 'old boys club', some of it is down to the gender roles that still impact the way in which women are treated in the workplace.

These factors definitely have an impact on the way the law is interpreted and applied, but these laws themselves are generally a product of an even more old-fashioned worldview from decades and generations in the past. While things today are certainly not perfect, they are an improvement on the attitudes that existed in the time of the current generation's great-grandparents. Yet, many laws which have a strong impact on women's lives date from this period. When it comes to South Africa and India, I am sure there are similar problems in the present day, but in the case of legal standards are the laws more modern, in the sense that they were either drafted recently or are subject to regular revision or update, or are they more akin to Japan, where in 2017 the laws on sexual violence received their first significant revision in 100 years?

**Shrivastava:** That's a good question, Gavan. Indian rape laws are rooted in colonial laws dated back to the time when India was colonised for 200 years. The treatment of rape victim-survivor during court trials, where the defence lawyers prod through a woman's sexual history, are practices that date back to this period. In fact, to this day, a hundred-year-old book by Jaising Modi on jurisprudence and rape called *Medical Jurisprudence and Technology* is considered a law bible in India. During the research for the coming chapter, I looked it up and it was still in print in India. Students were praising the work, without realising that it is problematic in terms of the practices the author encourages. For example, Modi problematically assumes that if a woman is a virgin, she is of a 'good character'. Thus, it is more likely that her rape happened, and her testimony can be trusted. Elizabeth Kolsky mentions in her research the case of *King vs. Patha Kala* from the early twentieth century, where a young woman named Viru was raped by someone from a lower caste. Feeling shameful, Viru attempted to commit suicide by jumping into the well. The judge in this case, punished Patha Kala by sentencing him to four years of imprisonment. Kolsky observes that although Viru was not on trial, the trial was about her because her non-consent, her appearance and caste, and her sexual history took centre stage. Because she fought back and later tried to 'save her honour' by attempting to kill herself, she became a model for defining a 'good' rape victim. Years later, in 1972, during the Mathura rape case – Mathura had been raped by two policemen – even the Indian Supreme Court refused to believe her because they doubted her character.

**Gray:** This goes back to the treatment of women in the sex industry I explored in my first chapter. So much apathy, and failure to provide protection or support, is excused based upon attacks on the character or moral quality of the women involved.

**Shrivastava:** Exactly. Of course, there is pressure for change and feminist organisations and lawyers have advocated for the courts to give more credence to the testimony of rape survivors. Yet, changes that occurred in 1983 were dismissed by many of these groups as purely symbolic. After an infamous gang-rape case in Delhi in 2012, there was another wave of pressure from scholars and this finally led to the 2013 amendments of rape laws. Some of the noticeable changes were that the legal term for 'rape' changed to 'sexual assault' to include different types of sexual offences including penetration by objects, as happened during the 2012 rape case. The government also established a Nirbaya fund to help empower and provide resources to rape victim-survivors. Even so, sexist, patriarchal and often misogynistic attitudes towards rape victim-survivors are still quite widespread.

**Gray:** When it comes to legal punishments, the Japanese system can veer from excessively harsh to overly lenient without any seeming common standards as to what determines the severity. In actuality, the set punishments are clearly defined by fairly rigid laws that leave quite wide ranges for possible sentences. Murder, for example can result in sentences of from 5 to 20 years, or in extreme cases, the death penalty. This leaves a lot of leeway for judicial discretion, but in practice, the actual punishment will be strongly affected by precedents that take into account things like remorse, motive, apologies, settlement payments, the offender's age and character etc. In the same way, the treatment of violent sexual crime is often handled in a formal, by-rote manner that focuses on precedent and established standards rather than the specifics of each individual case and the impact the events have on the actual people involved.

The Japanese courts, in my view, have become, or perhaps always were, a very cold, bureaucratic system in which true justice takes a back seat to 'proper procedure'. One unfortunate outcome of this is that the system as it is currently applied often allows offenders to evade formal punishment by reaching out-of-court settlements with victims. It's a system that I feel, in the case of crimes of sexual violence, does too little to generate true justice for the victim, adequately punish offenders, or maintain the safety of the general public. It is improving but, at present, if I were to hear of an incident of sexual violence, I would not hold high hopes that the offender, even after being identified, would be properly punished by Japanese courts. Do you think that standards or procedures are significantly different in either South Africa or India? In other words, do you think that offenders in sex crimes, once they have been identified by the police or court, are more likely than not to receive a custodial sentence?

**Dayal:** If I can address that Gavan, there is quite a disparity in South Africa between what the legal system enshrines versus what the lived realities of citizens are. Because of my research interest, I will use an example that focuses on the experience of LGBTQ+ groups. In 1994, South Africans from all racial groups helped give birth to a new democracy that was meant to allow freedom, equality, social justice and opportunities for all. Due to this, South Africa has often been presented as a regional model for hope, social rebirth and democracy. However, today, more than two decades post-democracy, a paradox exists where, despite numerous policies and legislation guaranteeing the preservation of human rights, there are still significant levels of crime and human rights violations.

For example, the new South African Constitution marked it as one of the first countries in the world to prohibit discrimination based on gender identity and sexual orientation. There are also provisions for same-sex partners to marry, adopt and be legally recognised in deceased estates. Yet, as was discussed in the first section of this book, even when things seem to be moving in a progressive direction, deep flaws can remain and LGBTQ+ individuals in South Africa still experience high rates of overt and covert violence. They can be said to straddle two worlds, one with intricate legal protections and another of continuing, often hidden, persecution. Part of the persistence of this problem can be attributed to the 'un-African' label that is assigned to LGBTQ+ individuals and the dominant themes of conservative community values, heteronormativity, heterosexism and patriarchy in South African societies. Gavan, I am wondering what the repercussions of sexual violence in Japan are?

**Gray:** Japan also has a somewhat deserved reputation for entrenched sexism, which many write off as misogyny. In my personal experience, this is not true at the broader level. There are certainly many misogynists and some of them rise to high positions where their public gaffs can create an impression that Japan's political system is still completely unconcerned with the welfare of women. In practice though, I find that most Japanese men, whether young or old, have the basic level of concern for the welfare of all social groups that you would expect from a society that places such strong emphasis on egalitarianism and social harmony.

The problem, from my perspective, is that very few have a strong knowledge of the actual problems which women face, both in terms of their awareness of the extent of the problems that exist and their understanding of the way that these problems affect women. For example, in regard to sexual violence, many may think that rape is terrible but they might consider it as not being very common, considerably underestimating its rate of occurrence. Then, in terms of impact, they may view it as a crime of violence and consider that arrest and punishment of perpetrators is sufficient, believing the fact that Japan has strong laws against such offences will be enough to resolve the problem. Their lack of awareness of the flaws in the system, or the way in which the system itself can harm victims, does not mean they do not care; many Japanese men, I would say the great majority, find sexual violence against women utterly abhorrent but they are frequently lacking awareness of the scope, severity and impact of the problem.

What this means is that there is a fundamental problem in terms of understanding and education and that public attitudes to such issues have not yet caught up with what experts, activists and the victims themselves know about the subject. I'm curious whether general awareness levels and education about sexual violence and its impact on victims are widespread in Indian and South African institutions, especially among the police and courts, and also in systems like hospitals.

**Shrivastava:** Yes, there is definitely a need for deep, structural change in the Indian law enforcement system. In fact, rape survivor-victims are often hesitant to file First Information Reports (FIRs) because they are discouraged by the police officers themselves. The police in India are often viewed as corrupt and bureaucratic and as holding entrenched patriarchal and misogynistic attitudes. I mentioned the Mathura rape case earlier, and it was only the response to this that saw 'custodial rape' – in other words: sexual assault by police or jailers – as being a punishable crime, and this only happened in 1983. There are female police officers but even in popular culture, they are portrayed as unsupportive and corrupt.

**Gray:** Do you think there is room to improve this issue through greater training and awareness? Personally, I had initially thought that increasing the number of women involved directly in each element of the system was the way to go. However, when looking at the level of female representation in the police I was left wondering whether this is necessarily true. In Japan, only 10% of police officers are female and I thought this was terribly low, especially when you compare it with places like England and Wales where the level is over 30%. I was surprised to learn, though, that the level in the United States is only about 12% and, while this may be a problem, the United States still leads the field in many areas of responding to sexual violence.

One other factor that influenced my views is that there is sometimes a misconception that female victims of sexual violence will prefer to deal with female officers. In some cases, this is not true, and the victims prefer male officers who give them a greater sense of physical security. According to some experts, it is not the gender that is most important but rather the training the responders have received and, ideally, the use of non-police experts in forensic interviewing skills.

**Dayal:** Gavan, I think it is true that deeper reforms are required. As you said, the system itself can be very cold, impersonal and unsupportive. The objective of a criminal justice system is to ensure that criminal cases are processed speedily and that lawbreakers are handed appropriate punishments. But, in the case of South Africa, the criminal justice system has not been operating optimally. The Victims of Crime Surveys in South Africa for many years keeps revealing concerning statistics that show household satisfaction with the courts and the criminal justice system is constantly decreasing. Many households believe that the courts are too lenient on criminals when passing sentences, that court proceedings take far too long and the people who are at the receiving end of discrimination and violence suffer even more due to this. People lose trust in the legal system and this leads to a decease in crime reporting because people who are affected by crimes, who are often part of a marginalised group, feel that their reports will not be given the attention they deserve. Some members of society also fear that they may experience secondary victimisation if they report crimes.

**Shrivastava:** I think, Gavan, you make a great point about if training and education can change/help with the issue of gender-based violence. However, while I do think they are great starting points for India, I believe that it will take re-learning of certain cultural attitudes and letting go of problematic ideologies such as favouring boys over girls, the reduction in the statistics of female infanticide and also acceptance of women's education and freedom to travel in public space that will reduce gender-based violence in India. India as a country is multi-layered, multi-religious and also shaped by the class and caste issues that shape it. Therefore, I think the solution to reduce gender-based violence will have to come from different avenues working together to change cultural attitudes in the country.

In the film, *Damini*, which I explore in this chapter, for example, the main character witnesses and reports the gang rape of a family servant by some of her relatives. She ends up having to fight against not just the perpetrators but corrupt police officers, biased lawyers and an uncaring legal system. Although she is ultimately successful, we kind of see that it is the main character who has been leading this fight, not the victim herself, who is actually murdered and discarded, both physically and metaphorically, halfway through the movie. In one way this highlights a troubling fact that often the activists and reform-minded lawyers have more influence than the actual victims of these crimes. Is this something you see in either Japan or South Africa?

**Gray:** Well, in Japan most of the women who work in the sex industry tend to come from economically fragile groups. They are from small rural towns with few economic opportunities, women who left the education system early, single mothers and so on. So, it's not so much an issue of social class, as you can be relatively high class in Japan without having a lot of money, but of economic stability, or rather, of the lack thereof. So, in terms of the sex industry, economic class certainly leaves these women vulnerable to exploitation. In other areas, though, such as crimes of sexual assault, those who are affected can come from a much wider segment of society and it is not so much that the system disenfranchises the poor, as it is the way it privileges the wealthy and allows them to pervert justice. I think this is a common problem internationally, where higher economic classes have a greater variety of ways to exploit the weaknesses of the system and often at an individual level it is impossible to generate change. You need either a larger activist organisation or major media coverage to create the required pressure.

**Shrivastava:** Yes, they are meant to be support systems for all people but often the poor have limited access to them. This is represented in movies like *Damini* where victims of rape, where they are poor, are often unable to get justice when the perpetrators come from a higher class. So, there is a question too, of whether the same legal support exists for victims who are poor, middle and upper class and whether the systems have a classist element wherein victims of different types receive very different treatments.

**Dayal:** I feel that there are dynamics of class and economic status in my study on South African Indian LGBTQ+ people. Sometimes society assumes that because people are from a population group that is seen to be economically active, that they are immune to gender identity and sexual orientation discrimination. However, this is not the case. As per my research findings, LGBTQ+ people of Indian descent in South Africa experience gender identity and sexual orientation discrimination regardless of their economic backgrounds. However, in South Africa, many studies have confirmed that people who are in lower-income groups may experience higher levels of crimes, regardless of race.

**Shrivastava:** One other aspect of this is the specific economic reality of women as a social group. In India, for example, women are becoming much more independent, more involved in business, more career-oriented and are leaving their family homes and occupying public spaces. This empowerment is actually doing the opposite for men because they are starting to feel intimidated by such women. We sometimes forget how much masculinity is tied to the economy and personal economic performance. Even to the extent that in some cultures women are still seen as an economic burden because they are not expected to become financially independent. So there is an issue where middle-class women are finding new opportunities due to these opening doors but for women from working-class or rural backgrounds, often the social mobility is significantly less open and so social class can be a huge factor in the problems we see. I'm assuming that something similar might exist in Japan?

**Gray:** I think that's right. The voices that are heard are those that come from the middle class, the professors, the politicians, the media personalities, and while they might be transmitting the stories of women from lower economic classes, those women still lack the power to advocate for their own stories.

**Dayal:** Yes, I see that too in communities where, due to a lack of money, people who experience discrimination feel silenced. Their lack of financial resources prevents them from entering a different social class where they would possibly have more open expression. Without economic independence, some people at the receiving end of discrimination and violence feel trapped in a community that can be very threatening to them and which might react in a very unsupportive or even negative way.

**Shrivastava:** It also works the other way, as Gavan mentioned. While poverty can restrict some people's access to support systems, wealth can give other people unfair access to, or the ability to buy, the justice system. But this not only happens in negative ways. There are stories like in *Damini*, where the main character's wealth gives her the privilege to highlight an injustice that the victim's poverty prevented her from addressing.

**Dayal:** That resonates completely with some beliefs in South Africa, in that a lot of the activist organisations are found in more middle to upper-class communities, and people from the low-income communities come to these people for representation. As a result, you have a class dynamic where people feel that their story will only be taken seriously if it is told by someone who is in a position of authority. There are also research studies that mention that events, such as Pride, that create visibility for LGBTQ+ people and their experiences often take place in areas that are not inclusive of people from all social groups.

**Gray:** When I was doing research in Thailand, it was often exactly that situation, where people from very, very poor communities had no way of interacting with the courts or with other agencies, except through these activist-intermediaries who were almost always middle class. In Japan, it is a little different though, as it is largely a middle-class society. There is poverty, of course, but it is far less clearly delineated. Wealth and poverty are often separate from superficial distinctions of high and low class so that someone who looks like they might be from a wealthy family might be living on the borderline of serious poverty, while someone who appears poor might have significant cash hidden away. When it comes to the justice system, it would definitely be money rather than social class which has the stronger influence. Victims will frequently be pressured to accept out of court settlements as the best way to resolve cases of sexual violence and one result is that the richer you are, the easier it is to escape more significant punishments by utilising your wealth.

**Shrivastava:** Yes, I think I can relate to that, as in my research I came across many scenarios where rich criminals would be able to buy off the victims. But I wonder whether it is money or gender norms that have the bigger influence because I see very often that courts have certain expectations of women in these cases, where if they did not act in a proper manner they are automatically treated more like they encouraged the crime. There was one case where a lawyer was speaking to a victim of assault and he was trying to say that because she had a painting in her room which showed a semi-nude woman who had her hands bound – just because of the presence of this painting – the victim-survivor had been playing the role of the seductress and that she, rather than the man who had attacked her, was the immoral one. So if you're not prim and proper and quiet and meek then you are not the right kind of woman. But of course, if you are quiet and meek you will not make a fuss about the crime. And yet, at the same time, they expect women to fight back, and if they do not have marks on their body to show they resisted, then this is also used against them.

**Gray:** You mentioned this earlier and I was thinking how similar that is to Japan where, if there's no evidence that you've actually been fighting, then, it's suggestive of you being complicit to whatever happened. This issue has been highlighted by a few recent cases where people took advantage of positions of authority to abuse girls who were too frightened or traumatised to resist physically in such a manner.

**Shrivastava:** Sometimes it feels like the courts have a particular image of what an 'acceptable' victim is and what an 'unacceptable' victim is and, regardless of the crime, if you do not fit into the right bracket you will have a harder time achieving justice.

**Gray:** And, of course, we have to be careful with the terms we use. Typically when referring to women who suffered sexual crimes we will call them 'survivors', but it gets a little difficult when you are talking about the legal system, which still refers to perpetrators and victims. I just want to point out that if we talk about victims of crime it is not meant in any way other than to refer to the legal designations.

**Shrivastava:** In my research, I use Robin E. Field's term 'victim-survivors' to describe the people who have encountered rape and gender-based violence. The term victim-survivors, in a nutshell, means that we cannot define an individual's traumatic experience in one manner. Rather, it is up to them to decide whether they want to be addressed as a victim (as someone whose trauma needs to be acknowledged and supported) or as a survivor (where they have come to terms with the traumatic experience). The term – victim-survivor – allows the individual to exist in a liminal or third space and lets them define their experience the way in which they want to address it, rather than letting society decide for them. It is so difficult to find the correct term to describe them. How do you think courts, lawyers and society should describe them? Often, labels can also take away power from the person experiencing the trauma. How are labels handled in South Africa and Japan?

**Dayal:** Words have great power when speaking about gender. Because gender is seen as being on a spectrum, some people feel as though you shouldn't use the term homosexual, as it polarises the sexuality of the people involved. Yet, whereas language in some areas is so progressive and constantly changing, legal terminology is much more rigid and slow to change. There are a lot of researchers writing about how the wrong labels can take power away from people, so perhaps that is something that needs to change in terms of the law.

**Gray:** I agree completely. I mentioned earlier the problem of the system being too cold and impersonal and here is one area where there is room for relatively easy and quick changes. Does there need to be a single catch-all term to refer to either 'survivors' or 'victims' or can we instead allow some flexibility and human interest to enter into things, leave room for those involved to reclaim their own agency and determine how they would like to be referred to in court proceedings?

**Dayal:** I think we may be moving in that direction but we are certainly not there yet. And I think we might expect attitudes to change much quicker than legal procedures. As Gavan mentioned, Japan only recently changed some sex crime laws and in many places, there are still such outdated systems in place. As long as awareness of the problems continues to increase, we are at least moving the right way.

# Chapter 4

# The Insidious Culture of Fear in Indian Courts

*Nidhi Shrivastava*

## Abstract

On 20 March 2020, the four adult convicts of the 2012 Delhi rape case were executed after a long debate regarding the punishment for their crime. The Delhi rape case, unlike others, was also given to the fast track court because of the worldwide outrage India received in its aftermath. Otherwise, most rape survivors rarely speak out and if they do, their lives are often endangered and threatened, depending on the severity of the case itself and the perpetrator's rank in the society. Through the analysis of Aniruddha Roy Chowdhury's, 2016 film *Pink*, and Ajay Bahl's film *Section 375* (2019), this chapter explores the different ways in which mainstream Hindi cinema deals with such questions, especially in its depictions of courts. Both these films foreground India's contemporary cultural systems of fear that silence the rape survivors. They also imply that in the court cases, unless the specific court case faces intense global publicity, as was the case of the Delhi gang rape, rape survivors will *never* want to speak out. Moreover, the rape survivors will also hesitate to file a First Information Report (FIR) – a document that records crimes by the police against their perpetrators – limiting any possibility for justice for them. The laws surrounding rape cases are obscure and complex and finding justice for a rape victim (unless it is on a global level) is not an easy venture in India. At the time of the #metoo movement, the rape laws in India are not designed in such a way to arguably encourage victim-survivors to *speak up*. Instead, if rape survivors do decide to confront their perpetrators, they not only face ostracisation from society but also the danger of losing loved ones and endanger their lives as well.

Gender Violence, the Law, and Society, 79–89

doi:10.1108/978-1-80117-127-420221007

*Keywords*: Rape; sexual assault; Indian court; Unnao gang rape; Hindi cinema; rape law

The 2019 Unnao gang rape paints a complex picture of the Indian justice system, police attitudes and enforcement (or lack thereof) of rape laws in the midst of the #MeToo movement in India. On 5 December 2019, a twenty-three-year-old woman was set on fire in the Unnao district in Uttar Pradesh (Sagar, 2019). She did not survive the heinous attack and succumbed to her injuries the next day (Kumar, 2019).

A year earlier, she had accused two men of raping her, had testified against them in a court in Rae Bareli, and had filed a case report against them. In 2018, she reported that both Shivam and his friend Shubham raped her again at gunpoint, which led her to file a report in Lalganj police station in Rae Barelli (Sagar, 2019). She struggled to get the attention of the police who did not take any action against the accused, such that she was compelled to reach out to the Police Superintendent, who also did not show any interest in pursuing the case further. It was not until March 2019, after she had filed a case report in the District Court, that the police recorded her first information report (FIR) against the two men she had accused of rape. Shivam was arrested and released two months later, in November 2019.

In the aftermath of the rape victim's untimely death, the political leadership of Uttar Pradesh claimed that there would be a fast-track court set up to deliver justice to the victim and her family (Siddiqui, Bhardwaj, & Phartiyal, 2019). However, the authors of *Reuters* note that the judicial system in India, especially for rape cases, involves 'lengthy trials' that 'delay convictions leaving poor, disillusioned victims with little money or patience to pursue the case' (Siddiqui et al., 2019). Moreover, they add that 'long trials result in bails to the accused who often intimidate victims and their witnesses, and try tampering with evidence' (Siddiqui et al., 2019).

This case makes visible that despite the recent amendments to the rape laws in 2013 – initiated in the aftermath of the 2012 Delhi rape case – the current system ultimately does *not* support the rape victim-survivor, rendering her helpless and re-traumatising her in the process. Since the colonial era, the rape laws in India have been shaped by fundamentals rooted in patriarchal attitudes. The resulting system scrutinises the rape victim-survivor if she decides to pursue the case in court to get justice for the violent crime that has been committed against her.

Through a chronological examination of films that were released between the 1980s and present times, in this chapter I explore not only how the Hindi film industry depicts rape victim-survivors during court trials and attempts to problematise the treatment of them in court but I also argue that such cultural representations embody the contradictions that exist within the Indian judicial system. These discourage rape victim-survivors from speaking up against their perpetrators and filing the FIR. Many women are afraid to come to the forefront and seek justice for themselves because they experience a fear for their lives, and humiliation and shame for both themselves and their loved ones. Therefore, it is in these judicial spaces that the 'culture of fear' exists. The term – culture of fear – can be defined as social and political conditions that prevent or discourage rape victim-survivors from coming forward into the public sphere to share their traumatic experiences and reporting their cases to the law systems to get social justice. We will see examples of 'culture of fear' in the filmic representations that I explore in this chapter.

Feminist scholar Skylab Sahu (2012) contends that the '[Indian] law exercises power and disqualifies women's experiences and or knowledge' (Sahu, 2021, p. 165) and that 'when the laws and policies followed and formulated in a state often or at times help the state to retain its hegemony and the dominance of particular groups within society, it then helps in maintaining an unjust status quo of power instead of ensuring justice to the vulnerable' (Sahu, 2021, p. 166). Similarly, Swapna Mukhopadhyay (1999) argues that there is 'the disenchantment with the potential of law as an instrument of social transformation' (p. 11) because feminist human rights lawyer, Flavia Agnes, in her meticulous research, demonstrates 'that laws, old and new, are structured to operate against the larger interests of women'. (p. 12) Indeed, the journey to get justice is tumultuous and often considered a shameful and humiliating event not only for the rape survivor-victim but also for her family members.

As we will see, the trials that are represented in the films reduce the rape victim-survivors (usually women) to the essentialised figures of 'good' or 'bad' women – depending on their past sexual history, behaviour and lifestyle. In most cases when the trial takes place, the rape victim is judged based on her previous sexual history, her behaviour and education. Second, the victim's testimony is also often used against her. If she is disenfranchised and poor, then she is further unable to seek justice for herself as the cultural and legal systems are often powerful enough to silence her in the process. Moreover, the rape victim-survivor's body is sexualised during the rape trial as her sexual history is brought forward. While filmmakers in Hindi cinema problematise and highlight these issues within Indian judicial system, the treatment of rape victim-survivors and patriarchal attitudes that silence them continues to remain unchanged even today, as evidenced by the 2019 Unnao gang rape case. It also further highlights that while such rape laws and their amendments aim to act as instruments of social change, they are not enforced because of the socio-political and cultural structures that exist – whether it's shame, lack of awareness of rights and deployment of further violence through abuse of power that prevents the rape victim-survivor from speaking up, filing a report or fighting for justice in courts.

## The History of Indian Rape Laws, the 1983 Amendment, B.R. Chopra's *Insaaf ka Tarazu* (1980) and Rajkumar Joshi's *Damini* (1993)

Historically, the Indian rape laws are rooted in its colonial era and were established vis-à-vis the Indian Penal code (IPC) 1860. Informed by reports from Thomas Macaulay's Indian Law Commission in 1837, the law defined 'the crime of rape as sexual intercourse by a man with a woman against her will and without her consent, except in cases involving girls under nine years of age where consent was immaterial' (Kolsky, 2010, p. 109). In 1860, the age of consent was raised to 10 years and the sentencing was either life or up to 10 years (Kolsky, 2010, p. 109). Indian women faced a dual challenge in colonial courtrooms because they were not only 'subjected to British legal presumptions about false charges, they also had to contend with specifically colonial ideas about the unreliability of native witnesses and other prejudicial ideas about Indian culture' (Kolsky, 2010, p. 111). Instead of deterring from these archaic rape laws, Indian law practitioners embraced them.

Jaising Modi's *Medical Jurisprudence and Toxicology* (1920) continues to remain an established text that is referred to in Indian courts to this day. Modi's text, according to Kolsky, echoes the sentiments of colonial predecessors who always already view the rape victim-survivor as a hostile witness unless she proves otherwise. Elizabeth Kolsky's (2010) study of rape trials in colonial India between 1860 and 1947 indicates that the 'colonial criminal jurisprudence was markedly hostile to rape victims who sought judicial remedy in court' (p. 122). 'A woman's charge', Kolsky writes, 'required some form of material corroboration, preferably a body evidencing the crime, although assumptions about class and culture sometimes trumped proof of bodily injury and broken bodice strings' (p. 123). Kolsky further observes that 'strict evidentiary requirements were established by the courts according to the presumption that the doubly doubtful complainant (the native woman) was a non-credible witness whose testimony could not be trusted' (p. 123). In other words, the rape victim-survivor had to 'corroborate her charge and prove non-consent' by providing additional evidence such as 'a fresh complaint, class and caste background, prior sexual activity, and, most importantly, physical marks of violent resistance on the body evidencing the crime' (p. 123).

These colonial rape laws continue to influence the contemporary rape laws even today, though the famous 1972 Mathura rape case led to 1983 amendments in the rape laws. A sixteen-year-old girl, Mathura, was repeatedly raped by a head police constable and his colleague while she was in police custody. When her case was tried, the Supreme court concluded that Mathura was responsible for the alleged rape because there was an 'absence of injuries on her body' (Kolsky, 2010, p. 124) which showed no evidence of resistance. Thus, her perpetrators were acquitted. Flavia Agnes (1992) further adds that Mathura's character was decided based on the fact that she 'had eloped with her boyfriend' and was 'habituated to sexual intercourse and hence could not be raped' (p. WS-20).

The Supreme Court's judgement led to nation-wide outrage and protests by feminists and other lawmakers who intervened and demanded a review of the court's judgement in Mathura's rape case in 1979 (Sahu, 2021, p. 61). Ultimately, the Criminal Law (Amendment) Act 1983 was established, which states that 'if the victim says that she did not consent to sexual intercourse, the court shall presume that she did not consent' (Sahu, 2021, p. 61). Renowned women's rights lawyer Flavia Agnes (1992), cultural anthropologist Veena Das (1996), feminist scholars of law and sociology Pratiksha Baxi (2014) and Skylab Sahu (2021) have stated that although there were some positive changes associated with these amendments, they were largely symbolic.

A cult classic, B.R. Chopra's *Insaaf ka Tarazu* (1980) was released in the aftermath of the Mathura rape case. Film critic Deepa Ghalot (2016) has called this film 'bold for its time' and said that it was considered 'progressive at a time when rape victims in Hindi films usually committed suicide or were sometimes "accepted" by a noble man who did not hold her non-virgin status against her'. The film's plot explores society and law's patriarchal attitudes that shaped the judge and lawyer's perception of the rape victim. Bharti (Zeenat Aman) is a popular model who attracts attention not only for her beauty but also because she is modern, assertive and not afraid to take on modelling projects which at the time would have been considered risqué (photo shoots in swimming costumes and other revealing westernised outfits). Although she has a boyfriend, Ashok (Deepak Parashar), she encounters Ramesh (Raj Babbar) during one of her modelling events. He finds himself obsessed with Bharti and turns up at several of her modelling shoots, eventually holding a party for her. Ultimately, he rapes her during a visit. There are two trials that take place in the film. In the first one, Ramesh is acquitted after the defence lawyer shames Bharti for her lifestyle and career choices. In the second half of the film, Ramesh humiliates and rapes Bharti's sister, Neeta (Padmini Kohlapure). In anger, Bharti shoots and kills Ramesh. The film suggests that a raped survivor-victim has to take laws into her own hands to gain justice, as the judicial system does not support them.

The representation of both trials is insightful. At the beginning of the first trial, Bharti is warned by her female lawyer that many women do not file charges of rape – because often they are humiliated and shamed but the perpetrator is not convicted. This gender bias is made visible during the covering of the rape itself: whenever she denies his claims, the defence lawyer speaks to her in a dismissive tone. Chandra dissects different aspects of Bharti's culturally un-traditional and modern behaviour. During the cross-examination, we see that Chandra uses Bharti's lifestyle and career choices for choosing to adopt a modelling career over a secretary job (which he considers to be more decent for a young woman) as a way to discredit her. Throughout the trial, he shows that Bharti is responsible for the rape and not Ramesh because she is a woman of a 'loose' and indecent character (Chopra, 1980, pp. 1:14:43–1:20:00). In contrast, the second trial is noticeably different because Bharti is no longer clad in a western dress. Instead, she is wearing a sari with her head covered. The attitudes of the judges and lawyers change remarkably at this time. In the initial ruling against her in the first trial, the judge's decision resulted in Bharti's social ostracisation in her society where she was not only viewed with hateful and disgusted eyes but was also spit on. Whilst being examined, she says that her trial became an example of the consequences that rape survivors face if they choose to step forward. This is a pivotal moment in the film for two reasons. First, we hear Bharti, the rape survivor-victim's testimony as she admonishes the judge and defence lawyers who shamed and obliterated her case in the first trial. The film seems to argue that the patriarchal and misogynistic attitudes permeate the justice system creating conditions that prevent a rape survivor from seeking justice. Ultimately, she is *forced to take the law into her own hands* to punish the rapist. It is no wonder that this film is still considered to be a cult classic. At the end of the film, the judge and the defence lawyer, Chandra, are ashamed such that the judge even steps down from his position because he could not deliver Bharti justice. Her honour is also restored after her boyfriend Ashok's family accepts her and her sister back into their lives after the trial, as if the rape and murder had never happened. The film, therefore, suggests that for a raped woman to regain her honour, she is left with no choice but to seek justice on her own terms whether it be by breaking laws.

Although *Insaaf ka Tarazu* shows a progressive representation of a rape victim-survivor, it is important to note that Bharti, who was a model by profession, belonged to middle/upper middle class, even though the defence lawyer disparaged her work in court. She still had a further privileged position that enabled her to speak up and condemn the court. In Rajkumar Joshi's *Damini* (1993), however, that is not the case because the rape victim-survivor belongs to a lower class and works as a domestic servant. The film reveals complex power structures that continue to silence and erase the narratives of rape survivor-victims, especially those who would be considered poor.

The film follows the story of Gupta family who use their power to cover up the brutal gang-rape of Uma, their domestic servant, that Rakesh, Damini's brother-in-law, and his friends are responsible for. Throughout the film, we see instances of different avenues of power and law: police, prosecuting lawyers and even Damini's wealthy father-in-law are working to silence Uma. At first, Uma is admitted to the hospital where none of the Gupta family members come to visit her. Eventually, she is murdered by the police. The narrative then shifts to Damini, who begins the journey to fight for her justice. We do not see Uma at all during the trial: although it is *her* rape case that is at the heart of the film, the focus is not on her. It is implied that she has been murdered by the corrupt policemen who have been bribed by the perpetrator's family to do away with the case. Instead, the film focusses on Damini and the forces that work to silence her for speaking and advocating for the rape victim. Ironically, Damini was also the name given to the 2012 Delhi gang rape victim. But, in the film, Damini is the victim's advocate/activist, *not* the rape victim herself. The common thread that both these films share is the disparaging and humiliating line of questioning that rape survivors and their witnesses are asked to humiliate and shame them. During the trial, the devious prosecuting lawyer questions Damini about the details of Uma's rape, asking her where the men were and which parts of her body were they holding.

*Damini* also shows instances of 'compromise' – a method that has been used to put pressure on the rape victim-survivor and her family outside of the court. In other words, Pratiksha Bakshi (2014) explains that 'it becomes apparent that the pressure to compromise is enforced through networks of powerful middlemen including lawyers, policemen and local politicians who act on the behalf of the accused. Refusal to compromise often results in tragic consequences [for the rape victim and her families]' (p. 182). Sahu also adds further that, 'in many cases, compromise could be possible and trials can be curtailed, or the witness may turn hostile. There are several cases that depict the grim consequences for women who are raped, assaulted, murdered or were forced to commit suicide by the men who raped them (especially when the rapists were from socio-economically and politically powerful groups) and because they refused to compromise' (p. 69). Indeed, this tactic is used often by the perpetrators and their families to settle the rape case outside of the court/ by persuading the rape victim to marry the man who raped her or by threatening to harm her and her family members as I discussed earlier in 2019 Unnao rape case as well. It becomes apparent, then, that if the rape victim belongs to the (upper) middle class or higher, she is given a platform to challenge and, ultimately, is able to claim justice while the women who belong to the lower echelons of the society are left silenced and powerless in these same courts.

## The 2013 Amendments to the Rape Laws, Aniruddha Roy Chowdhury's *Pink* (2016), and Ajay Bahl's Section *375* (2019)

The 2012 Delhi gang-rape case was so heinous that it led to another amendment in the rape laws, after a twenty-three-year-old student was brutally gang-raped on a moving bus in Delhi. In 2013, the committee on Amendments to the Criminal Law, also known as the Justice Verma committee, was asked to guide and advise the Indian government as national and international protests sparked in the aftermath of the Delhi gang rape case.

The 2012 Delhi gang-rape case was so heinous that Indian government established the Criminal Law (Amendment) Act, 2013, resulting in significant changes to the rape laws in the form of section 375, to ensure quicker trials and stricter punishment. Sahu highlights that, 'the amended law bars the use of sexual history in determining the consent of woman and bars cross examination as the way to prove the general immoral character of the victim'. If the victim states in the court that she did not give consent, the court will presume that it is so (p. 66). The 2012 gang-rape case also prompted the justice Verma committee to reframe the definition of rape. As a result, the 'penetration of a woman's vagina, urethra, anus or mouth by a penis and penetration of the vagina, urethra or anus by finger(s), object(s), body part(s) is considered "rape". Acts of cunnilingus and fellatio are also covered within the definition' (Satish, 2016). By calling it 'sexual assault', the law now recognises that penetration by objects will also be considered rape. The Ministry of Women and Child Development also established the $113m Nirbhaya fund to ensure empowerment, safety and security initiatives dedicated to help victims of gender and sexual violence. One of their schemes under this fund was the creation of One Stop Centres that were designed to aid rape survivors and victim-survivors medically. However, media critics have noted that the one stop centres have been inefficient in providing the appropriate services to the rape victim-survivors (Bajoria, 2017). Additionally, the current rape laws in India problematically acknowledge *only* the sexual violence experienced by people who are assigned female at birth. These laws do not recognise the gender-based violence that young men and transgender people experience in India. Aayush Akar and Shubhank Suman (2020) note that, at most, Indian rape laws refer to the act of sodomisation under section 377 [10] of the Indian Penal Code, but beyond that there is an assumption that the rape victim-survivors are primarily women, in the Indian court of law.

Since 2013, the state and government, as well as the judicial government, have in fact created and designed laws that do support the victims of gender and sexual violence. Social-political and cultural realities prevent the rape and sexual violence survivor from receiving the support she needs as she is reeling from the trauma of the crime. Sahu reports, 'lack of coordination between the one-stop centre, the police, the magistrate, medical service and the magistrate creates hurdles for the rape survivor' (p. 176). Rupal Oza, a feminist geographer who has worked on sexual and gender-based violence in Haryana, has also argued that 'despite amendments to the 2013 Code of Criminal Procedure, which holds the police accountable for not filling a first information report, Human Rights Watch found that the police resist filing cases, especially if the accused is from a dominant caste or community' (p. 104).

In the aftermath of the 2012 Delhi gang-rape case, there was a significant cultural response from filmmakers, activists and feminist groups. Among them were the films, Aniruddha Roy Chowdhury's *Pink* (2016) and Ajay Bahl's *Section 375* (2019). *Pink* begins *in media res* as three female roommates – Minal, Falak and Andrea – are seen escaping from a dangerous situation. At the same time, we see three men – Raunak, Vishwajyoti and Rajveer – who are injured and being rushed to the hospital. As the plot thickens, we learn that the group of men and women had met up for drinks after a concert they had attended. It becomes evident that Minal has caused a head injury to Rajveer. As the women try to put the incident behind them, Rajveer's friend Ankit begins to send threats to Minal and desires revenge for his friend's injury. Falak loses her job after a scandalous photo of hers is sent to her boss and the men also start to harass her landlord to discourage her from filing a court case. The local police are aware that the men have connections with political leaders and are afraid to charge them. We see an instance of compromise as the men eventually kidnap Minal and threaten and molest her in a moving car, which leaves her shaken. Because of Rajveer's uncle's connections, it is Minal who is arrested for attempted murder. Andrea and Falak seek the help of Deepak, a reputed lawyer who has retired. He vows to fight for her as her trial begins. In this trial, Rajveer's lawyer, like Barrister Chandra, also attacks Minal's character and reputation because she is an independent girl living in Delhi: he suggests that the women prostituted themselves to the men and demanded money for their company. Intent on deriding Minal's moral character, the defence implies once again that it is the victim who is responsible for the rape attempt. As the trial continues, the women argue that it was the men who had tried to sexually assault and rape them. Thus, Minal had hit Rajveer with a bottle in self-defence. Deepak argues that the trial is about consent – when a woman says no, it means no – and their clothes, drinking habits and lifestyle should *not* be determining factors. *Pink*, like *Insaaf ka Tarazu*, shows a progressive representation of a rape survivor who also had to take the law into her own hands because the conditions were so perverse that she had no choice but to act in defense.

Unlike Bharti, who killed her perpetrator, Minal is ostracised, blamed for the events that have unfolded, and had her arrested.

It becomes clear that even if the rape laws have been changed to recognise a woman's testimony, the cultural systems and society's patriarchal often misogynistic attitudes continue to seep into the court room trials. In fact, the final film, *Section 375*, is arguably a regressive representation in this genre of films and ultimately foregrounds the problematic notion that women are filing false rape cases for revenge. Released amidst the #MeToo movement, the film explores a rape case in the entertainment industry. Notable film director Rohan Kurana (Rahul Bhat) is accused of rape by costume designer Anjali Dangle (Meera Chopra). The court case is taken up by prosecutor Tarun Saluja (Akshaye Khanna) and Hiral Gandhi (Richa Chaddha), his former mentee who is passionate about social justice. Saluja has a very troubling belief: essentially that law is business, and not an instrument of social justice. He argues that Anjali had created this story of rape as a way to take revenge on Rohan after their relationship soured. While Hiral tries to follow the law and argues that consent is still relevant even if a relationship has taken place where two people were mutually involved, the film implies that the judges are under pressure to support the rape victim even though evidence seems to suggest that she is doing this for revenge. The most frustrating part of this film, as a viewer, is the ending, because Anjali confesses that she had indeed filed the rape charge to avenge Rohan for breaking up with her.

Films such as *Section 375* show that women often file false rape charges and problematically revert back to the old and archaic colonial laws that were doubtful of a woman's testimony. Although this chapter only briefly surveys a selection of four films, it becomes clear that even in the Hindi film industry, rape victim-survivors are viewed with ambivalence and doubt. The rape survivors are compelled to take justice and law into their own hands (which is one extreme) if they belong to (upper) middle or elite classes, which is when there is a danger that they can also file a false rape charge because of their bad and immoral character. If they are poor or marginalised, then they are unable to even stand trial and are silenced before they enter the court, as we saw in Uma's case in *Damini*.

## Conclusion

This chapter has been perhaps one of the most challenging and emotionally devastating ones to write because it becomes apparent that there have been significant and noticeable shift in rape laws since India's inception in 1947. Yet, rape victim-survivors continue to be questioned. Oza sees in her work that 'even when they [the rape victim-survivors] are discouraged from filing a case, the very attempt at lodging a complaint is an act of defiance' (2020, p. 105). Although it is indeed true that more women and rape survivors are coming forward, the cultural and societal systems continue to influence the judicial system which does not enforce the laws and often works against the rape survivor. The 2019 Unnao gang-rape case is a clear example of this. Finally, the film industry, which itself has had to reckon with #MeToo movement, has been able to create and construct narratives of empowered rape survivors, though within the industry itself, the justice for many rape-survivors remains unachievable as their own reputation is put in jeopardy if they come forward.

# References

Aayush, A., & Shubhank, S. (2020, April 16). Critical analysis of male rape in India. *iPleaders*. Retrieved from https://blog.ipleaders.in/critical-analysis-of-rape-of-male-in-india/

Agnes, F. (1992). Protecting women against violence? Review of a decade of legislation, 1980–1989. *Economic and Political Weekly, 27*(17), WS19–WS33.

Bahl, A. (director). (2019). Section 375 [film]. SCIPL.

Bajoria, J. (2017, November 10). One-stop centres for rape survivors in India are now resolving marital disputes. *Scroll*. Retrieved from https://scroll.in/article/857370/one-stop-centres-for-rape-survivors-in-india-are-now-resolving-marital-disputes

Baxi, P. (2014). *Public secrets of law: Rape trials in India*. New Delhi: Oxford University Press.

Chopra, B. R. (director). (1980). *Insaaf ka Tarazu* (balance of justice) [film]. Youtube, B.R. Films.

Chowdhury, A. R. (director). (2016). Pink [film]. Netflix, Rashmi Sharma Telefilms.

Das, V. (1996). Sexual violence, discursive formations and the state. *Economic and Political Weekly, 31*(35/37), 2411–2423.

Ghalot, D. (2016, September 18). 36 years ago, Insaaf Ka Tarazu was as bold as Pink. *Daily O*. Retrieved from https://www.dailyo.in/arts/insaf-ka-tarazu-pink-good-women-patriarchy-lipstick-zeenat-aman/story/1/12973.html

Kolsky, E. (2010). 'The body evidencing the crime': Rape on trial in colonial India, 1860–1947. *Gender & History, 22*(1), 109–130. doi:10.1111/j.1468-0424.2009.01581.x

Kumar, K. (2019, December 7). Unnao rape victim, set on fire a year after being brutalised, dies. *India Today*. Retrieved from https://www.indiatoday.in/india/story/unnao-rape-victim-set-on-fire-a-year-after-being-brutalised-dies-1626035-2019-12-07

Mukhopadhyay, S. (1999). Law as an instrument of social change: The feminist dilemma. In S. Mukhopadhyay (Ed.), *In the name of justice: Women and law in society* (pp. 9–14). New Delhi: Manohar.

Oza, R. (2020). Sexual subjectivity in rape narratives: Consent, credibility, and coercion in Rural Haryana. *Signs: Journal of Women in Culture and Society, 46*(1), 103–125. doi:10.1086/709214

Sagar. (2019, December 7). Gang raped, filmed, blackmailed and murdered: The long and tortured road of the Unnao rape victim. *Caravan*. Retrieved from https://caravanmagazine.in/crime/gang-raped-filmed-blackmailed-murdered-long-tortured-road-unnao-rape-victim

Sahu, S. (2021). *Gender, violence and governmentality: Legal and policy initiatives in India*. London: Routledge.

Santoshi, R. (director). (1993). *Damini* (lightning) [film]. Cineyugg Entertainment.

Satish, M. (2016, August 22). Forget the chatter to the contrary, the 2013 rape law amendments are a step forward. *The Wire*. Retrieved from https://thewire.in/gender/rape-law-amendments-2013

Siddiqui, Z., Bhardwaj, M., & Phartiyal, S. (2019, December 6). Unnao rape victim dies in hospital after being set ablaze. *Reuters*. Retrieved from https://www.reuters.com/article/india-rape-idINKBN1YB02W

Chapter 5

# Legal Responses to Sexual Violence in Japan: First Steps in a Lengthy Process of Rehabilitation

*Gavan Patrick Gray*

## Abstract

The Japanese legal system has several significant, deep-rooted and widely recognised flaws, one of which has been a history of weak support for the needs of victims of sexual violence. This structure of prosecutorial apathy has meant that female victims, and wider society, have been insufficiently protected from all but the most extreme cases of abuse and assault. However, a growing political interest in gender equality and the nascent development of a Japanese #MeToo movement has brought more pressure for reforms, with 2017 seeing the first significant change of Japan's sex crime laws in 110 years. Despite this, many serious flaws remain to be addressed, including: concerns over the statute of limitations for sexual crimes, the manner in which vague legal definitions can prevent the law from being effectively applied, the lack of support for victims, and the often arbitrary standards for prosecution and the settlement system that allows the wealthy to avoid more than cursory punishment. This chapter examines the efforts to introduce reforms and the extent to which such changes are likely to have a positive impact on the well-being, safety and legal rights of Japanese women.

*Keywords*: Japan; Sexual violence; gender violence; rape; women's rights; sexual assault

Gender Violence, the Law, and Society, 91–103
doi:10.1108/978-1-80117-127-420221008

Japan is, rightfully, recognised as one of the safest countries in the world, and its level of violent crime consistently ranks among the very lowest.[1] However, no country has yet established a perfect system of justice and, like all others, Japan has its weaknesses and areas where reforms are badly needed. One of these is the manner in which women are protected and served by the law. Unlike the generally proactive and effective nature of its approach to crime, in this area, Japan has failed to achieve the kind of gender equality that many other developed countries have demonstrated. Outmoded gender attitudes are reflected in archaic laws which, despite some recent revisions, remain unsuitable for addressing the requirements of women in respect to protection from violent crime, especially that of a sexual nature. Fortunately, public attitudes are changing and there is a growing wave of support for further change that could bring Japan more in line with its international peers and safeguard the rights and welfare of its female citizens. Perhaps the most important issue, though, is whether such changes will be purely superficial, aimed at changing laws alone as a symbolic gesture towards gender parity, or whether they will focus on some of the deeper, structural elements of the Japanese legal system which have been instrumental in preventing a more equitable application of justice in many cases of sexual violence.

## Current Situation

Given Japan's low level of crime, many are often surprised by how strict its legal system is, with relatively severe punishments being common for offences that in other countries might be considered minor. In fact, Japan has been frequently criticised for failing to protect the rights of criminal suspects by subjecting them to harsh interrogations, spartan jail conditions and extended periods of detention without bail, based on flimsy evidence (HRW, 2019).

However, in some areas, its protection of victims also leaves a lot to be desired. In terms of gender equality, Japan ranks 110th out of 149 countries (WEF, 2018), and signs of this disparity can be seen in many elements of an otherwise admirable social system. One of these is the response toward sexual crimes against women. Considering the low level of other violent crimes, it is significant that 7.8% of Japanese women report that they have experienced forced sexual intercourse at some point (GoJ, 2017, p. 68). It is also notable that while roughly 20% of crimes in Japan are committed by minors, when it comes to the offences of rape and sexual assault they are the primary victims in 41.6% and 52.5% of cases, respectively (Ogasawara, 2011, p. 164).

It has been widely recognised for some time that such crimes, and the disproportionate targeting of minors, has been a shameful smear on Japan's national image and various campaigns – from women-only train cars to apps designed to protect young girls from molesters – have been part of the pushback against the problem. In recent years there have been more significant

[1]This work was supported by a Kaken grant (18K13005) from the Japan Society for the Promotion of Science.

improvements, including the introduction of prefectural sexual assault hotlines, increased training of female investigators with a focus on victim awareness and greater collaboration with private support groups that offer specialised training and victim counselling. However, the demand for wider reform has been building, and many hoped that the worldwide #MeToo movement would play a part in helping Japan initiate such change. Initially, however, the movement was primarily localised around professional support networks that highlighted the problems faced in individual, high-profile cases, and many women still faced a backlash that included victim-blaming and social and professional ostracisation for those who challenged the system. The impact of the popular movement was not as visibly impactful as in neighbouring South Korea. Where it led directly to a significant policy change regarding gender-based violence (Hasunuma & Shin, 2019).

Despite the less forceful nature of the Japanese movement, since its beginning a series of court cases that resulted in the dismissal of charges for sexual crimes have reignited public anger over what is perceived as a failure to protect vulnerable women and generated a series of 'flower demos', public protests organised by a network of women's rights groups. Their goal has been to highlight specific outstanding weaknesses in the legal system and put increased pressure on the government to respond with concrete policies that would address these long-standing failures (Osaki, 2020).

If anything, the COVID pandemic exacerbated the problems faced by women and created a higher impetus for change to occur sooner rather than later. From the beginning of the pandemic in late 2019, there were reports that levels of domestic violence were significantly higher than the previous year (Ando, 2020), while in late 2020 Seiko Hashimoto, the Minister for Gender Equality, announced that the number of consultations at support centres for sexual violence had increased 15.5% year on year (Tokyo Shinbun, 2021).

## Recent Legal Changes

In 2017, Japan made the first major changes to its penal code on sex crimes in more than 110 years. These revisions increased the penalty for many crimes, altered the definition of 'rape' to move beyond vaginal penetration by a penis and allowed crimes such as rape and sexual assault to be prosecuted even where victims do not file charges (Osaki, 2017).

While these changes were both needed and welcome, they perhaps served a greater value in showing that after more than a century of intransigent resistance to the demands of modernity, meaningful change in the legal system was actually possible. They did not, however, go nearly far enough in addressing the myriad problems that still remain. The fact that these problems are so wide-ranging means that efforts to address them will likely involve a long campaign of incremental battles, rather than something that can be achieved in a single set of sweeping revisions. These include things like coercive exploitation in the pornography industry, where abolitionists and industry groups fight a back and forth struggle over the balance between commercial freedom and the protection of human rights (Norma & Morita, 2020). It also involved the Joshi-Kousei elements of the sex trade, which commodify the sexualisation of schoolgirls (Ogaki, 2018). This is an industry with strong ties to the ongoing problem of domestic human trafficking in Japan where, despite the introduction of regional laws aimed at curtailing their exploitation, significant numbers of minors are inducted into the sex industry each year (Acadimia, 2018). However, these issues – tied as they are to the culturally embedded, and highly profitable, sex industry – will likely see a slower rate of change and the requirement of a general public shift in attitudes toward commercialised sex. In the short term, there exists far more potential to generate significant change in the way the legal system addresses the crimes of sexual violence. When the 2017 reforms were introduced, they included a provision that required a review of the sex crimes laws within three years, and many activist groups see this as an opportunity to focus on some key areas which the 2017 revisions failed to address (Sieg, 2019).

## Outstanding Issues

Following the 2017 revisions, the key driver of public desire for further reforms was a series of highly publicised court cases in 2019 in which several, apparently clear-cut, cases of abuse and assault were dismissed due to the outstanding weaknesses in the legal system. In one of these cases, a man on trial for repeatedly raping his teenage daughter was acquitted on the grounds that she had not exhibited sufficient physical resistance to the attacks (Eiraku & Aizawa, 2019). While this might, on the face of it, seem like a lapse in judicial oversight, in this case the judge was merely following the written laws. Japan has long held the view that rape is inherently an act of violence and thus to show an incidence of rape there should be evidence that force or threats were used (Egawa, 2019). However, as has become abundantly clear as our understanding of such crimes has evolved, rape can be carried out in certain cases without non-sexual violence or the threat thereof – for example, where a victim is rendered drunk or insensible, is too terrified to resist physically or is in a relationship with the perpetrator where non-physical coercive control can be exerted, such as a family member, or teacher. Japan's failure to recognise such nuances led directly to the above instances of acquittal, but they also helped to focus a growing sense of public dissatisfaction with the outdated legal strictures. The problems that exist are, however, quite varied in nature and in scope, with some primarily requiring changes to the poorly worded or overly lenient laws. Others require broader change in how the laws themselves are applied, for example, the manner in which the prosecution system treats victims generally, and the role played in the prosecution process by Japan's 'settlement' system.

One area where revision of laws alone might suffice is the statute of limitations which applies to sex crimes. In 2010, the statute of limitations for murder and other capital crimes, which was previously 25 years, was abolished. Yet, the 10-year limit for rape charges, and the 7-year limit for sexual assault, remains fixed.

A 2019 case brought attention to their limitations when a suspect in a rape case was identified by DNA tests for a separate crime, just four days after the statute of limitations had expired. Luckily, in Japan the statute is suspended during any time the suspect is outside Japan, and in that case the suspect's international travel during the intervening years created a two-month extension that allowed charges to be made. Nonetheless, it ably highlighted the weakness of the current limits and the need, if not for abolition, then for a significantly extended period of potential arrest and prosecution (Sankei, 2019b).

A similar problem of insufficient legal regulation exists in the definition of, or failure to define, certain crimes. For example, voyeurism, the illicit observance, photography or recording of women without their knowledge, is a common problem in Japan, yet there is no actual crime that fits this action. As a result, offenders are instead charged under a variety of minor crime laws such as Trespassing, Nuisance Prevention or, in the case of minors being involved, the more serious Child Pornography Law (Maeda, 2016).

The vagaries of lax definition were further highlighted in a case where a man was arrested for 'splashing bodily fluid' onto the arm of a schoolgirl. Again, there was difficulty knowing what to charge him with. Indecent assault required the use of violence or threats and so was deemed inadmissible. The Nuisance Prevention Law could have been used but this would have limited the maximum punishment to one year of jail. Instead, the charge was deemed to be Common Assault, with a potential two-year sentence. If the act had been deemed to have damaged the girl's clothing, however, the law for Criminal Damage to Property could have been applied with a possible three-year prison sentence (Maeda, 2020).

The fact that it can be so unclear on what grounds sexual offenders should be charged, as well as the fact that damage to property is deemed more serious than both assault and sexual molestation, are clear signs that some fundamental changes in the wording of laws and their sentencing guidelines are still required.

## Standards of Prosecution

Moving away from the definition of the crimes themselves, there exist several deeper problems with the manner in which the laws are applied, one of the most serious of which is the nature of prosecution in Japan. For a long time, Japan was regarded as a 'prosecutor's paradise' where the Office of Public Prosecutor enjoyed considerable leeway in deciding which cases to pursue and how to handle their enforcement. Since the 1990s there has been a general increase in transparency and victim's rights, yet, the influence of the prosecutor on criminal cases is still very powerful (Johnson, 2012, p. 37). One way that this comes into play with cases of sexual violence is that many such cases resolve with a decision to forgo prosecution. The most problematic aspect is that in such instances there is almost no transparency, there is no public record of the reasons for non-prosecution and even victims have only very limited opportunity, in cases involving death or injury, to access these records (Kamon, 2019, p. 53).

This is an especially critical issue as the prosecutors' office represents the last in a long line of hurdles that must be cleared for a sex crime to be brought to open court. The first barrier is the victim actually reporting the incident; the second is the police making an official crime report; the third is apprehending the suspect and the last, the prosecutors deciding to formally indict them on the criminal charges. The lack of transparency means that not only is it true that very few sex crimes are ever brought to court, we generally never learn why this failed to occur in the other instances, a situation that does a disservice to both victims' need for closure and the general public's need for understanding of the system's efficacy and its impact on public safety (Maita, 2020).

Considering the size of the Japanese population and the aforementioned government surveys that suggest one in 13 women are victims of rape or sexual assault, one can estimate that there are at least 66,000 incidents per year.[2] Yet, government records account for slightly less than 6,000 officially recognised cases (GoJ, 2019, p. 2), suggesting that, at a minimum, less than 10% of incidents are reported. Then, only a third of these are actually prosecuted, which would mean that, at most, only 3% of serious sexual crimes in Japan are prosecuted. The level of prosecutions has also been steadily declining, from 43.4% in 2014 to 34.2% in 2019 (GoJ, 2019, p. 5).

While we do not know the specific reasons for non-prosecution in individual cases, the government does release statistics that give a breakdown of reasons for choosing not to indict suspects where the grounds are 'insufficient evidence'. Between 2018 and 2019 there were 380 such cases related to sexual offences. The statistics reveal that, by far, the most common reasons for claiming insufficient evidence are the possibility that sex may have been consensual (47% of cases) or that the perpetrator may have believed it to be consensual (40% of cases), and that there was doubt regarding the truthfulness of the victim's statement in 89% of the former and 61% of the latter cases (GoJ, 2021, p. 3). This raises the question of whether such subjective judgements should be made at such a preliminary stage of the legal process, but it also shows, perhaps more importantly, that the majority of cases where non-indictment occurs are for other reasons than a lack of evidence and, while there has been little hard data generated on the numbers involved, the primary reasons appear to be victim hesitancy and the use of settlements.

## Treatment of Victims

In any circumstances, there are numerous reasons why undergoing the lengthy and draining process of a criminal prosecution can be an undesirable ordeal on the part of a victim of sexual crimes: discomfort regarding the level of public disclosure, a sense of shame, fear of revenge on the part of the perpetrator or the effects of post-traumatic stress, among others. In Japan, these factors can be exacerbated by normative expectations to conform to certain social morals and

---

[2]In comparison, RAINN estimates 433,648 rapes and sexual assaults in the United States each year. https://www.rainn.org/statistics/victims-sexual-violence.

the fear that any involvement in such criminal proceedings, even as the victim, might tarnish one's reputation (Kamiya, 2019).

Victims also have to face interactions with police and prosecutors that can range from indifferent, to cold or even hostile. In one case a young woman was taken advantage of while in a severe state of intoxication and immediately went to the police to report a crime. However, prosecutors refused to indict the suspect because, during the man's recording of the act, the girl had said 'stop filming me' instead of 'stop raping me'. The possibility that the girl may have been resolved to her inability to stop the assault but still concerned about it being made a public spectacle was dismissed in favour of the common view that lack of direct, physical resistance negated possible conviction for rape (Ito, 2019).

There is also a seemingly widespread reluctance among police to pursue sexual assault aggressively, and stories of casual indifference to such crimes are commonplace (Maeda, 2019). The author has personally spoken with several lawyers representing victims of such crimes who reported that the police actively pressured their clients to forgo making a formal criminal report.[3] A common barrier that any victim will have to cross at an early stage is being asked 'what did you do to resist', with the implicit message that if they did not do enough, then the inability of police or prosecutors to proceed is down to the victim's failure to act. This is only the beginning of a process that, for the victim, can be long, highly stressful and demeaning.

Given the history of poor treatment of victims, it is perhaps unsurprising that a 2020 survey of victims of sexual violence in Japan found that only 15% actually contact the police at all. Less than half of these, just 7%, were actually accepted as criminal reports, and a mere 10th of these, 0.7% of all cases, ended with convictions (Mainichi, 2020).

These outdated, and seemingly uncaring, attitudes towards victims extend beyond the justice system. Many victims are denied access to abortions by hospitals due to health regulations that require the consent of the father for the procedure to occur. No consideration is allowed for victims of rape, and in the absence of explicit guidelines on the matter, the common response is to simply refuse them the option (Oshiro, 2020).

The introduction of a lay-judge system to Japanese courts in 2009 allowed members of the public to serve as judges alongside several professionals (typically, six of the former and three of the latter). This system led to a general increase in the number of suspended sentences and greater leniency towards suspects, except in cases of sexual violence, where the average sentence increased (Johnson, 2012, p. 37). Professional judges openly welcomed these changes in a manner that suggested they were previously restricted from imposing what they felt were just sentences due to outdated procedural guidelines (Hirayama, 2012, p. 7). This certainly represents a positive development for victims. However, one weakness of

---

[3]In some cases, the same lawyers told me that criminal reports they submitted to the police on behalf of clients were returned to them without being filed, something that goes directly against the letter of the law.

the lay-judge system, in regard to the handling of cases of sexual violence, is that victims are often reluctant to take part in a court system in which key members of the court may not be public officials but figures from their own community. Matters of victim protection and anonymity still need to be addressed but steps have already begun such as the ability of victims to exclude candidate judges who may be known to them, and for pseudonyms to be used by victims (Hirayama, 2012, p. 12).

While some of the above may suggest that the Japanese system has a callous attitude toward victims, this is generally not the case. Rather, the current laws are written, and the system structured, in a way that fails to accommodate their needs or take account of their vulnerabilities. Often the reluctance of police or prosecutors to accept or proceed with cases is based entirely upon their knowledge of the likelihood of the case failing to reach a satisfactory conclusion for the victim. The primary problem on their part is that they take a purely responsive role, seeing it as their duty merely to enforce what is stipulated in law, rather than actively pressing for change from within. Thankfully, external forces have begun to consolidate efforts to promote victim rights, and principles of restorative justice and pressure for better patterns of response is building through a network of human rights groups and victim support groups (Ito & Ishii, 2020).

## The Settlement Industry

One factor which some consider a significant impediment to the process of justice, especially in cases of sexual violence, is the Japanese system of settlements known as jidan (示談). The Japanese cultural preference for avoiding conflict favours, wherever possible, out-of-court agreements that will negate the need for a trial. As a result of this, in many cases, apologies and settlement payments are sufficient to bring matters to a resolution. There is a widespread public perception that this process means that to be wealthy means you will be able to skirt the law simply by paying the appropriate settlement. Some net commentators have referred to its application in sexual assault cases as 'erasing rape with money',[4] and a 2019 case involving a student at a prestigious university, who was arrested on five separate occasions for crimes of sexual assault yet failed to be indicted every time, led many to question whether his continued freedom was entirely due to his family's extensive wealth (Sankei, 2019a).

Of course, we have already seen that other reasons do exist for such failure to prosecute, whether reluctance of the victims to undergo the difficulty of the trial process or a lack of reliable evidence. However, we know these factors play a role only in a minority of cases. Meanwhile, week after week news stories announce the non-prosecution of suspects for unspecified reasons, raising constant questions

---

[4]For an example, see the following article on the Mag2News news blogging site, Mr. Keio, as expected 'erasing rape with money.' Why is Japan so soft on sex crimes? (ミスター慶応、予想通り「金でレイプもみ消し」完了。なぜ日本は性犯罪に甘いのか). https://www.mag2.com/p/news/478270.

of whether the suspects involved escaped more significant punishment through the use of a simple disbursement of cash. In the space of fewer than two weeks surrounding the writing of this piece, stories reported a man avoiding indictment over the suspected rape of a female acquaintance (Kumanichi, 2021), a former director of a talent agency avoiding indictment over the suspected rape of an aspiring model (Yahoo News, 2021a) and a former town councillor avoiding indictment over suspicion of exposing himself to a woman in a coffee shop (Yahoo News, 2021b). There may well have been others during the same period as such stories are a constant element of the news cycle and rarely merit more than a brief paragraph, despite the serious nature of the crimes they may refer to only in passing.

Law offices in Japan can make significant profits from the part they play in this cycle of payment and absolvence and are eager to highlight their proficiency in achieving settlement of such matters. There is, in fact, a 'Settlement Market', wherein lawyers generally know how much they will have to pay to get someone to drop the charges in specific cases, e.g. a case of molestation above clothes will require X amount of Yen, while if the offender moves below clothing the cost will be a little higher, etc. (Tabata, 2020).

In this manner, skilled lawyers will be able to estimate how much a 'get out of jail free' card is likely to cost their prospective clients. One public defender's office claims an 81% settlement rate for indecent assault cases, with an average settlement amount of ¥1,554,683 (roughly $14,000) (Atom, 2020). Often, not only the lawyers, but the system as a whole acts to put pressure on victims to accept such settlements.

One improvement of the 2017 revisions was the introduction of a 'non-confidential offence' categorisation that allowed prosecutors to indict crimes of sexual violence even without the victims' participation. In practice though, the support of the victim is generally crucial for the successful prosecution of such crimes, and it seems highly unlikely that we will see a significant increase in cases where suspects are convicted after a victim has agreed to a settlement (Maeda, 2017).

This settlement system is a difficult problem to address, though. On the one hand, it seems important that offenders should not be able to escape punishment simply by the payment of monetary amounts that might, to them, be relatively small. On the other hand, where the process of a criminal trial is too onerous for victims to endure, the settlement system does allow them some recourse for achieving a form of closure and limited justice. Perhaps one flaw in the current system is the notion that there is a 'standard' settlement price for specific offences. Rather than gauging such payments by the crime involved, it might be more equitable to have them mandated as either a set amount related to the crime or as a portion of the offender's assets, whichever is higher. The latter, if set sufficiently high, might be one way to eliminate the possibility of wealthy individuals flaunting the system.

## Movements Toward Reform

While Japan's legal system does have a long and very poor history in regard to its treatment of women in general and victims of sexual violence in particular, the 2017 revisions to the penal code are a strong sign that pressure for change has generated a response that is more than mere superficial, face-saving. The changes made were meaningful and fell short only in regard to the fact that the problems which exist are too widespread and varied to be fixed in a single burst of proactive zeal. As we saw with the issue of settlements, some of the problems still have no clear, single solution and the potential options need to be properly evaluated to ensure they will produce the greatest benefit.

Among the key issues that remain to be addressed is the revision of the age of consent to suitably reflect the impact of sexual crimes on minors. While all Japanese prefectures have superseding local laws that set higher ages, the national age remains 13, and this affects how several laws categorise crimes against minors. Another issue is that several crimes need to be properly defined, including the overly broad obscenity charge and the absence of a charge for voyeurism, among others. Perhaps one of the largest outstanding revisions is the issue of consent and an end to the prerequisite use of physical violence or threats to qualify a crime as rape or sexual assault. These and other key issues are, thankfully, being kept in the political spotlight by a variety of rights groups and political activists (HRN, 2020). Media coverage is also helping to raise public awareness of the nature of the problem and shine a spotlight on some of the key areas of needed change.

This is one potential danger regarding ongoing reform, namely that, by necessity, only a small portion of the required changes are properly highlighted in the public sphere. The full list of desirable changes is too long, too varied and too complex to easily explain to the general public, or political leaders, in a comprehensive fashion. The government review process that began after the 2017 revisions has now seen the 14th meeting of its fact-finding working group, which has laid out several of the areas it hopes to target in the next wave of revisions. In addition to those mentioned above, the group has shown an interest in examining the use of hormone therapy, medication and GPS tracking in dealing with repeat offenders. They have also worked with experts from Finland and Sweden to assess how those countries' approaches to sex crimes might be adapted for Japan (GoJ, 2020). In particular, it has focused on the 'Yes means Yes' form of explicit, consent-based sex that is endorsed in those countries, something that is very distinct from the 'No means No' form, requiring clear, demonstrable rejection to nullify consent, which underlies some of Japan's problematic laws (Mochizuki, 2020).

It remains to be seen what final set of recommendations this working group will deliver and whether they will, in fact, be accepted into law. Some scholars have expressed concerns, however, that attempts to impose standards that work in other cultures might not have, for all their good intentions, the same success in Japan (Kamon, 2019, p. 71). Once again, changing the laws is relatively easy, but if the structures and culture surrounding those laws have deeper flaws, then it may be that greater and more long-term change is required, and it is important to focus on such change as a continuing process with deeper structural goals.

## Conclusion

Japanese activism in the area of sexual violence has developed new strength in recent years, but the changes in awareness and legislation that have occurred do not represent a highpoint. Instead, it is merely the beginning of a long-overdue reassessment of a flawed system. While it has the power to initiate meaningful change – especially in specific issues such as the nature of consent and a better understanding of the plight of victims – it must not be a simple adjustment to the wording and impact of individual laws. The treatment of victims of sexual violence, by police, prosecutors, the courts and other institutions such as hospitals, needs to be comprehensively reviewed and revised. The fundamental nature of the system needs to shift in a manner that recognises and accounts for the underlying vulnerability of victims and the difficulty they have in negotiating the legal process without specially tailored support.

From the other end of the process, that of ensuring offenders are properly punished, the system of settlements and the manner in which it can exploit victims' reluctance to engage in stressful legal proceedings, needs to be examined. The extensive and profitable system of legal services that can reliably promise the avoidance of trials in the majority of sexual assault cases must have sufficient oversight to ensure it does not offer loopholes that can be used by wealthy offenders to escape meaningful justice.

Such assessment and revision is an ongoing process and one which requires careful consideration of the complexities involved, not simply to protect victims but to do so in a manner that ensures potentially innocent suspects continue to receive suitable legal protection. It is not a battle that can be won in a single day, and while further revisions of individual laws, such as those that occurred in 2017, are both welcome and necessary, the overall process must involve a level of deeper structural and societal analysis with the goal of constant improvement.

## References

Acadimia, K. (2018). Human trafficking in Japan through the use of schoolgirls. *International ResearchScape Journal, 5.* doi:10.25035/irj.05.01.05

Ando, R. (2020). Domestic violence and Japan's COVID-19 pandemic. *Asia Pacific Journal, 18*(18), 5475.

Atom. (2020, April 29). 強制わいせつの起訴/不起訴率 [Sexual assault prosecution/ nonprosecution rates]. アトム法律事務所 (Atom Law Office). Retrieved from https://atombengo.com/db/c/kyouseiwaisetsu/t/kiso

Egawa, S. (2019, April 9). 性犯罪で無罪判決が続いたのはなぜか [Why have there been so many acquittals for sex crimes?]. *Business Journal.*

Eiraku, M., & Aizawa, Y. (2019, May 23). *Public alarmed by sexual assault acquittals in Japan.* NHK.

GoJ. (2017). 男女間における暴力に関する調査 [*Survey on violence between men and women*]. Gender Equality Bureau, Cabinet Office, Government of Japan.

GoJ. (2019). 年度年報-検察統計: 結果の概要 [*Ministry of justice annual statistical report, prosecution statistics overview*]. Japanese Ministry of Justice, Government of Japan.

GoJ. (2020). 第14回性犯罪に関する施策検討に向けた実態調査ワーキンググループ [*The 14th fact-finding working group for examining measures for sex crime*]. Gender Equality Bureau of the Cabinet Office, Government of Japan.

GoJ. (2021). 性犯罪に係る不起訴事件調査 [*Investigation of non-indictment cases related to sex crimes*]. Japanese Ministry of Justice, Government of Japan.

Hasunuma, L., & Shin, K. (2019). #MeToo in Japan and South Korea: #WeToo, #WithYou. *Journal of Women, Politics & Policy*, *40*(1), 97–111.

Hirayama, M. (2012). Lay judge decisions in sex crime cases: The most controversial area of saiban-in trials. *Yonsei Law Journal*, *3*(1), 128.

HRN. (2020). Proposed amendments to the sexual offenses provisions of the penal code. *Human Rights Now*.

HRW. (2019, April 10). Call to eliminate Japan's "hostage justice" system by Japanese legal professionals. *Human Rights Watch*.

Ito, K. (2019, September 13). "無理やり性交＆動画撮影"が不起訴となる理由 [Why "forcible intercourse & video recording" is not prosecuted]. *President*.

Ito, F., & Ishii, R. (2020, June). The current status and issues in crime victim support in Japan. *Sophia University Social Welfare Research Bulletin*, *45*, 41–52.

Johnson, D. T. (2012). Prosecutors and Politics: A comparative perspective. *Crime and Justice*, *41*(1), 35–74.

Kamiya, S. (2019, February 21). なぜレイプ事件が「不起訴」になるのか、その理由をすべて説く [All the reasons why rape cases are "not prosecuted"]. *Ironna*.

Kamon, Y. (2019). 性犯罪規定の見直しに向けて [Toward a review of sexual offenses regulations]. 立命館法学 [*Ritsumeikan Law Journal*], *5*(387), 52–72.

Kumanichi. (2021, April 8). 強制性交疑いの男性不起訴処分 [Non-prosecution of man suspected of sexual assault]. *Kumamoto Hi Nichi Shinbun*.

Maeda, T. (2017, July 24). 実際にどこまで性犯罪の厳罰化が進むのか [How much will sexual crimes actually be punished?]. *Yahoo News*.

Maeda, T. (2016, July 3). 横行するハレンチな盗撮の「罪と罰」 ["Sin and punishment" of shameless voyeurism]. *Yahoo News*.

Maeda, T. (2019, July 17). 深夜の駅で泥酔女性の胸を触る男を目撃し通報 それでも警察は真剣に捜査しないという悲劇 [Police fail to take seriously a report that a man groped a woman at train station]. *Yahoo News*.

Maeda, T. (2020, November 11). なぜ電車内で中1女子に体液をかけた小学校教頭が「暴行罪」で逮捕されたか？ [Why was the vice-principal of an elementary school who sprinkled body fluids on a middle school girl on the train arrested for "assault"?]. *Yahoo News*.

Mainichi. (2020, November 24). Many sexual violence victims in Japan do not report assaults to police. *Mainichi Japan*.

Maita, T. (2020, February 26). 法廷で裁かれる性犯罪はごくわずか......法治国家とは思えない日本の実態 [Very few sex crimes are brought to justice in court...... The reality of Japan's lack of rule of law]. *Newsweek Japan*.

Mochizuki, T. (2020, March 8). Sweden's sexual offense law holds key to amending Japan's law. *Kyodo News*.

Norma, C., & Morita, S. (2020). Feminist action against pornography in Japan: Unexpected success in an unlikely place. *Dignity*, *4*(4), 4.

Ogaki, M. (2018). Theoretical explanations of joshi kousei ("JK business") in Japan. *Dignity*, *3*(1), 1–13.

Ogasawara, K. (2011). Current status of sex crimes and measures for the victims in Japan. *Japan Medical Association Journal*, *54*(3), 164–167.

Osaki, T. (2017, June 16). Diet makes historic revision to century-old sex-crime laws. *Japan Times*.

Osaki, T. (2020, July 14). Fight against sexual abuse in Japan gains strength. *Japan Times*.

Oshiro, N. (2020, October 20). Japan's abortion rule: Get consent from your sexual predator. Nikkei.

Sankei. (2019a, January 25). 性的乱暴で5度逮捕の慶応大生ら全員不起訴 [Keio University student arrested 5 times for sexual violence not prosecuted]. *Sankei Shimbun*.

Sankei. (2019b, November 11). 時効目前、自営業の男を強姦容疑で逮捕 [Before the statute of limitations, a self-employed man was arrested on suspicion of rape]. *Sankei Shinbun*.

Sieg, L. (2019, June 12). Rape acquittals spark calls to fix law in Japan, where prosecutors must prove victim 'incapable of resistance'. *Japan Times*.

Tabata, A. (2020, December 10). 多発する性犯罪……"示談の相場"はいくら？ 弁護士が解説する「ドキュメント 示談の現場」 [Many sex crimes……How much is a settlement? I'm not sure if you've heard of it or not]. *Yahoo News*.

Tokyo Shinbun. (2021, January 12). コロナと性暴力:多様な対策で防ぎたい [Corona and sexual violence: Various means should be used to prevent it]. *Tokyo Shinbun*.

WEF. (2018). *The global gender gap report 2018*. World Economic Forum.

Yahoo News. (2021a, April 20). 元豊郷町議の男性不起訴 自分の下半身触った疑い [Former Town Councillor not prosecuted over suspicion of exposing himself]. *Yahoo News*.

Yahoo News. (2021b, April 19). 女優志望者にわいせつ 容疑で逮捕の男、不起訴処分 [A man arrested on suspicion of obscenity for an aspiring actress, not prosecuted]. *Yahoo News*.

Chapter 6

# The Paradox of Constitutional Protection and Prejudice Experienced by LGBTQ+ People in South Africa

*Deepesh Nirmaldas Dayal*

## Abstract

South Africa attained democracy over 24 years ago. The changes in South Africa's Constitution allowed for protection for all citizens. Despite these freedoms and the promise of change, the country is plagued by violence, corruption and crime. These crimes affect the LGBTQ+ people of the South African population. These citizens have been protected by the Constitution; however, they continue to live their lives in a paradox, between protection and prejudice. LGBTQ+ people experience high levels of hate crimes which extend to violence, assault, bullying and cyberbullying. This chapter focuses on the legal protection and challenges experienced by South African LGBTQ+ people.

*Keywords*: South African Indian; LGBTQ+; hate crimes; overt discrimination; discrimination; South African law

South African people from all walks of life rejoiced at the birth of a new democracy by voting on the 27th of April 1994. This new democracy would allow for equal opportunities for all citizens, in terms of freedom, social justice and general equality (Bennett & Reddy, 2015). It signalled South Africa's reign as a regional example of hope and social rebirth. However, more than two decades after the birth of the democracy, a paradox exists within South Africa, where citizens are offered legislative freedom and protection, while there are still high

Gender Violence, the Law, and Society, 105–120
doi:10.1108/978-1-80117-127-420221009

levels of crime, corruption and human rights violations. Through the Gini coefficient used by the World Bank, South Africa is recognised as one of the most inequitable countries in the world (Keeton, 2014). Along with inequality, failures in the public sector and rampant crime, the levels of social cohesion, productivity and the confidence of citizens in the public sector have decreased (Eagle, Benn, Fletcher, & Sibisi, 2013). Despite the existence of some denialist lobbyists who claim that high levels of crimes are normal for developing counties, there is sufficient evidence to show that South Africa's crime rate is higher than the global average and that citizens feel vulnerable to victimisation and violence (Statistics South Africa, 2017, 2020).

The internationally aligned policies in South Africa aim to protect, promote and safeguard the rights of all citizens, including those who identify as lesbian, gay, bisexual, transgender, queer and additional sexual orientation or gender identities (LGBTQ+) (Hirsch, 2005; Mkhize, Bennett, Reddy, & Moletsane, 2010). A milestone move in 2006 saw South Africa becoming one of the first countries in the world to Constitutionally protect citizens against discrimination based on sexual orientation (Bhana, 2012; Thoreson, 2008). This offered citizens adoption rights, estate rights and rights to marry (Thoreson, 2008). Despite these advanced and intricate legal protections, LGBTQ+ people in South Africa continue to face discrimination and violent persecution, mainly due to the 'un-African' label of identifying as LGBTQ+ (Francis & Brown, 2017). The reported experiences of LGBTQ+ people have emphasised a disconnect between the Constitutional protection and people's real-life experiences, which range from discrimination and homophobia to acceptance (Bhana, 2012). Discrimination against LGBTQ+ people is also caused by notions of heteronormativity, patriarchy and conservative culture which exist within South Africa's diverse communities (Ratele & Suffla, 2010). Despite the legal protections, many South African people continue to believe that same-sex relationships are morally wrong (Sutherland, Roberts, Gabriel, Struwig, & Gordon, 2016).

South Africa consists of societies rich in cultural diversity, and within these societies, LGBTQ+ people have diverging experiences (Coopoosamy, 2018). While there have been aspects of positive change with regards to the experiences of LGBTQ+ people, many qualitative and empirical studies have highlighted the difficulties that LGBTQ+ people continue to face (Khan, 2017; Mkhize et al., 2010; OUT, 2016). A large-scale study focusing on crime in South Africa, the Victims of Crime Survey, revealed that 9.3% of respondents felt unsafe expressing their sexual orientation freely (Statistics South Africa, 2017). Within this statistical report, South African people of Indian descent are very limitedly represented. There has also been only a very small focus on South African LGBTQ+ people of Indian descent in other research studies (Dave, 2011; Dayal, 2021; Moonsammy, 2009).

Some media representations of sexual orientation-based discrimination experiences of South African Indian LGBTQ+ people are highlighted in this chapter. In a round-up of some of these media representations, this chapter first explores the historical and causal aspects of crime and violence in South Africa. It then proceeds to identify the prevalence of hate crimes, before unpacking the legal rights and cultural context of the LGBTQ+ communities.

## Hate Crimes in South Africa

Hate crimes are acts of prejudice that are committed against individuals, groups or organisations based on the groups they belong to (IACP, 1998; Marais, Nel, & Govender, 2022). These acts include hate speech, intentional unfair discrimination and other hate crimes, which occur across a variety of different settings (Triangle Project, 2006). These hate crimes are intended to dehumanise and demean individuals and groups of people (IACP, 1998). They also lead to mental health challenges and experiences of trauma on the part of the victims (Marais et al., 2022). Hate crime is a global challenge.

Within South Africa specifically, 7.3% of citizens who participated in the 2017 Victims of Crime Survey revealed that they feared being at the receiving end of hate crimes (Statistics South Africa, 2017). Hate crimes that occur most prevalently in South Africa include those that are based on nationality, race and sexual orientation. Within South Africa, homophobic views and vocalisations of hate speech against LGBTQ+ people are still prevalent, and some studies even reveal that there may be a rise of these negative views towards LGBTQ+ people (TMG Digital, 2016). Hate crimes against female-presenting people with LGBTQ+ identities are also seen to be higher than those against others (Nel & Judge, 2008). These hate crimes against women mostly occur in the form of corrective rape, murder and abuse of lesbian women (OUT, 2016).

In South Africa, hate crimes are criminal offences, and the National Policy Guideline for Victim Empowerment has introduced frameworks that address them. Due to the range of hate crimes present, legislature is constantly evolving, and currently, there exist some gaps in the frameworks which address them (Department of Justice and Constitutional Development, 2008; Department of Social Development, 2009; Nel & Judge, 2008). In 2016, updated hate crimes legislation was presented for passage (De Barros, 2018). These legislations have led to legal punishments for those who are perpetrators of hate crimes; which in turn led to renewed faith of citizens in the criminal justice system (Mitchley, 2018).

## Causes of Hate Crimes in South Africa

Hate crimes in South Africa occur due to a myriad of reasons (Demombynes & Özler, 2005; Statistics South Africa, 2017). Within this section, some of the debates surrounding the causes of hate crimes will be introduced. South Africa's history of Apartheid forms the backdrop of hate crimes and victimisation: from the mid-1950s to the late-1980s, rights of citizens were categorised in a racial hierarchy and the freedoms of certain race groups were restricted (Schönteich & Louw, 1999). Apartheid presented many challenges for citizens, such as the prevention of interracial marriages, the prevention of cohabitation among different races as well as limitations to the political expression of citizens (Kane-Berman, 1993). Around 1993, a period of transition occurred, which signalled the end of Apartheid (Schönteich & Louw, 1999). During this time, tensions existed within communities in South Africa, with a heightened amount of protests and crime (Schönteich & Louw, 1999). The intra-community conflict that occurred during Apartheid and towards the transition period led to an increase in the levels of crimes in under-resourced areas (Christopher, 1994; Ramphele, 1993). What's more, as Apartheid was rooted in Christian Calvinism, during this time the country saw an overvaluing of identities that aligned with values presented by patriarchy, traditional gender roles and conservatism (Cameron, 2001; Potgieter, 2006). Due to these factors, same-sex marriages and relationships were considered illegal, with sex between men being criminalised and identified as 'sodomy' (Cameron, 2001; Gunkel, 2010). People in same-sex relationships were often discriminated against, and if they openly expressed their identities, they were likely to experience job losses and family rejection (Wells & Polders, 2006).

The lack of legislative recognition by policymakers and authorities in South Africa has made the reporting and prosecuting of hate crimes challenging (De Barros, 2018). This legislative lack of recognition has been compounded by other challenging aspects such as socioeconomic status and lack of resources of citizens. Through the onset of urbanisation, crime rates in cities exceed crime in rural settings, with the crime rate increasing with the size of the city (Roelofse, 2009; Statistics South Africa, 2020). In larger cities factors such as unemployment, overcrowding and the rise in consumerism are believed to be factors that contribute towards higher crime rates (Chalfin & McCrary, 2017; Hsieh & Pugh, 1993; Pratt & Cullen, 2005; Rufrancos, Power, Pickett, & Wilkinson, 2013). The South African economy sees very high unemployment rates. All these factors have played intersectional roles in the perpetration of hate crimes. What's more, empirical evidence has shown that South African people are apprehensive to report hate crimes, where the Victims of Crime Survey of 2016/2017 state that a decline was noted (from 64.2% in 2011 to 57.3% in 2016/2017) in satisfaction levels experienced by the public in the South African Police Service (Statistics South Africa, 2017). Currently, only 7.7% of citizens have trust in the police services (Statistics South Africa, 2017). It will be unsurprising then, that the 2020 Victims of Crime Survey (Statistics South Africa, 2020) showed that not all crimes experienced get reported to the police.

In order to reduce hate crimes, an optimal criminal justice system that responds quickly to reported crimes is needed. This criminal justice system needs staff members who are fully equipped with knowledge on the updated legislation, in order to effectively apprehend and prosecute lawbreakers for their actions (Chalfin & McCrary, 2017). However, though efforts have been made on a national scale, this ideal justice system has not yet come into existence.

The 2016/2017 Victims of Crime Survey reveals that there is low satisfaction of South African citizens with the criminal justice system. The households' satisfaction with courts decreased from 64.5% in 2011 to only 44.9% in 2016/2017. Only 20.9% of the households felt that there was no corruption within South African courts, and the majority of households (45.8%) believed that sentences that were passed in courts were too lenient (Statistics South Africa, 2017). The Victims of Crime survey also revealed that South African people were disappointed that cases involving violent crimes took too long to finalise, which did not give people who reported these crimes effective justice (Statistics South Africa, 2017). These factors result in a decreased level of crime reporting, which in the case of hate crimes would result in a reduction in the prosecution of hate crime perpetrators. Within a province in Gauteng, Nel and Judge (2008) found that a staggering 73% of hate crimes do not get reported by people who experience them, due to a lack of confidence in the justice system and a belief that the reporting of hate crimes would not be given the attention that it needed. People who experience hate crimes also fear that during the process of reporting the hate crimes, they will be at the receiving end of secondary victimisation by a system that should ultimately be safeguarding them (Nel & Judge, 2008).

To promote a culture where hate speech and hate crimes are stopped, the media's role in showing the importance of seeking support is essential (Khan, 2018). Therefore, I'll go on to explore some of the media representations in South African online news and lifestyle platforms.

## Media Representations of Discrimination

Gender and sexual orientation–based discrimination experienced by South African LGBTQ+ people have been written about in many opinion pieces in the media. These articles display how these experiences negatively affect the lives of people who are at the receiving end of gender and sexual orientation–based discrimination. As the focus on these experiences of South African Indian LGBTQ+ people has not been emphasised as much in media, in this chapter an attempt is made to provide a focus on South African Indian LGBTQ+ people, by using media articles from the South African *Indian Spice, Independent Online* and *Mamba Onlinee-zines*.

### *"Calling Me a Faggot Is Not OK"*

The non-acceptance of LGBTQ+ people is often based on factors related to patriarchy, conservative cultures, heterosexism and religion (Ratele & Suffla, 2010). LGBTQ+ people walk the tightrope of fear and acceptance – where they are sometimes free to express themselves, and at other times experience overt and covert discrimination (Bhana, 2012). It is noteworthy that there are intersectional influences that lead to these experiences of discrimination of LGBTQ+ people (De Waal & Manion, 2006). In addition to legal attitudes that criminalise sexual orientation expression – a barrier which in theory has been overcome in South Africa – aspects such as community values, race, biological sex, economic background and other key identities, all play a role in how discrimination or freedom is experienced by LGBTQ+ people in South Africa and in other places (De Waal & Manion, 2006). In understanding the experiences of hate crimes, these key identities play a role in helping us understand how hate crimes are experienced, reported and processed, with each person relating to hate crimes in different ways (Meyer, 2008).

Naufal Khan, the openly gay publisher of *Indian Spice* e-zine, expressed that he has been openly experiencing sexual orientation–based discrimination throughout his life. He reveals: 'I have over the years been called a number of distasteful names due to…my sexual orientation' (Khan, 2018). And, 'Calling me a faggot is not ok' (Khan, 2018). Khan (2018) shares that derogatory names were used to make him feel uncomfortable in social settings. Within the South African context, several other names are used to discriminate against gay men, such as ungqingili, inkwili, moffie and faggot (Graham & Kiguwa, 2004).

LGBTQ+ discrimination happens at interpersonal, personal, institutional and community levels (Thompson & Zoloth, 1990). Victimisation experienced by LGBTQ+ people is not only verbal, but physical violence may also occur. LGBTQ+ people are beaten up, have objects thrown at them or objects used to harm them (OUT, 2016). Other forms of physical violence may be extreme forms of sexual violence such as corrective rape and sexual assault (Morris, 2017). Another reason LGBTQ+ people report for feeling unsafe is that their homes and property may be damaged due to spiteful hate crimes directed at them (Morris, 2017). A large-scale study focusing on the beliefs of residents in Gauteng, a South African province which is densely populated, found that 12% of participants believed that hate crimes were an appropriate way of dealing with people who identified as gay (Mahomed & Trangoš, 2016).

OUT LGBTQ+ Well-Being (an LGBTQ+ advocacy, research and healthcare organisation based in South Africa) conducted a large-scale study called the Hate Crimes Against LGBTQ+ people in a South Africa Survey (OUT, 2016). Their study revealed that 44% of the participants experienced all possible forms of discrimination. Of these forms of discrimination, the most common form of discrimination they experienced was verbal insults (20%), followed by being threatened with physical violence (17%). The study also revealed that the minority LGBTQ+ people of Indian descent experienced particularly high levels of discrimination, with 38% of them experiencing verbal insults, 17% being threatened with physical violence, 11% being sexually harmed and also 11% being abused by members of their families (OUT, 2016) – making studies on LGBTQ+ people of ethnic minorities, such as this one, especially relevant. These experiences of bullying of LGBTQ+ people, in varied settings, including schools, are often written about in media articles. One such example is an article by Jagmohan (2017), who interviewed the mother of a South African Indian gay man. The interviewee revealed that her son had experienced bullying regularly, which made him struggle with his sexual orientation. In the interview, she mentioned that her 'child had battled with constant bullying [...] and a struggle to accept his gay identity' (Jagmohan, 2017). She also says: 'At high school he had a torturous life and was physically beaten' (Jagmohan, 2017).

LGBTQ+ discrimination within South African school settings is noted by many researchers (Bhana, 2012; Francis & Reygan, 2016; Siwela, Sikhwari, & Mutshaeni, 2018). In the OUT (2016) survey, 56% of LGBTQ+ participants reportedly experienced sexual orientation bullying in schools. The bullying is often tied to the idea that within school heteronormative teaching methodologies perpetuate gender binaries, which results in students taking on traditional gender roles (Francis, 2017). Students who do not align with these traditional roles are often picked on (Francis, 2017).

The mechanics of LGBTQ+ bullying can be explained using the social identity theory: LGBTQ+ people are seen as an out-group, making them targets of discrimination and persecution as their identities are seen as incompatible with that of the in-group. The latter then resort to discriminatory methods to make the lives of the out-group members challenging (Terry & Hogg, 2001).

## *"People Don't Trust the System"*

The process of reporting hate crimes in South Africa presents unique challenges to people experiencing them, and there is often hesitation in reaching out to law enforcement officers when reporting these crimes.

One of these unique challenges is the difficulties present in the categorisation of hate crimes and the policies that are directly applicable to these crimes. Until changes in hate crimes legislation, which took effect in 2016, and were amended in 2018, policymakers were 'flying blind' when it came to processing hate crime reports (De Barros, 2018). Due to this, crimes that were reported were often classified in a different way, resulting in data related to hate crimes being incomplete or inconclusive (Lepodise, 2018). The existent empirical data were usually presented in studies done by South African non-governmental organizations (NGOs), who assisted those who experienced hate crimes by offering support in reporting and dealing with the impact of hate crimes (Lepodise, 2018). A five-year report by the Hate Crimes Working Group (HCWG) states that NGOs are at the frontline in terms of supporting those who experience hate crimes, with 43% of those who experience hate crimes contacting NGOs first, and only 26% going directly to the police, with the remainder contacting other organisations or healthcare facilities (Lepodise, 2018).

A legal victory linked to the reporting of hate crimes emerged in 2016, and again in 2018, when the South African Department of Justice revised a Bill designed to protect individuals from hate crimes, which was then approved by Cabinet (De Barros, 2018). This Bill was named the *Prevention and Combating of Hate Crimes and Hate Speech Bill,* and it has the criminalisation of hate crimes as its focus (De Barros, 2018). The Bill hopes to ensure swift punishment for those who perpetrate hate crimes, and it also aims to reduce the confusion surrounding the reporting of hate crimes. What's more, this Bill aims to provide improved training and knowledge to law enforcement officers when it comes to the managing and prosecution of people who commit hate crimes. According to an online news article by De Barros (2018), the Bill defines hate speech as the infliction of hate 'on the basis of age, albinism, birth, colour, culture, disability, ethnic or social origin, gender or gender identity, HIV status, language, nationality, migrant or refugee status, race, religion, or sex, which includes intersex or sexual orientation'.

Despite formalisation in hate crimes legislation, LGBTQ+ people continue to face challenges in reporting hate crimes. The OUT survey from 2016, the same year the Bill was introduced, reported that an astounding 88% of LGBTQ+ people do not report discrimination experiences to the police. Most LGBTQ+ people polled mention that this is often due to the fact that they do not believe that their reports will be taken seriously. What's more, some LGBTQ+ people do not openly reveal their sexualities in their communities, and they fear that reporting incidents of discrimination may cause their hidden sexualities to become known by members of the community they live in (OUT, 2016).

In an article in *Indian Spice* e-zine, Khan (2018) encourages LGBTQ+ people in South Africa to reach out for help and persevere in reporting hate crimes. He believes that often, people do not know how to report hate crimes, and they need to be educated. This is where he sees an important role for himself: the sharing of information and knowledge on experiences and legislation related to hate crimes. 'I want the LGBTQ+ community to know that you DO have a voice and there are options [... to] protect yourself from hate speech and much more' (Khan, 2018).

Another reason for the under-reporting of hate crimes remains the scepticism from South African citizens, who believe that what exists on paper does not always translate to real-life experiences (De Barros, 2016). In an online news article about the reporting of discrimination experiences, De Barros (2016) argues: 'Discrimination is experienced in everyday life and I don't know if this will stop it. [...] They pass these Bills but implementation is the problem'.

LGBTQ+ people also believe that they may be discriminated against by the court systems, which are meant to be protecting them (OUT, 2016). The OUT (2016) survey, which has a special section focusing on the experiences of LGBTQ+ people with the justice system, states that 25% of LGBTQ+ people withdrew cases of hate crimes, and a further 7% were too afraid to report to court. Those who withdrew cases or failed to report to courts may fear secondary victimisation. The reporting of hate crimes may also lead to secondary victimisation if they are not handled correctly (Nel & Judge, 2008). This secondary victimisation occurs when those who report hate crimes and discrimination are blamed by community members for the crimes that are reported, leading to social, emotional and psychological effects (Campbell & Raja, 2005). But it does not stop there: in addition to these personal and legal challenges, there are also reports that some LGBTQ+ people feel discriminated against when using healthcare services (OUT, 2016; Polders & Wells, 2004).

In essence, Lerato Phalakatshela, Hate Crime Manager at OUT LGBTQ+ Well-Being, in an interview with De Barros (2016), simply states the sad reality that: 'People don't trust the system' (De Barros, 2016). This was further affirmed by Dawie Nel, the Director of OUT LGBTQ+ Well-Being, who also mentioned the very long response time for receiving assistance from law enforcement officers (De Barros, 2016). '...it took more than 30 phone calls to get hold of the investigating officer' (De Barros, 2016).

Upon reporting hate crimes, LGBTQ+ people further mention that they did not find the police very helpful (OUT, 2016), and this led to low confidence in reporting hate crimes. In an older study by Polders and Wells (2004), 33% of LGBTQ+ people reported negative experiences when reporting hate crimes at police stations. Judging by the statistics from these two separate studies, it appears that not much has changed between 2004 and 2016, and that South African LGBTQ+ people continue to experience difficulties when reporting hate crimes – despite the major legal reforms.

### *"Fear, Humiliation, Shame"*

The problems with reporting hate crimes may be due to institutional limitations. However, there are also personal factors at play that impact hate crime reporting, and a person's inhibitions and fears during the reporting process may restrict one from seeking assistance after incidents of discrimination (De Barros, 2018). The fear of reporting hate crimes is high among LGBTQ+ people: OUT (2016) reported that 55% of LGBTQ+ people displayed high levels of fear of being discriminated against due to their sexual orientation. De Barros, based on the views of those assisting those who experience hate crimes, writes: 'emotional changes were noted, including fear, humiliation, shame, loss of trust and powerlessness' (De Barros, 2018).

Hate crimes are also reported differently by people of different genders, as especially men who experienced hate crimes felt embarrassed about reporting them (Louw, 2014). These men felt that there are social pressures to behave in strong and assertive ways, and reporting experiences of discrimination causes these men to feel ashamed and 'lesser than' (Louw, 2014). People who experience hate crimes may also experience self-blaming attitudes, where they may start to believe that they are the cause of their negative experiences, which results in them being embarrassed to speak to other people (Hill & Zautra, 1989).

The fear of reprisals from those who perpetrate hate crimes is also a constant fear of people reporting hate crimes (OUT, 2016; Sampson & Phillips, 1996). People who report crimes feel exhausted by the fact that they may need to challenge societal views and community attitudes in the process of seeking justice. They believe that they may not be able to cope with repeated victimisation and trauma, should they be discriminated against (Louw, 2014). What is evident is that discrimination against LGBTQ+ people leads to emotional and self-esteem difficulties in people who experience them (OUT, 2016), often leading to very serious life challenges.

### *"It All Starts With a Joke…Next…Someone Has Committed Suicide"*

The negative psychological, emotional and interpersonal challenges faced by LGBTQ+ people due to discrimination have been noted in many studies across different countries. Hate crimes may involve threatening messages which cause LGBTQ+ people to feel unsafe and unwanted in their communities, and LGBTQ+ people feel restricted and inhibited in their daily interpersonal relationships due to the negative impacts of hate crimes. The South African Hate

Crimes Working Group concluded that 50% of people experiencing hate crimes experienced emotional challenges; 7% experienced mental health effects; 35% experienced economic impacts and among 27% of LGBTQ+ people, negative living environments were experienced (Lepodise, 2018).

Muhsin Hendricks, a religious leader from South Africa, shares in an interview with Sheldon (2016), that hate crimes lead to challenges within communities, testing social cohesion and leading to a threatened feeling of physical and psychological well-being. Muhsin speaks of the impact of religion as well: 'There are a lot of lives being destroyed based on sexuality and religion, and that needs to change' (Sheldon, 2016). Though the legal changes are necessary and commendable, there needs to be constructive change within communities in order to allow for LGBTQ+ people to feel safer and accepted within their communities.

Most LGBTQ+ people live in communities that are heterosexist, and they are surrounded by symbols and attitudes that often marginalise them (Herek, Gillis, & Cogan, 1999). This marginalisation can also lead to feelings of internalised homophobia. This type of homophobia is defined as 'the gay person's direction of negative social attitudes toward the self, leading to a devaluation of the self and resultant internal conflicts and poor self-regard' (Meyer & Dean, 1998, p. 161). This internalised homophobia is often learned before LGBTQ+ people may be aware of their sexual orientation, as they may be raised in societies where they come into contact with homophobic messages; and the experiences of levels of self-devaluation is an inevitable part of identity development (Herek et al., 1999; Meyer, 1995). For LGBTQ+ people who are affiliated with communities that do not affirm different sexual orientations, a higher level of internalised homophobia is noted (Barnes & Meyer, 2012).

Internalised homophobia is also shown to decrease self-esteem, reduce motivation and may also affect intimacy and affection (Gormley & Lopez, 2010; Meyer & Dean, 1998). An extreme psychological challenge of internalised homophobia is its tendency to cause depersonalisation, where people who experience discrimination may feel detached and isolated from others (Rosenberg, 2000). The Right to Care organisation, an NGO in South Africa, echoes the view of researchers that LGBTQ+ people are more prone to suffering mental health challenges, substance abuse and extreme stress (Igual, 2018). It has also been identified that discrimination and microaggressions lead to workplace challenges among South African gay men (Dayal, 2021). A 2019 study on 27 South African corporate companies and multinational organisations highlighted that despite progressive company policies protecting LGBTQ+ people, many of the policies are administrative and that practically, work needs to continuously be done to ensure that diversity policies are being implemented (The South African LGBTQ+ Management Forum, 2018, 2019). This, again, shows the paradox of institutional progressiveness and cultural resistance.

The damaging impact of media in perpetuating discrimination against LGBTQ+ people was highlighted by Khan (2018), in his online review of a recent South African movie focusing on the South African Indian community. The movie, *Broken Promises*, showcased examples of heteronormativity and homonegative dialogues, in which gay men were used for comic relief. Using gay men in overly effeminate roles tends to create narrow views of gay men. These gay men are made out to be out-group members, and seen as deviant and subordinate. Negative associations with LGBTQ+ characters were also identified with movies made in India's Bollywood cinema (Kaur, 2017). This may lead to incidents of discrimination and hate speech, and even emotional challenges. Khan (2018) vehemently states: 'It all starts with a joke and the next thing you know someone has committed suicide' (Khan, 2018). In another news article, a South African Indian mother speaks of the emotional pain her son endured due to homophobic abuse and repeated bullying: '[He] attempted suicide twice. He consumed all of his anti-depressants' (Jagmohan, 2017).

The South African Human Science Research Council in a 2016 study revealed that 31% of LGBTQ+ people have thought of suicide, and this statistic is well above the national average, further indicating the vulnerability of LGBTQ+ people (Igual, 2018). The South African Depression and Anxiety Group, an NGO providing counselling and support, reveals that LGBTQ+ people may be twice as likely to attempt suicide (SADAG, 2017). Among those who have thoughts of suicide, SADAG (2017) believes that Indian gay men experience cultural pressures and pressures from Indian media representations of men and gay men, that make them more vulnerable to mental health challenges. Many NGOs and other support organisations in South Africa work together to encourage a culture of support and reduced discrimination. However, it is also important for parents to note the damaging impact of discrimination on their children. As a concerned South African mother states in an interview with *Independent Online:* 'Parents need to listen to their children. We need to stop criticising and let people live' (Jagmohan, 2017).

Families have an important role to play in promoting self-acceptance among LGBTQ+ people. Family support allows for a positive self-image and greater psychological well-being (Ryan, Russell, Huebner, Diaz, & Sanchez, 2010). LGBTQ+ people show a reduction of mental health challenges if they have a safe space to live in. Family members and community members have an instrumental role to play in creating this safe space.

## Conclusion

South Africa's history of violence and oppression is well documented in all forms of academic literature and mainstream media (Hirsch, 2005). During the time of South Africa's democratic transition, South Africa served as a beacon of hope for many nations. However, over two decades post-democracy, South Africa continues to experience crime and violence at a high rate. Despite sound legislation and Constitutional protection, South African citizens continue to face difficulties. Among South African citizens experiencing challenges, LGBTQ+ people in South Africa are particularly vulnerable (Khan, 2017). Hate crimes against LGBTQ+ people happen at alarming rates (OUT, 2016). These hate crimes result in a sense of fear and humiliation, and intense mental health and emotional challenges among those who experience hate crimes. Due to infrastructure concerns and a lack of confidence in the justice system (OUT, 2016; Statistics South Africa, 2017), there are a lower amount of crimes being reported. In order to sustain social cohesion and remedy tears in the social fabric, societies need to stand together in promoting the acceptance of all members.

# References

Barnes, D. M., & Meyer, I. H. (2012). Religious affiliation, internalized homophobia, and mental health in lesbians, gay men, and bisexuals. *American Journal of Orthopsychiatry, 82*(4), 505–515. doi:10.1111/j.1939-0025.2012.01185.x

Bennett, J., & Reddy, V. (2015). African positionings: South African relationships with continental questions of LGBTI justice and rights. *Agenda, 29*(1), 37–41. doi: 10.1080/10130950.2015.1015829

Bhana, D. (2012). Understanding and addressing homophobia in schools: A view from teachers. *South African Journal of Education, 32*, 307–318. doi:10.15700/saje. v32n3a659

Cameron, E. (2001). Constitutional protection of sexual orientation and African conceptions of humanity. *South African Law Journal, 118*, 628.

Campbell, R., & Raja, S. (2005). The sexual assault and secondary victimization of female veterans: Help-seeking experiences in military and civilian social systems. *Psychology of Women Quarterly, 29*, 97–106. doi:10.1111/j.1471-6402.2005.00171.x

Chalfin, A., & McCrary, J. (2017). Criminal deterrence: A review of the literature. *Journal of Economic Literature, 55*(1), 5–48. doi:10.1257/jel.20141147

Christopher, A. J. (1994). *The Atlas of Apartheid*. London: Routledge.

Coopoosamy, D. (2018, March 4). Same sex marriage in the SA Indian community. *Indian Spice*. Retrieved from https://www.indianspice.co.za/2018/03/04/same-sex-marriage-in-the-sa-indian-community-religious-leaders-speak-out/

Dave, P. (2011). *Experiences of Indian gay and lesbian individuals*. Honours thesis, University of Cape Town, Cape Town, South Africa. Retrieved from http://www. psychology.uct.ac.za/sites/default/files/image_tool/images/117/Punam.Dave.pdf

Dayal, D. N. (2021). *Microaggressions against South African gay Indian men*. Master's thesis, University of Johannesburg, Johannesburg, South Africa. Retrieved from https://ujcontent.uj.ac.za/vital/%20access/manager/Repository/uj:43235? view=null&f0=sm_creator%3A%22Dayal%2C+Deepesh+Nirmaldas%22&sort= sort_ss_title%2F

De Barros, L. (2016, November 29). Shocking scale of LGBT discrimination in South Africa revealed. *Mamba Online*. Retrieved from http://www.mambaonline.com/ 2016/11/29/shocking-scale-lgbt-discrimination-south-africa-revealed/

De Barros, L. (2018, February 9). New report reveals critical need for hate crimes law in SA. *Mamba Online*. Retrieved from http://www.mambaonline.com/2018/02/09/ new-report-reveals-desperate-need-hate-crimes-bill-sa/

De Waal, A., & Manion, A. (2006). *Pride: Protest and celebration*. Johannesburg: Fanele.

Demombynes, G., & Özler, B. (2005). Crime and local inequality in South Africa. *Journal of Development Economics, 76*(2), 265–292.

Department of Justice and Constitutional Development. (2008). *Equality for all. Promotion of equality and prevention of unfair discrimination Act No 4 of 2000.* Information brochure.

Department of Social Development. (2009). *Integrated victim empowerment policy.* Pretoria: Department of Social Development.

Eagle, G., Benn, M., Fletcher, T., & Sibisi, H. (2013). Engaging with intergroup prejudice in victims of violent crime/attack. *Peace and Conflict: Journal of Peace Psychology, 19*(3), 240–252. doi:10.1037/a0033685

Francis, D. A. (2017). Homophobia and sexuality diversity in South African schools: A review. *Journal of LGBT Youth, 14*(4), 359–379. doi:10.1080/19361653.2017.1326868

Francis, D., & Brown, A. (2017). 'To correct, punish and praise' LRC leaders experiences and expressions of non-heterosexuality in Namibian schools. *International Journal of Inclusive Education, 21*(12), 1–18. doi:10.1080/13603116.2.017.1336577

Francis, D., & Reygan, F. (2016). Let's see if it won't go away by itself: LGBT microaggressions among teachers in South Africa. *Education as Change, 20*(3), 180–201. doi:10.17159/1947-9417/2016/1124

Gormley, B., & Lopez, F. G. (2010). Psychological abuse perpetration in college dating relationships. *Journal of Interpersonal Violence, 25*(2), 204–218. doi:10.1177/0886260509334404

Graham, T., & Kiguwa, S. (2004). *Experiences of black LGBT youth in peri-urban communities in South Africa.* Cape Town: CMFD Productions and The Institute for Democracy in South Africa (IDASA).

Gunkel, H. (2010). *The cultural politics of female sexuality in South Africa.* New York, NY: Routledge.

Herek, G. M., Gillis, J. R., & Cogan, J. C. (1999). Psychological sequelae of hate crime victimization among lesbian, gay, and bisexual adults. *Journal of Consulting and Clinical Psychology, 67*, 945–951. doi:10.1037/0022-006X.67.6.945

Hill, J. L., & Zautra, A. J. (1989). Self-blame attributions and unique vulnerability as predictors of post-rape demoralization. *Journal of Social and Clinical Psychology, 8*, 368–375. doi:10.1521/jscp.1989.8.4.368

Hirsch, A. (2005). *Season of hope: Economic reform under Mandela and Mbeki.* Pietermaritzburg: University of KwaZulu-Natal Press.

Hsieh, C., & Pugh, M. D. (1993). Poverty, income inequality, and violent crime: A meta- analysis of recent aggregate data studies. *Criminal Justice Review, 18*(2), 182–202. doi:10.1177/073401689301800203

Igual, R. (2018, July 31). Local film Broken Promises 4-ever accused of insulting gay community. *Mamba Online.* Retrieved from http://www.mambaonline.com/2018/07/31/local-film-broken-promises-4-ever-accused-of-insulting-gay-community/

International Association of Chiefs of Police (IACP). (1998). Responding to hate crimes: A police officer's guide to investigation and prevention. Retrieved from http://www.theiacp.org/documents. Accessed onApril 18, 2018.

Jagmohan, K. (2017, November 26). Mother's heartache after gay son's death. IOL. Retrieved from https://www.iol.co.za/sunday-tribune/news/mothers-heartache-after-gay-sons-death-12156567

Kane-Berman, J. (1993). *Political violence in South Africa.* Johannesburg: South African Institute of Race Relations.

Kaur, P. (2017). Gender, sexuality and (be) longing: The representation of queer (LGBT) in Hindi cinema. *Amity Journal of Media and Communication Studies*, *7*(1), 22–30. Retrieved from https://ajmcs.blogspot.com/

Keeton, G. (2014). Inequality in South Africa. *The Journal of the Helen Suzman Foundation*, *74*, 26–31.

Khan, N. (2017, March 30). What's it like being gay in the South African Indian community? *Indian Spice*. Retrieved from https://www.indianspice.co.za/2017/07/whats-it-like-being-gay-in-the-indian-community/

Khan, N. (2018, February 9). Calling me a faggot is not ok. *Indian Spice*. Retrieved from https://www.indianspice.co.za/2018/03/30/calling-me-a-faggot-is-not-okay-says-naufal-khan/

Lepodise, O. (2018, February 9). Hate crimes: New report cites policing, lack of records as main problems to addressing the issue. *Daily Maverick*. Retrieved from https://www.dailymaverick.co.za/article/2018-02-09-hate-crimes-new-report-cites-policing-lack-of-records-as-main-problems-to-addressing-the-issue/

Louw, A. (2014, April 11). Men are also corrective rape victims. Bhekisisa. Retrieved from https://bhekisisa.org/article/2014-04-11-men-are-also-corrective-rape-victims

Mahomed, F., & Trangoš, G. (2016). An exploration of public attitudes toward LGBTI rights in the Gauteng city-region of South Africa. *Journal of Homosexuality*, *63*(10), 1400–1421. doi:10.1080/00918369.2016.1157999

Marais, A., Nel, J. A., & Govender, R. (2022). Emotional consequences of hate incidents: Experiences of a South African cohort. *South African Journal of Psychology*, *52*(1), 122–134. doi:10.1177/0081246320985343

Meyer, I. H. (1995). Minority stress and mental health in gay men. *Journal of Health and Social Behavior*, *36*, 38–56.

Meyer, D. (2008). Interpreting and experiencing anti-queer violence: Race, class and gender difference among LGBT hate crime victims. *Race, gender and class*, *15*(3/4), 262–282.

Meyer, I., & Dean, L. (1998). Internalized homophobia, intimacy and sexual behavior among gay and bisexual men. In G. Herek (Ed.), *Stigma and sexual orientation* (pp. 160–186). Thousand Oaks, CA: Sage.

Mitchley, A. (2018, April 4). The Vicki Momberg case: Equality court vs criminal court. *news24*. Retrieved from https://www.news24.com/SouthAfrica/News/the-vicki-momberg-case-equality-court-vs-criminal-court-,0404

Mkhize, N., Bennett, J., Reddy, V., & Moletsane, R. (2010). *The country we want to live in: Hate crimes and homophobia in the lives of black lesbian South Africans.* Cape Town: HRSC Press.

Moonsammy, D. (2009). *What will people say? Three stories of Indian women loving women in Jozi.* Master's thesis, University of the Witwatersrand, Johannesburg, South Africa. Retrieved from http://wiredspace.wits.ac.za/handle/10539/45/browse?value=Moonsammy%2C+Davina&type=author

Morris, M. (2017, April 12). LGBT community still faces high levels of violence. *news24*. Retrieved from https://www.news24.com/Analysis/LGBT-community-still-faces-high-levels-of-violence-report-20171204

Nel, J. A., & Judge, M. (2008). Exploring homophobic victimisation in Gauteng, South Africa: Issues, impacts and responses. *Acta Criminologica*, *21*(3), 19–36.

OUT. (2016). Hate crimes survey. Retrieved from https://out.org.za/library/reports/

Potgieter, C. (2006). The imagined future for gays and lesbians in South Africa: Is this it? *Agenda: Empowering Women for Gender Equity, 67,* 4–7.

Pratt, T. C., & Cullen, F. T. (2005). Assessing macro-level predictors and theories of crime: A meta-analysis. *Crime and Justice, 32,* 373–450.

Polders, L., & Wells, H. (2004). *Overall research findings on levels of empowerment among LGBT people in Gauteng, South Africa.* Pretoria: Out LGBT Well-being.

Ramphele, M. (1993). *A bed called home: Life in the migrant labour hostels of Cape Town.* Cape Town: David Phillip.

Ratele, K., & Suffla, S. (2010). Men, masculinity and cultures of violence and peace in South Africa. In C. Blazina & D. S. Shen-Miller (Eds.), *An international psychology of men: Theoretical advances, case studies, and clinical innovations.* New York, NY: Routledge.

Roelofse, C. J. (2009). *Organised crime in South Africa. Urbanization, policing and security: Global perspectives.* London: CRC Press.

Rosenberg, L. G. (2000). Phase oriented psychotherapy for gay men recovering from trauma. *Journal of Gay & Lesbian Social Services, 12*(1–2), 37–73. doi:10.1300/J041v12n01_03

Rufrancos, H. G., Power, M., Pickett, K. E., & Wilkinson, R. (2013). Income inequality and crime: A review and explanation of the time-series evidence. *Social Criminology, 1*(1), 1–9.

Ryan, C., Russell, S. T., Huebner, D., Diaz, R., & Sanchez, J. (2010). Family acceptance in adolescence and the health of LGBT young adults. *Journal of Child and Adolescent Psychiatric Nursing, 23*(4), 205–213. doi:10.1111/j.1744-6171.2010.00246.x

SADAG. (2017, September 12). Homosexuals, depression and suicide. Retrieved from http://sadag.org/index.php?option=com_content&view=article&id=169:homosexuals-depression-and-suicide&catid=61&Itemid=143

Sampson, A., & Phillips, C. (1996). *Reducing repeat victimisation on an East London Estate.* Police research group crime prevention unit crime prevention and detection paper 67. Home Office, London, England.

Schönteich, M., & Louw, A. (1999). Crime trends in South Africa 1985–1998. In Paper commissioned by the Centre for the Study of Violence and Reconciliation as part of a review of the National Crime Prevention Strategy carried out for the Department of Safety and Security, June.

Sheldon, R. (2016, October 31). Inside Cape Town's gay mosque. *IOL.* Retrieved from https://www.iol.co.za/news/south-africa/western-cape/inside-cape-towns-gay-mosque-2085211

Siwela, V. G., Sikhwari, T. D., & Mutshaeni, N. H. (2018). Exploring challenges faced by homosexual youths and their parents in Driekoppies, Enhlanzeni district, Mpumalanga province, South Africa. *Gender & Behaviour, 16*(1), 10677–10685. Retrieved from https://www.ajol.info/index.php/gab

Statistics South Africa. (2017). *Victims of crime survey 2016/2017.* Pretoria: Statistics South Africa.

Statistics South Africa. (2020). *Victims of crime survey 2019/2020.* Pretoria: Statistics South Africa.

Sutherland, C., Roberts, B., Gabriel, N., Struwig, J., & Gordon, S. (2016). *Progressive prudes: A survey of attitudes towards homosexuality & gender non-conformity in*

*South Africa*. Retrieved from http://ecommons.hsrc.ac.za/handle/20.500.11910/ 10161

Terry, D. J., & Hogg, M. A. (2001). Attitudes, behaviour, and social context: The role of norms and group membership in social influence processes. In J. P. Forgas & K. D. Williams (Eds.), *Social influence: Direct and indirect processes* (pp. 253–270). New York, NY: Psychology Press.

The South African LGBT Management Forum. (2018). *South African workplace equality Index 2018*. Retrieved from http://LGBTforum.org/resources

The South African LGBT Management Forum. (2019). *South African workplace equality Index 2019*. Retrieved from http://LGBTforum.org/resources

Thompson, C., & Zoloth, B. (1990). *Homophobia, a pamphlet produced by the campaign to end homophobia*. Cambridge, MA.

Thoreson, R. (2008). Somewhere over the rainbow nation: Gay, lesbian and bisexual activism in South Africa. *Journal of Southern African Studies, 34*(3), 679–697. doi: 10.1080/03057070802259969

TMG Digital. (2016, November 29). Majority of LGBT South Africans live in fear of discrimination. *Times Live*. Retrieved from https://www.timeslive.co.za/news/ south-africa/2016-11-29-majority-of-LGBT-south-africans-live-in-fear-of-discrimination/

Triangle Project. (2006). *Sometimes X, Sometimes Y (always me). An anthology of lesbian writing from South Africa*. E-book. Cape Town: Triangle Project.

Wells, H., & Polders, L. (2006). Anti-gay hate crimes in South Africa: Prevalence, reporting practices, and experiences of the police. *Agenda, 20*(67), 20–28. doi:10. 1080/10130950.2006.9674694

# Gender-Based Violence and Society

# Section III: Gender-Based Violence and Society

*Gavan Patrick Gray, Nidhi Shrivastava and Deepesh Nirmaldas Dayal*

## Abstract

This chapter is a transcript of an open-ended discussion that occurred between the authors when they met to discuss the subject matter of the third section of the book, which focuses on cultural and normative attitudes toward the problem of gender violence. As with the previous introductory dialogues, the discussion takes place after preliminary drafts have been completed and the authors share their thoughts on the subjects that they will each discuss in more detail in the following chapters. These include the culture of silence surrounding rape in India, the way masculine gender norms impact the treatment of women in Japan and the cultural factors that drive microaggressions targeted at LGBTQ+ people in South Africa.

*Keywords*: Gender violence; gender norms; society; Japan; India; South Africa

**Gray:** Nidhi, in an earlier chapter you asked me to comment on the commodification of the 'lolita' culture. It's something I examine in more depth in the upcoming chapter, but there is very definitely a sexualisation and commodification of schoolgirls that is extremely bad for Japan's international image. It has a reputation for this highly sexualised 'lolita' imagery, whether in books, games, animation or its music industry. However, this element of fetishisation is very localised to specific cultural groups, and sexual elements of it are rarely seen in general daily life. While Japan does have a semi-open sex industry, everyday life is far less sexualised than the West in terms of music, television and advertising.

Gender Violence, the Law, and Society, 123–129

doi:10.1108/978-1-80117-127-420221010

Japan has a far higher degree of purity and innocence in its 'daytime' life, a stark contrast to the commodified sex of its 'nighttime' life.

**Shrivastava:** Is there a specific reason for the overt sexualisation of youth?

**Gray:** Well, that's a key factor that is often overlooked, the focus on 'youth' is not always sexual. There is an element of Japanese culture that simply prizes youth and views the high school years in particular as one of the ideal stages of life. As a result, the commodification of this age, which is the focus of some of the country's most popular TV shows and pop groups, is not simply about sexuality but about people's emotional connection to that period. This extends to things such as Papa Katsu,[1] insofar as it is not always a sexual exchange that is involved but sometimes a purely emotional one, i.e. the men involved pay for the facade of an emotional relationship, rather than simply for sex, often as a response to an inability to form emotionally open relationships in their 'real' lives.

This does not, of course, make it healthier for either party, but it does make the situation a little more complex than it is often portrayed. At one extreme you have the focus on youth, which has its own genre called *seishun* in Japan, as a period of innocence, strong emotional bonds and boundless possibility, which is the selling point of so many TV dramas and idol groups. Then, at a mid-point of commodification, you have Papa Katsu, which is an exchange that can be either emotionally or sexually motivated. At the alternate far end, you have the more extreme sexual commodification of youth that can be seen in sexually explicit animation and DVDs featuring young children in skimpy clothes.

**Dayal:** And, is this, these products, are they legal in Japan?

**Gray:** Part of the problem is that the issue has yet to be treated, at a legal or political level, with the severity that it deserves. Possession of child pornography was only banned in Japan in 2015 and a casual attitude toward the sexualisation of children still seems commonplace, something I would personally ascribe to widespread ignorance of the extent of the problem rather than indifference to its effects. This links back to what I mentioned at the beginning of this book; Japan is generally a very safe and relatively chaste society, and people tend to avoid looking into or examining the more shadowy areas where problematic behaviour is often rampant. Like many elements of Japanese culture, its more extreme segments tend to get more attention overseas than they do in Japan itself. So, while most Japanese people do not often see the dark side of this area, it is something that international audiences have come to associate with Japan. In all likelihood, it will be these international views that generate sufficient pressure for the government to finally take stronger action in protecting young people from sexual predation.

**Dayal:** There are many places in the world that do not share the same view on sexual and gender violence. It is important that all countries equally consider the seriousness of these crimes.

**Gray:** That's right. And it's one of the key reasons why we're looking at these alternative perspectives. In the European Union and United States, discussions of

---

[1] A form of commodified dating discussed in more detail in Chapter 8.

gender violence or sexual crimes – while still dark and sensitive – have become relatively easy to examine in both social and institutional terms. But, in so many other parts of the world, there are these extra barriers where the social stigma is still placed on the victim and where there can be a distinct lack of support services to provide mental and emotional care for them.

**Shrivastava:** Actually, that's the common thread for all three of us, I think: that there are additional factors in some societies and cultures, things like shame, family honour or collective identity that can place additional burdens and stress upon women and that are not necessarily taken into account by standard Western approaches to these issues.

**Dayal:** Some families seem almost embarrassed when a member tells them what happened to them and the most important thing is that they don't want anybody to know about it.

**Shrivastava:** This reminds me of my dissertation work, where I came across the story of a son, who was mad at his mother for not killing herself as a way to protect the family honour. So he just refused to acknowledge her existence. But it's another kind of silencing, the failure of not just communities but families to acknowledge victimhood.

**Dayal:** I feel, for me, with the studies that I look at regarding South African gay men, there's this idea of just being a man or, rather, that you're less of a man, if you speak about any kind of problem with sexual or gender violence. They are told that they're 'being a sissy' or to 'man up'. Even when they just want to be open with their family they're not even given that relief due to the social barriers that can prevent basic discussion of some topics. It's such a tragedy.

**Shrivastava:** With sexual violence, another problem, in India at least, is that against young girls it is always private and usually with a relative, within the extended family. And, in these cases, it is the family's reputation that can be seen as the most important thing to protect, which gives power to the perpetrator. It can even empower them to do it again or to feel comfortable doing similar things to other people.

**Dayal:** Focusing on the perpetrator. Because, obviously, one has to go into 'why do they behave the way that they do' and, I think, some of these perpetrators say 'you know, well, this is just how we were brought up' or 'this is just the way society moulded' and they reject any personal responsibility for their behaviour.

**Gray:** And, of course, that rings false because, if it was true, you'd have an entire generation who were brought up under those social values all acting the same way, and they don't. Some develop quite liberal, open-minded views, and it's only a small group of them that end up with these warped patterns of behaviour. But these social forces can certainly influence people in these directions, create pressure to follow negative patterns or hold negative views of women and minorities. And they can certainly be used by them to justify their behaviour rather than reflecting upon it as a personal failing.

**Shrivastava:** This links to what I focus on in my chapter, which is that there is a culture of silence in India, again regarding certain elements of society that people like to avoid looking at. And recently there has emerged a trend in terms of how filmmakers are trying to change the conversation on rape victim-survivors. There are multiple ways in which the silence exists, both in the public and private sphere, and one is that the media tend to be quiet about the names or identities of rape survivors, even where they have publicly spoken out, and so feminists argue that they are taking away the identity of the women and reducing them to just statistics which isn't fair to them.

There is often an attitude of, like, whatever happened to you, it's a personal thing and we don't want to hear about it and don't need to think about it. As though it will be harmful to them or for society for awareness of these crimes to become more widely known. The same thing happens with child sexual abuse, even more so in that case because usually the criminal is someone the victim knows, and so there is more pressure to keep things quiet. This is something that filmmakers are trying to disrupt by showing that these problems exist, and that they exist everywhere, across caste and class.

**Gray:** Where I'm coming from in this section is a little different. For my final chapter, I'm looking at how male gender norms, or specific variants of them, affect the way that women are treated both on an individual and institutional level. People often talk about 'toxic masculinity', but it's incredibly reductive as there are many types of masculinity, many of which are culturally specific, and more than one of which can be quite negative in the way it views or treats women.

**Shrivastava:** I'm actually reading a book at the moment called *The Damage* by Caitlin Wahrer, and it looks at the issue of rape among gay men, so I think it's both an example of what you mean by different types of harmful masculinity but also another culture of silence where the majority of people are still so uncomfortable with this topic and don't know how to discuss it openly.

**Gray:** That's part of what I'm looking at, in that some topics are silenced at the social level, where you are affecting others, or at least others feel you are affecting them, by speaking about it. But some topics are silenced at the personal level because we don't learn how to express ourselves or engage with the issues on an emotional level. In Japan, with many instances of men who have poor connections with women, it seems to stem from the social pressures that relegate the development of male emotional bonds to an insignificant level of priority.

When this kind of thing becomes generational you have young men growing up with emotionally removed father figures and so they see wives as being the same as mothers and having a very specific social role. The idea of treating them as equals, whether as friends, lovers or colleagues, becomes somewhat alien to them, and when they encounter a new type of woman who is less traditional and more assertive, they react with discomfort, fear or anger. And the real problem is that they don't have the emotional or communicative toolset to deal with these issues in an open and healthy manner. Again, this doesn't apply to all men, but it is common enough in Japan to be noticeable.

**Dayal:** This inability to communicate and to understand or properly express their emotions is something that I have also come across in relation to my research on microaggressions. When you see men who react negatively to gay men, often it is because the subject of homosexuality itself was taboo so there was never any discussion about it. And so when they encounter not just gay men, but even men who are comfortable emotionally, they react by being nasty and labelling them as effeminate or unmasculine because they feel they can show they are not gay by being nasty to anyone who is gay or even displays femininity.

**Gray:** It's exactly the same with men showing more misogynist tendencies, an inability to interact comfortably with women, I think due to a lack of emotionally open male role models, creates hostility toward women.

**Dayal:** The idea of men communicating in an emotional way needs to be normalised.

**Gray:** I wonder, Nidhi, you focus on the use of media more than either of us, do you think there is a shift in how media is addressing these issues? Do you feel it is helping raise awareness, or helping break open the Overton Window in a way that lets young people access or discuss topics that were formerly taboo?

**Shrivastava:** Well, some of the films I actually look at address this topic in a way, for example the 2014 film called *Highway*, in which the daughter of a wealthy industrialist is kidnapped by a gang of lower-class men. However, the girl develops a bond with one of them and they share their tales of how they both experienced childhood abuse. In the end, this gives the girl the confidence to confront her family and her abuser and to challenge the culture of silence they had supported.

Another film is called *Article 15* from 2019, which is an even darker story about two girls who were gang-raped and murdered and how caste differences affect attitudes toward and investigation of the crimes. Finally, I also look at *Bombay Begums*, a recent TV drama on Netflix about a group of women who each have personal challenges to overcome, which highlights social problems affecting women that rarely get this kind of coverage in the media. So, you can kind of see that media, especially more international types like Netflix, are touching on topics that would have been hard to do in the past.

**Gray:** And this, again, kind of goes back to something we mentioned in the last section, which was that you have a middle-class who are highlighting problems that are affecting less well-off groups, or, in some cases, which are universal.

**Shrivastava:** Yes, I suppose that the awareness raised by these movies and shows, especially through Netflix, are accessible, though somewhat middle-class, in India at least. So, it is good in that it might be creating a wider understanding of different issues, or even creating a new set of future activists, but it is probably not doing a lot to change attitudes or cultural norms at lower economic levels. But maybe there is a chance that they might disrupt the silence. So while there are some problems with the pathway, I think it can be good if it can change the audience from being passive into being activists, not just being aware of the problems but actually doing something to address them.

**Gray:** In your case, you see media as a way of broadening this awareness. In my own chapter, I highlight education as the way to improve and inform people's understanding, especially young people. But it's clear, I think, that there are multiple paths that these messages can take and that, ideally, they would be reinforcing one another.

**Dayal:** Actually, that's precisely what I am looking at in my final chapter: the intersectionality of the messages and pressures that produce these problems – coming from family, from culture, from religion – and how they kind of work upon each other to put down these layers that can end up silencing people. I guess you are looking in the opposite direction, at how positive layers of messaging can help lift that blanket of silence and give people a greater voice or more freedom.

**Gray:** Well, this is one area where education, I think, has a greater reach than media. In Japan, there is a very low level of effective sex education in schools. I think there might be a conservative view that if junior high school kids begin learning about sex then they will start having sex and teen pregnancies will increase, when, generally, the opposite is true and better education tends to prevent that. More importantly, it's an area, encompassing human relationships and emotional ties, that is frequently overlooked in education and which offers huge potential for preemptively addressing many social problems.

**Dayal:** Yes, if I can just pick up on that regarding microaggressions. It is an area that is still not clearly defined, and it is not something people really speak about. Instead, hate crimes and hate speech are far more common, and there is still such a lack of understanding of the other forms of abuse that are expressed more covertly. I think these undercurrents of discrimination are an area where education can be used to raise awareness.

**Gray:** Is there, do you think, a danger in that the media often focuses on more dramatic instances of abuse or discrimination, and that sometimes the more subtle forms get overlooked or even dismissed as being 'less important', even though, as we are well aware, the subtle and constant pervasive effect can be equally harmful over the long term?

**Dayal:** Well, I think there is that element of the overt and covert forms, and that the former definitely receives more attention. But you also tend to see issues of sexual discrimination being lumped in with gender discrimination, and in the latter field, the focus tends to be less on the experiences of men. So, to some extent, the stories of men, whether gay men or male rape, tend to be a little more silenced in that they don't receive the same kind of media attention, at least.

**Shrivastava:** Just to touch on that, perhaps you are speaking about news media, but I wanted to mention a show I saw called *Made in Heaven*, which is one of the few entertainment representations of gay Indian men that I have seen. It includes things like harassment from the police and also, I think, the subject of rape. I think this is part of that movement by activists or feminist filmmakers to tackle these kinds of untouched subjects. This show was made by Amazon, and I think these online services are offering room for more of this kind of activist entertainment to be introduced.

**Gray:** From what I have seen as well, I only really know of Netflix, but they seem to be doing a good job of finding and nurturing regional talent. So they can introduce more liberal issues, but do it in a way that it is coming more organically from within the region and made by people who properly understand the region and its complexities.

**Shrivastava:** Yes, the online platforms allow for less censorship and regulation, although now the Indian Government is trying to catch up on it. They're starting to kind of say, 'Okay, we want you to know we'll start banning Netflix or whatever, or some of your shows, if you don't make these changes'. And it's things like, in *Bombay Begums* there was a whole section on menstruation and the government. Some media were saying it has a negative effect on women by sexualising them faster, which is obviously nonsense. What it is doing is creating a space for dialogue and education that wasn't there when I was growing up. I certainly couldn't speak to my mother comfortably about anything connected to sex when I was younger, and that is changing. But, it may be that it is changing mostly for the middle class and the urban residents, and that the lower class and rural people are still trapped by these kinds of barriers and old-fashioned attitudes.

**Gray:** We have been speaking a lot of the importance of Western researchers and activists being aware of the complexities of other regions and cultures, but it's good that you point out how important it is to remember that even where successful efforts are being made to introduce more progressive values in a culturally informed manner, there are still groups locally that are unlikely to have access to those messages. It's so important to build direct connections with the people who are most directly affected, and I think one of the privileges we have is that while those people often cannot travel to other countries or meet the people in them who might share their problems or live in similar circumstances, we can act as a bridge of sorts, to help build connections and share information on those underreported areas.

**Shrivastava:** This is why speaking like this, or meeting at conferences, is so important: it allows us to really explore and understand the issues in a more complete way that really brings the focus back to the human element of the issues and the fact that it is not an abstract problem but things that affect real people each and every day.

**Dayal:** I couldn't agree more. I know I can learn a lot from reading the chapters that you have written, but having a chance to speak with you and explore these issues in a more natural manner makes a huge difference, both in helping to understand the topic and also in bringing home its reality.

Chapter 7

# India – Rape and the Prevalent Culture of Silence in Indian Cinema and Television

*Nidhi Shrivastava*

## Abstract

In this chapter, I explore two media texts, Imtiaz Ali's *Highway* and Alankrita Shrivastava's Netflix original series *Bombay Begums* (2021). I contend that recent filmmakers have begun to arguably reframe the narratives of rape victim-survivors and disrupting the cultural of silence described above. They offer progressive and multi-faceted representations of these experiences, such that there is an opportunity for a dialogue within both private and public spheres. What I mean when I say that they are 'progressive representations' is that the rape victim-survivors are not merely reduced to helpless women in distress, nor painted as vengeful, aggressive characters. Instead, their characterisation shows that they have agency and autonomy, but at the same time struggle with the repercussions of speaking out against their perpetrators in a society that does not support them wholly.

*Keywords*: #MeToo movement; India; caste system; class; honour; silence

In a thought-provoking article, Krupa Shandilya (2015) calls attention to the construction of Jyoti Singh Pandey aka Nirbhaya, the victim of the 2012 Delhi rape case 'both as "everywoman" and as a middle-class, upper-caste, Hindu woman' (p. 465). She then furthers her argument that 'despite feminist interventions that call attention to the intersections of caste, class and gender, the bodies of lower-caste, lower-class, non-Hindu rural women are excluded from protest movements' (p. 406). For Shandilya, the reason for their exclusion is that 'mainstream Indian feminist demand for legal reform is premised on a normative subject – the Hindu, middle-class women. Subjects who fall outside this category

Gender Violence, the Law, and Society, 131–141
doi:10.1108/978-1-80117-127-420221011

have struggled to navigate the structural inequalities of the legal system' (p. 466). According to her research, the media channels have reported rape cases all across the country but 'within a few days each specific case disappeared, only to be replaced by yet another story of sexual assault' (Shandilya, p. 479). Her study, thus, makes 'evident that none of these cases have captured the public imagination in the same way as the Nirbhaya rape case' (Shandilya, p. 479). Shandilya's study underscores that contemporary Indian rape culture rests on the intersection of caste, class, gender, honour and shame, but that mainstream movements and popular culture tend to exclude lower caste/class women and rape victim/survivors who exist on the margins. Debolina Dutta and Oishik Sircar (2013), in agreement with Shandilya, further observe, 'location and identity thus seem to be essential qualifiers in determining whose rape is worth being the subject of urban, middle-class concern and rage' (p. 298).

Shandilya, Dutta and Sircar convey the notion that rape discourses in the Indian public privilege certain narratives – such as the Nirbhaya gang-rape case – in the mainstream media and popular culture. While they are correct in pointing out that the narratives of rape survivor-victims who exist are silenced, I would further add that their analysis demonstrates that by the proliferation of the Nirbhaya rape case in the national and international mediascapes, there is a problematic circulation of the notion that rapists and perpetrators primarily belong to the downtrodden, economically disadvantaged and less educated classes. Here, we see the culture of silence manifest on mainstream media channels where urban, upper and middle-class rapists and paedophiles are protected from being held responsible for their crimes. This type of silence exists especially in private spheres; there is often no recognition or acknowledgement of the rape and/or sexual assault by the families of the rape victim-survivors, as if the crime never occurred at the first place. In turn, the rape victim-survivors are re-traumatised again after the incident. Often, family members persuade and coax them to remain quiet, and, if they choose to speak up, they blame them for bringing dishonour and shame to the family. Because of this, the perpetrator's crimes never come to the forefront and, thus, they are not held responsible for their crimes.

In this chapter, I contend that recently filmmakers have begun reframing the narratives of rape victim-survivors and disrupting the cultural of silence described above. They offer progressive and multi-faceted representations of these experiences, such that there is an opportunity for a dialogue within both private and public spheres. What I mean when I say that they are 'progressive representations' is that the rape victim-survivors are not merely reduced to helpless women in distress, nor painted as vengeful, aggressive characters. Instead, their characterisation shows that they have agency and autonomy, but at the same time struggle with the repercussions of speaking out against their perpetrators in a society that does not support them wholly. The two media texts I explore are Imtiaz Ali's *Highway* (2014) and Alankrita Shrivastava's Netflix original series *Bombay Begums* (2021).

There has been a noticeable shift in the way in which rape victim-survivors are represented in mainstream popular culture. In the 1970s and 1980s, rape victims were either depicted as archetypical poor, helpless, lower class women or as vigilantes who sought violent revenge for their trauma (Gopalan, 2008; Karki, 2019; Virdi, 2003). These films also saw the creation of the main protagonist who was fighting the system (government, rich and corrupt landlords and bandits) for social justice and represented the ordinary/everyday man or woman. Pascal Zinck (2019) observes that such films are

> located in remote rural areas governed by zamindar/thakur [Hindi: feudal landlords]. In these films, the message is to frame violence against women as a critique of patriarchy and feudalism versus modernity. The danger with this binary is to consciously or subconsciously manufacture a consensus in middle-class viewing audience that avoids antagonizing masculinity, and ultimately, *exonerates urban sex abusers*
>
> (p. 273; emphasis added).

In the two media texts that I examine in this chapter, we see that the film-makers focus on the figure of the urban rapist and perpetrator and shifts away from the common representation of gender-based violence as an issue that is faced by people who exist on society's margins. By doing this, both Shrivastava's and Ali's messages remain that child sexual abuse and gender-based violence are not relegated to the poor, lower class parts of the society. Rather, they take place in both the public and private spheres of the elite and upper middle classes. At the same time, both filmmakers also re-imagine the rape victim-survivor, who is characterised with complexities and nuance as she confronts the perpetrator in both media texts. It is apparent that these filmmakers are trying to shift the conversation to draw attention to the culture of silence surrounding rape and gender-based violence that exists within the upper and upper-middle class spheres. While the filmmakers do not elide the viewers from the violence that women from lower-class experience and encounter, they are not afraid to show that upper-caste/class men are equally responsible but are often able to escape conviction or recognition of their crime because of the culture of silence that protects them.

## Re-imagining the Vengeful Rape Victim-Survivor: Imtiaz Ali's *Highway*

Imtiaz Ali's *Highway* paints a multi-layered picture of rape victim-survivors. The film begins with Veera Tripathi (Alia Bhatt), a rich tycoon's daughter, meeting secretly with her fiancée to escape the ongoing wedding celebrations in her home. They drive too far and bear witness to a robbery. In a frenzy, the criminals kidnap her and take her with them to the crevices of India's poor neighbourhoods. His fellow criminals reprimand the kidnapper – Mahabir (Randeep Hooda) – for abducting Veera, and fear reprisal from her wealthy family. Mahabir is an angry and frustrated man, tired of the atrocities he had to face because he belongs to the lower class in India. He sees Tripathi as a consignment – a method by which he can make the rich class suffer. As their relationship develops, he reminds her that he is a man with a criminal past who has committed three murders and is on the run. Although initially Veera makes desperate attempts to escape from Mahabir's grip and is accosted sexually by one of the kidnappers in his group, we see a strong bond develop between Mahabir and Veera as the plot thickens. Towards the end of the film, Veera and Mahabir escape the society that has caused them trauma and grief and create a utopic home for themselves in the mountains. Their happiness is short-lived as the police team is able to locate Veera and shoot Mahabir on the spot. He is declared dead upon arrival at the police hospital. Veera, in a shock, begs her family members to allow her to see Mahabir but she is given a tranquilizer and brought back to Delhi to recover.

At the heart of this powerful film is a very sensitive issue that many people fear to speak about. Unfortunately, rape and sexual abuse of young children are unspoken commonalities in India. No one speaks about them publicly because it can tarnish reputation and honour of families. The perpetrators are not held accountable for their criminal offense and in order to protect the honour of families rich or poor, women and men grow up traumatised, unable to comprehend the contradictions that are before them. Both Veera's and Mahabir's mothers are victims of such a society. Veera's uncle and family friend had raped Veera since the age of nine, luring her with chocolates and gifts. Her own mother stops her from speaking the truth and forces her into behaving as if everything is normal. Mahabir, on the other hand, bears witness to his mother's abuse when she is prostituted by his own father to cater to the needs of rich men. While we hear of Mahabir's upbringing and his mother's sexual abuse, we do not hear from her and can only access her through Mahabir's memories.

The film alludes to a glaring issue that rarely gets taken up in the socio-political fabric of India: it suggests that rape and sexual abuse over-rides class complexities within India because women and young girls are subjected to it *regardless* of their class status. Perhaps the most powerful moment in the film is when Veera confronts her family. She says, 'growing up, you told me to be careful of strangers outside our home but you never told me that I should be careful inside my home too' (Ali & Nadiadwala, 2014, 1:58:56–1:59:31). This is a defining moment because Veera's confrontation takes place within the home when her family is re-introducing her to her fiancée in the hope that she will marry him regardless of the trauma that she experienced. At that moment, she realises that her perpetrator, Shukla Uncle, is also in the same room. She is not afraid to speak of the abuse she suffered by his hand as a child and shares with her entire family and friends that he used to rape and molest her by tempting her with imported chocolates. When her rapist is put on the spot, he calls her crazy and flees from the house. The most touching moment is when she screams in pain as her childhood trauma manifests and breaks the silence that she is encountered all her life. Yet, her family is shown to be lost and confused – unable to handle the truth that she has confronted them with. This is a significant moment because it shows that due to the culture of silence within the upper classes, there is ambivalence and confusion about how to confront this sensitive subject matter. Eventually, Veera shares her decision to leave her family and start a new life working a regular job and leading an independent life where she, rather than her family or society, dictates the course of her life.

This is a significant shift in the representation of rape victim-survivors who, in the 1980s, belonged to the tradition of avenging women genre in Bollywood. The films *Insaaf Ka Tarazu* and *Pink*, which I discussed at length in the chapter on law, still explore the figure of the avenging rape victim-survivor. Isha Karki (2019) rightfully points out that although the rape-revenge device 'provided actresses with dominant roles' (p. 91), at the same time, 'a world of female agency was imagined where women became powerful, and utilised what is coded as masculine power, because of their violent initiation into victimhood – and even then, their rage had to be justified by their identity as a "good victim"' (p. 91). Unlike in the earlier films, *Highway* approaches the concept of rape revenge in a different manner. Rather than physically attacking or killing him, Veera shames and confronts her perpetrator in front of her family members, her fiancée and his family. Given the taboo and cultural silencing that exists within the Indian society, this is the first time we see that the rape survivor-victim is demanding justice vis-à-vis a conversation with her family members and relatives who have been quiet throughout the sexual abuse she suffered as a child. As mentioned earlier, Uncle Shukla quickly removes himself from the scene and disappears from the narrative so that as audiences, we do not know if he was punished for his pedophilic and criminal behavior. Interestingly, the film received mixed reviews from critics. Anupama Chopra (2014), for example only gave it a 2 and half stars and called it a 'problematic film' that left her 'dissatisfied' in her review. For Chopra, while the narratives of the 'damaged' characters is compelling, she fears that the film promotes the idea that 'kidnapping is therapy'. Ronnie Schieb (2014), on the other hand writes, 'abduction paradoxically results in liberation for both the sheltered daughter of an industrialist and her hardened criminal...' but he is more optimistic and suggests that the film 'should score with Indian aud [iences] globally, with arthouse cover as a distinct possibility'. From their reviews, it is apparent that the theme of kidnapping and abduction superseded the characterisation of both Veera and Mahabir. However, I do not agree with Chopra shows that kidnapping is an acceptable form of therapy – rather the abduction transforms both the characters and forces them to reflect on their respective lives. While Veera recognises that she does not want to depend on the wealth of her family members and wants to become autonomous, Mahabir softens and confronts his own demons that were caused by his father's horrifying actions.

*Highway*, therefore, portrays the rape survivor-victim as demanding justice by confronting her perpetrator in front of her family and even questioning her mother for silencing her. Veera's depiction is unlike other rape survivor-victims, who sought legal action and had no choice but to take the legal justice on their hands, as can be seen in films like *Insaaf ka Tarazu*. Rather, here, Veera is facing a situation that would have left her ostracised from her family members and brought shame to them. Instead, the film encourages rape survivor-victims to speak up and even confront family members who may have protected their rapists. Although a mainstream film, Ali speaks to a very current social issue that needs our attention. Honour and reputation are used as tools to silence voices of the innocent boys and girls who grow up in traumatic situations, not only as street kids who witness atrocities but also in the luxurious homes of the rich where sexual abuse and rape are kept under the rug to prevent shame and recognition of their trauma.

## #MeToo, Politics of Choice and Subjectivity in Alankrita Shrivastava's *Bombay Begums* (2021)

In the last decade, feminist filmmakers such as Alankrita Shrivastava, Anvita Dutt, Reema Kagti and Zoya Akhtar have produced and released movies like *Made in Heaven* (2019), *Bulbul* (2020) and, most recently, *Bombay Begums* (2021). Sharma and Sharma refers to the filmmakers who made the film *Bulbul*. These filmmakers and directors use the web-streaming platforms Amazon Prime and Netflix to represent social issues such as male rape and homosexuality in *Made in Heaven* and a re-telling of the *chudail* (female demon) myth – calling attention to sexual violence and child marriages in the colonial Bengal during the British Raj – in *Bulbul*. Bulbul, the main protagonist of the latter movie, is transformed into a demon after her brutal rape, then returns to her village to murder and kill the perpetrator to demand justice and better treatment for women. It is clear that Bollywood is moving towards a new direction with these recent feminist filmmakers who are not bound by the same censorship regulations as filmmakers in the earlier decades. Furthermore, these shows are not limited to primarily Indian audiences but make the stories accessible to audiences worldwide.

Released in March 2021, Alankrita Shrivastava's *Bombay Begums* focuses on the #MeToo movement and centers around narratives of ambitious women who have different struggles and desires as they come together to work at Royal Bank of Bombay. The television series is centered on Rani (Pooja Bhatt) who is the CEO of the Royal Bank. She is married to Naushad Irani and stepmother to the series' narrator, Shai (Aadhya Anand). The women in this show belong to various classes, including Lily (Amruta Subhash), a prostitute who desires a better life for herself and her son. We also meet Ayesha (Plabita Borthakur) who has moved from a small town to Bombay to pursue her dreams; as well as her boss Fatima (Shahana Goswami), who struggles with infertility, IVF, marriage and career ambitions. Although the television series deals with relevant issues such as bisexuality, stigma of menstruation and realisation of womanhood, it is an incident of workplace sexual violence and harassment between Ayesha and her boss, Deepak Sanghvi (Manish Choudhary), that brings these women together. Deepak has a fierce competition with Rani and wants to become the bank's next CEO. His family is also close to Fatima and her husband. These web of relationships also further complicate the events as they unfold when the issue of sexual violence and harassment come to light. The television web series also demonstrates how female friendships are tested when the issue of sexual abuse becomes apparent in a work place.

As audiences, we meet Ayesha when she is fired by Fatima in the first episode, after she miscalculates numbers that hinder Fatima's meeting with foreign clients. From a small town, Ayesha is a young, determined and enthusiastic career girl who wants to make it in the finance industry in Bombay – a cosmopolitan city akin to New York and London. The city culture does not favour single women living by themselves, best illustrated by her experiences living as a paying guest in a small home. After she is fired, she smokes and drinks to grieve and make sense of her job loss. Her landlady angrily throws her out of her home in the middle of night. Forced to find a place, Ayesha seeks shelter in her former office. In the morning, she encounters Rani in the bathroom. Being reminded of her earlier days in the city, Rani takes pity and re-hires Ayesha. She is put on a project to help create a scheme to help women like Lily, the sex worker, have a financially stable life and helps Lily realise her dream of opening a factory. Although Ayesha is initially happy with her job, she dreams of working with her mentor, Deepak Sanghvi.

When she meets Deepak at office party, she shares her desire to be mentored by him. Initially, he does not take her seriously, observes that she is drinking champagne, and treats like her like any other colleague. As the series continues, Deepak and Ayesha encounter each other again at another party. This time, Ayesha once again drinks and accepts the offer from Deepak to drop her off at her place of stay (her colleague Ron's place, where she is temporarily staying). When they are in the car, Deepak takes advantage of the situation and starts to touch her inappropriately. Lily, who by coincidence walks by, recognises Ayesha and witnesses the entire incident take place. At this time, for the audience, the extent of sexual violence that has occurred between them is unclear. We see Ayesha shakily coming out of the car. The next day Lily reports of the incident she witnessed but Ayesha denies any wrongdoing and tries her best to move on so as to not destroy her chances of moving up in the company. As she remains quiet about the events, Fatima suspects that Ayesha was having an affair with Deepak and shames every time she sees her. Then, Ayesha is notified that Deepak has asked for her to be transferred into his department. Shocked and uneasy about her job placement, she reaches out to the HR to withdraw her application, but the HR officer in charge is surprised and questions her decision. Ultimately, after another meeting with Deepak when she is out on a smoke with him, she is unable to keep the trauma in. In a panic, she runs into the bathroom where she hastily tears the sexual harassment posters and finally goes on a website where she reports the incident. To her surprise, another anonymous woman reaches out to her and validates her experience with Deepak. Being aware that Lily is her only witness, she gains courage to file a formal report in her company against Deepak. Fatima is still denial about the incident, knowing Deepak and his family intimately, and shows reluctance to believe Ayesha.

In episode five, titled 'The Golden Notebook', Ayesha files the report, causing the floodgates of investigation to open and transforming the relationships that were already fragile. In her testimony to her colleagues, she reveals that Deepak has forced her to perform oral sex on him and says that she had no choice but to give into Deepak's demands. She informs that she had resisted but it had been no avail: 'I was scared of upsetting him. I was scared of what else he might do. I just wanted it to be over' (Shrivastava, 2021, 10:29–11:01). Fatima and Rani deal with Ayesha's testimony in strongly diverging ways. Fatima behaves in a passive-aggressive manner, questioning Ayesha's motives and character for not coming forth earlier. In a conversation with Rani (who is insisting on following due process), Fatima shares her doubts that Deepak could be a sexual predator (Shrivastava, 2021, 12:14–12:16). In fact, she then starts to doubt Ayesha and accuses her of changing her story, saying that everyone's life is at stake (Shrivastava, 2021, 12:41–13:29). Rani, on the other hand, faces pressure from the board committee members who want the issue to disappear. They see the entire situation as a PR disaster and want Deepak's position to be restored. It is clear that the upper echelons of the bank do not consider Ayesha's case a significant issue but merely a case of reputation. Initially, Rani tries to coax Ayesha to retract her case, even asking Ayesha to move on and threatening her job for speaking up. Deepak's wife, Nalini, also harasses and tries to silence her in this episode. Ultimately, however, in the final episode we see that Rani reckons with her own experience of sexual harassment and pressures she faced from her own mentor when she shares her experience publicly at the end of the series. When Deepak's crimes come to light, he is arrested and taken to the police station, where he is shown finding ways to reveal secrets about Rani's past. Like *Highway*, this web series too highlights the privilege that upper-class perpetrators have. The protection they receive from their families and peers makes it extremely difficult for rape victim-survivors to fight for justice. However, unlike Uncle Shukla whose narrative fades at the end of the film, we witness Deepak's arrest before our eyes.

In the final episode titled 'A Room of One's Own' (the feminist filmmaker's nod to Virginia Woolf), the private space – which is usually where a woman's traumatic sexual experiences are silenced – transforms into a space where a mother shares her experiences of sexual assault and rape with her step daughter. Once again, we see filmmaker's refreshing approach to this salient issue. In this pivotal scene, Rani openly asks Shai to share it with her if boys at a party had touched her inappropriately. She then emphasises that her daughter must share it with her if she ever faces such a situation (Shrivastava, 2021, 33:04–33:21). Then, we see a rare scene in which Rani opens up about her own sexual assault and expresses her regret for not opening up and sharing this with anyone sooner due to shame. Rani says,

> I had just joined JDR bank. I was relatively new in Bombay. My boss – he expected me to spend time with him after work…and then he started touching me. When it happened the first time, I was really confused. I was really scared but I thought maybe that's just the way it is. I wanted success at any cost. No matter what. So, I kept shut. Just…But, then it didn't stop. It just went on and on and on. My husband thought I was having an affair with him. I just let him think that way. It was horrible, Shai. I can still feel his breath on my face. I can still feel him inside me. There is not a single day when that nightmare doesn't come back to haunt me!
>
> (Shrivastava, 2021, 35:38–38:00)

In this pivotal scene, we see a strong bond that develops between Rani and Shai. This is also the first time that a filmmaker has shown a mother not silencing her daughter, but encouraging her to talk about an issue that is typically considered tabooed. In *Highway*, for example when Veera was facing her perpetrator, her mother had attempted to shush her. But here, the filmmaker draws attention to the private space, showing that rape victim-survivors need to have the support of family members and loved ones rather than face the trauma by themselves. Once again, unlike the typical rape-revenge devices that have been used previously, here again the rape victim faces the society and her perpetrator.

While the television web series focusses primarily on the narratives of elite and upper/middle class men and women, Lily's narrative also deserves equal attention. Unlike the similar character in *Highway* – Mahabir's mother, whose trauma is shared through her son, and who herself is never seen or heard throughout the film – Lily is assertive, ambitious, a business owner and strives for a better future for her and her son. However, throughout the web series, she meets with obstacles that prevent her moving up on the social ladder. When Ayesha finds comfort with Lily after her traumatic experience, and says that they are both alike, Lily reminds her of a reality: 'you have a choice… I don't have the privilege. My destiny forbids it' (Shrivastava, 2021, 26:53–27:18). Initially, Lily who is the sole witness to Ayesha's traumatic experience of sexual assault, agrees to testify against the perpetrator to protect Ayesha. However, she changes her mind when the company offers her a chance to open a business. When Ayesha confronts her, Lily explains that for her survival supersedes the notion of social justice. In the wake of the #MeToo movement, *Bombay Begums* starts a crucial conversation: who can speak up against the perpetrators? Who is able to make themselves vulnerable? Who has access to resources and privilege to speak out? Whose story can be recognised in the public spheres?

This show was also well-received by audiences. Shubra Gupta (2021) writes, for instance, that 'Alankrita Shrivastava has been consistently pushing boundaries with her portrayal of women's sexuality…Flawed, real, hurting, laughing women who make you stay with them, and root for them'. V.S. Arvind (2021) calls the series 'a step in the right direction. Despite the flawed nature in which its story is presented the series has its heart in the right place and its representation of women is something new, even radical by Indian standards'. Ultimately, the show suggests that the rape victim-survivors – Ayesha, Lily and Rani – are complex and flawed characters. Because of this, the filmmaker shows that the big social changes necessary to subvert the structures that enable wide-spread sexual assault to persevere in a society like India are not easy to produce because of the repercussions that the rape victim-survivors face. Sometimes, despite being victims of sexual assault themselves, they are pressured into silencing others who may have suffered as well, because of career and societal expectations.

## Conclusion

Although there has been a noticeable shift in the way in which rape victim-survivors are portrayed in both Hindi commercial films and television web series, I do want to underscore that these visions by the filmmakers are equally a desire for a change that these filmmakers *want to see* in the society and arguably represent a utopic vision of what the outcome of the #MeToo movement would look like if it worked in the favour of the rape victim-survivor. Yet, at the same time, both Ali and Shrivastava should also be recognised for trying to start a dialogue with their show and film. This is an important effort to break the culture of silence (which continues to remain pertinent).

We also see that the filmmakers are no longer constructing a one-dimensional, helpless, rape victim-survivor who is unable to take charge of her situation. Rather, the rape victim-survivors are complex, multi-faceted women who are asserting their choices – Veera confronts her rapists and shames him in front of his entire family; Ayesha files charges against a man whom she considered her mentor; and Lily, who witnesses Ayesha's sexual assault, chooses to speak up against the crime but retracts it later.

Finally, both *Highway* and *Bombay Begums* represent the rapists/perpetrators as upper/middle class men who are of privilege and usually shielded from the crimes that they have committed. This is an important decision made by both filmmakers to go against the traditional representations of rapists as men who belong to the lower class. Their cinematic and television representations *shift* the conversation away from the perpetrators who belong to lower class/caste in the mainstream discourse, which continues to silence women who have been sexually assaulted and raped by upper-class men. To sum up, it is important to recognise the power and value of these media texts and the resulting conversations they create.

# References

Akhtar, Z., et al. (Producers). (2019). Made in heaven [Video]. *Amazon Prime*. Retrieved from http://www.amazonprime.com

Ali, I., & Nadiadwala, S. (Producers). (2014). Highway [Video]. *Netflix*. Retrieved from http://www.netflix.com

Aravind, V. S. (2021, March 21). 'Bombay Begums' review: A gripping drama about the plight of women in India's urban realm. *The Hindu*. Retrieved from https://www.thehindu.com/entertainment/movies/bombay-begums-review-a-gripping-drama-about-the-plight-of-women-in-indias-urban-realm/article62129919.ece

Chopra, A. (2014, February 25). Movie review by Anupama Chopra: Highway leaves you deeply dissatisfied. *Hinduism Today*. Retrieved from https://www.hindustantimes.com/movie-reviews/movie-review-by-anupama-chopra-highway-leaves-you-deeply-dissatisfied/story-2OnoP5ZWYGJeDf2SPv53jO.html

Dutta, D., & Sircar, O. (2013). India's winter of discontent: Some feminist dilemmas in the wake of a rape. *Feminist Studies*, *39*(1), 293–306.

Gopalan, L. (2008). Avenging women in Indian cinema. In J. Desai & R. K. Dudrah (Eds.), *The Bollywood reader* (pp. 97–108). New York, NY: McGraw-Hill.

Gupta, S. (2021, March 8). Bombay Begums review: Flawed, real and laughing women make this Netflix series come alive. *Indian Express*. Retrieved from https://indianexpress.com/article/entertainment/web-series/bombay-begums-review-flawed-real-laughing-women-make-this-netflix-series-come-alive-7219152/

Karki, I. (2019). Scripting resistance: Rape and the avenging woman in Hindi cinema. *Journal of International Women's Studies, 20*(4), 83–102.

Schieb, R. (2014, February 20). Film review: Highway. *Variety*. Retrieved from https://variety.com/2014/film/festivals/film-review-highway-1201114013/

Shandilya, K. (2015). Nirbhaya's body: The politics of protest in the aftermath of the 2012 Delhi gang rape. *Gender & History, 27*(2), 465–486. doi:10.1111/1468-0424.12134

Sharma, A., & Sharma, K. (Producers). (2020). Bulbul [Video]. *Netflix*. Retrieved from http://www.netlix.com

Shrivastava, A. (Producer). (2021–). Bombay Begums [Video]. *Netflix*. Retrieved from http://www.netflix.com

Virdi, J. (2003). *The cinematic imagination: Indian popular films as social history*. New Brunswick, NJ: Rutgers University Press.

Zinck, P. (2019). Disobedient bodies: Gendered violence in South Asian and desi film. *South Asian Popular Culture, 17*(3), 269–282. doi:10.1080/14746689.2019.1668590

# Chapter 8

# Japanese Gender Norms and Their Impact on Male Attitudes Toward Women

*Gavan Patrick Gray*

## Abstract

Japan is home to a relatively conservative and group-oriented culture in which social expectations can exert powerful pressure to conform to traditional patterns of behaviour. This includes gender norms, which have long been based around the common stereotypes of men as breadwinners and women as housewives. Social liberalisation and economic change in the late 20th century saw these patterns change as more women entered the workforce and, despite Japan's dismal standing in global equality rankings, began to make inroads into some positions of political and corporate leadership. Yet, the way in which women are treated by men is shaped not only by female gender norms but also by the social factors that determine male patterns of behaviour. This chapter considers how Japan's male gender norms, particularly the focus on man as economic labourers rather than active members of the family unit, have damaged many men's ability to connect, on an emotional level, with the women in their lives. It looks at the issue of misogyny; what is known as the Lolita Complex; the growing trend of herbivore men; and the concept of Ikumen, men who are active within the family. While some of these patterns of behaviour can be harmful – for women on the individual level, and for Japan as a whole, on the social level – there are some trends which suggest that gender norms in Japan can be directed in a manner which will allow for much healthier emotional relationships to develop between the genders in a manner that will help build a society that is more cognisant of and attentive to the needs of women.

Gender Violence, the Law, and Society, 143–159
doi:10.1108/978-1-80117-127-420221012

*Keywords*: Gender norms; misogyny; lolita complex; ikumen; Grasseaters; Japan

In collective cultures, of which Japan is a good example, behavioural expectations are often seen more as unspoken rules than loose guidelines, and people frequently exhibit severe discomfort – to a far greater degree than in the West – when stepping outside of social norms.[1] It is no surprise to find that these patterns extend to gender roles and, despite having eased considerably in past decades, these forces still have a powerful influence upon the patterns of social behaviour that both women and men feel obligated to conform to.

Although Japan had originally been a matriarchal culture, the introduction of first Buddhism, and later Confucian ideals, brought about a shift to a strictly patriarchal social structure from roughly the 6th century A.D. (Joyce, Paulson, & Powers, 1976, p. 4, Silva-Grodin, 2010). Despite this, during the later Tokugawa era (17th to 19th century), women's roles were not purely servile and depending upon social class, there were expectations that women would be well educated (Tocco, 2003, p. 194). It was during the Meiji era (1868–1912) that perhaps the most impactful gender norm came into existence, the concept of *ryōsai kenbo*, or 'good wife, wise mother', which was an injunction to women to use their education for the development of their children in a socially productive manner (Koyama, 2013).

During the early 20th century, this was explicitly taught to young women as a staple of education, even to the extent that they should see childbirth as a patriotic duty. This paradigm met resistance, however, from Japanese feminists and liberals who, by the 1980s, were making public calls for it to be replaced by greater standards of equality and increased female access to political and economic systems (Uno, 1993). Nonetheless, the underlying belief in the wise mother raising socially productive children still has a powerful influence over deep-rooted gender norms that affect men just as deeply as they do women. In particular, the notion that the family is the woman's domain, and that child-rearing is her responsibility, continues to support the equally rigid and outdated norm that the man's role is as the breadwinner and that work takes precedence over involvement in family affairs, whether marital or child-related.

This male gender stereotype, the industrious and productive, yet distant, breadwinner, has been a staple since the 1950s and, though it is beginning to slowly change, has created an emotional crisis among many Japanese men that deeply affects the way they view and treat women. When considering Japanese social attitudes towards women, it is therefore vital to understand the normative forces that shape men's interactions with them. Rather than seeing Japanese society as a patriarchal structure that marginalises women, it is important to recognise that a great many men have serious emotional problems that manifest in a variety of ways. I should make it clear that this by no means describes the

---

[1]This work was supported by a Kaken grant (18K13005) from the Japan Society for the Promotion of Science.

majority of Japanese men, very many of whom are emotionally well adjusted. However, the extreme cases are common enough to act as significant warning flags for underlying problems in the way many men relate to women. In some cases, this is inherently negative, where efforts to address emotional stress see men attempt to maintain a dominant role over subservient women (misogyny). In others it sees men fixate upon unthreatening juvenile women (*lolicon* or 'lolita complex'). In some cases, the stress of relationships sees men reject romantic entanglement of any kind (*sōshoku danshi*). Others choose a, seemingly, healthier path and attempt to reclaim a male role within the family dynamic by playing an active part in child-rearing (*ikumen*). Each of these is a direct response to emotional needs among Japanese men that are all too often neglected and each has a major impact upon how such men view and treat the women they know and encounter. Some are significant enough that they have a far-reaching effect on Japanese culture, including the way in which the 'ideal' woman is portrayed and how women, in general, are treated. Addressing gender equality in Japan, even if narrowly focused upon promoting the welfare of women, requires understanding the forces behind these differing patterns of male behaviour and the positive and negative impact they can have upon gender relations.

## Current Gender Norms

The late 19th-century industrialisation of the country failed to bring about any significant alteration in women's economic or legal status. It was really only the drafting of the post-WWII constitution that introduced a fundamental reordering of gender structures (Ochiai, 1997). In the following decades, some claim that there had been a steady displacement of the samurai ideal of masculinity, replaced instead by a feminine elevation of soft, cute imagery and a greater leaning towards passivity (Yano, 2009, p. 684).

There is no question, however, that men are still firmly in the driver's seat in political and economic terms. Recent laws have introduced guidelines for establishing gender parity in political candidates but women still made up less than a quarter of those gaining seats in recent elections (Johnston, 2020), while in the corporate world less than 8% of top executives are female (Kinouchi, 2021). There is a wide variety of factors that perpetuate these imbalances but Japan's deeply entrenched gender norms are one of the strongest. From expectations over life paths to the pervasive endurance of outdated idioms, such as *Otoko wa dokyō, onna wa aikyō* (men should be daring, women should be charming), they have an especially strong power in collective cultures to reinforce conformity to established patterns.

Yet, in comparison to the West, there has been far less hostile resistance to these norms. In the 20th century, Japanese women did not typically view the role of housewives as oppressive but rather as a separate and distinct source of power over both the family and society (Schultz, Tufis, & Alwin, 2010, p. 188). Such views persist, and in many cases, it is women who have more traditional outlooks than men. A 2012 government survey found that 50% of men believed it is better for their wives to do all the housework, while among women 60% held the same view. Similarly, while 75% of men said they expect husbands to be the main breadwinner, 80% of women held the same view. Asked whether women should continue to work after having children, 40% of men said they should not, compared to 55% of women. Of course, in some areas more patriarchal views were evident, such as 35% of men saying they feel housewives should follow their decisions, with only 20% of women agreeing (Cabinet Office, 2011, pp. 14–17).

Even these brief questions highlight some persistent trends in gender issues in Japan; women want more freedom from male decision-making but they do not feel this is necessarily connected to relinquishing established roles within the familial structure. What can we infer about men, though? The most dominant theme is that they are expected, by both sexes, to act as breadwinners and to have a focus on work. A separate and more recent survey highlighted the key factor even more clearly. When asked 'What society expects from being a man?', by far the most popular response (68%) was 'success at work and financial support for their family'. The next two most popular responses were 'not to cry or become emotional' (36%) and 'to show leadership' (29%). Among the least popular responses were 'to display empathy' (5.5%) and 'childcare' (5.5%) (Asahi, 2020). There is no question that Japan has deep gender imbalances, but it is equally true that the country's gender norms place severe restrictions on the manner in which men are expected to develop emotionally, and limitations on the role they are expected to play within the family structure.

## Emotional Development

It is understandable that cultural factors produce distinct patterns of emotional development when comparing a more collective society, such as Japan, and a more individualistic one, such as the United States (Kitayama, Mesquito, & Karasawa, 2006). A common factor, though, is that girls are generally expected to be more expressive and empathetic, while boys are expected to externalise their emotions. In Japan, boys are specifically expected to either hide emotion completely or to express it through 'displays of anger or disgust' (Saeki, Watanabe, & Kido, 2015, p. 30).

Traditionally, it was expected that these pressures would begin with the onset of elementary school and it was only in the period before that when boys could be emotionally free. With the father's role being highly career-focused, the child's emotional development was primarily tied to, and strongly influenced by, inter-actions with their mother who became the source of familial discipline (Benedict, 1989, pp. 254, 263). Miyamoto (1994, p. 186) saw this as a source of emotional dependency and reticence as well as the development of a skewed view of spousal relationships that was typically devoid of displays of affection, romance or physical attraction. For many men, this created an expectation that romantic partners and marriage partners were distinct things and that the idealised form of the latter was a traditional, asexual, mother-figure.

The notion of emotional dependency has taken a specific form in Japan through the concept of *Amae*, which Doi (1973, p. 167) defined as, 'the craving of a newborn child for close contact with its mother and the desire to deny the act of separation that is an inevitable part of human existence'. The concept has since been further studied and refined into distinct aspects and qualities that go beyond the preceding simplification (Behrens & Kondo-Ikemure, 2011). One common factor, however, was that insecurely attached children are the most affected by it, i.e. that it can exacerbate patterns of emotional fragility (Komatsu, 2011, p. v). The problematic aspect of this occurs when men consider future partners through the sole lens of being a suitable mother, rather than the additional aspects of either a romantic lover or an emotional friend. Success in finding the former can often result in deficits in other areas of their life that leave men with serious unsatisfied needs that they will, due to their own normative expectations, be reluctant to express openly.

The education system has done little to ease such problems, and in fact, is far more likely to exacerbate them where they exist. The implicit message that sexual relations within the family are purely a matter of procreation has generally been reinforced by limited sexual education curricula that focus purely on biological matters and disregard matters of emotion, sexuality or relationships (Hashimoto et al., 2017, pp. 391–395). Only recently have advocates begun to have some success in introducing the importance of exploring the latter subjects (Kuwahara, 2019), but it has already had a deep impact on the very nature of relationships for an extended period. Salamon (1974, p. 131) wrote that in Japan, apart from the courting and honeymoon period, sex was separate from home life and that, as a result, working men were alienated from their families and ill-equipped to interact with the opposite sex. A large part of why the sex industry became so deeply entrenched was that it provided both a sexual and emotional outlet for men. In the words of Allison (2009, p. 175): it allowed men, regardless of their station in life, to have a sense of worth. There are significant questions, however, regarding whether the worth derived from such sources is truly healthy for those involved.

Jolivet (1997, pp. 66–69) considered this rigid demarcation of boundaries something that risked men enduring an identity crisis when asked to take on roles of 'good father' or 'good husband', roles regarding which they had not received any prior guidance. Both Doi (1973, p. 153) and Iwao (1993) commented on the absence of men from family life, with the idea that Japan had, towards the end of the 20th century, become a 'fatherless society'. There are strong signs, as we shall see later, that efforts are being made to change this and to make men more active within the family structure. However, almost always the driving force behind these changes, though done in the name of gender equity, is from the perspective of balancing the workload of the female partner, in other words, a strong focus on male participation in childcare as an instance of burden-sharing. While this is worthwhile in its own right, it overlooks the, arguably, more significant aspect of male participation in the family unit, which is the healthy emotional growth, support and outlet that it provides.

The Japanese government found that women are open to men being more emotionally expressive, with 46% of women disagreeing that 'men should not be weak', compared to just 18% of men. Women were also far more likely to want men to express their private feelings although only 17% of men said that, 'when I have a problem, I feel I can talk to someone about it' (Cabinet Office, 2011, pp. 20–21). For all the restrictions that gender norms place upon Japanese women, these norms have also done considerable damage to men, particularly in terms of how they express themselves or fail to do so: patterns of behaviour that, in turn, can have a strong impact on the women they interact with.

## Misogyny

There is no doubt that persistent strands of misogynistic behaviour are a problem within Japanese society. There are, however, significant differences of opinion as to both the extent and the root causes of the problem. One perspective, as put forth by Ueno (2019), is that men hold an imbalance of power in society because to become a man means 'being accepted by men' while becoming a woman also requires 'being accepted by men'. This completely overlooks the fundamental importance of the key roles men can play, first as lover, then husband and finally father, and how much the acceptance of women means to so many men. Ueno also highlights money and economic success as being the primary determinant of a man's self-image, and how men determine their 'pecking order'. Once again, this grossly oversimplifies men and overlooks how important emotional bonds are to their identity and sense of self.

When we refer to misogyny we can look beyond simple hatred of women, to the more narrowly defined desire to control the social roles that they play. Manne's (2019, p. 33) definition is suitable, classifying it as 'a system that operates within a patriarchal social order to police and enforce women's subordination and to uphold male dominance'. Examples of this within Japan are boundless, with a recent one being the statements of Yoshiro Mori, former Chairman for the 2020 Tokyo Olympics, berating women for being noisy and taking up too much time at meetings with unnecessary comments (Asahi, 2021). Such pressure for 'noisy women' to assume a docile and subservient position in society seeks conformity with the traditional view of the housewife who will not contradict her husband's opinions on matters outside of family affairs. If, as Allison stated, many Japanese men use the sex industry as a substitute source of self-worth that they cannot find in their homes, it is understandable, though certainly not forgivable, that such men will feel challenged by women who threaten to undermine the self-worth they derive from their traditional, career-focused roles.

There is a pattern of behaviour that can occur within Japanese marriages known as *katenai rikon* (divorce within the household), wherein couples maintain the marriage purely as a matter of social convenience despite having no meaningful interpersonal communication or relationship. In some cases, this will persist until retirement, after which a real divorce can occur when the wife realises she no longer gains any financial benefit from the arrangement, something referred to as *teinen rikon* (retirement divorce) (Cherry, 2016, p. 19). Even during the marriage, the husband can lose control of his own finances with the term *sen-en teishu* (1,000 yen husband) referring to men who sacrifice their paychecks to their wives' control, receiving only a minuscule, and emasculating, stipend as pocket-money for the month (Cherry, 2016, p. 96).

It might be expected that these marital pressures would reveal themselves most in misogynistic behaviour among the older generation, in other words, men who have experienced many decades of gender-related, marital stress. However, surveys conducted on the question of 'Does Japan need to take gender equality more seriously?' found that support among men generally increased with age (Dentsu, 2021), with the lowest results being among those aged 30–39, typically the prime years of establishing a family. Divorce rates in Japan have been steadily increasing over the past four decades and more than 30% of marriages are estimated to end in divorce (Alexy, 2010, p. 238). Given this, it is perhaps understandable that those who are recently married are more concerned with traditional norms regarding family structure and career roles that might seem to offer a sense of greater stability.

The contradictory outcome of this mindset, however, is that women are relegated to one of two broad stereotypes, either the pure 'good girl' who adheres to the established rules, or the impure woman of 'loose moral character'. While the former is often envisioned as loving mother, dutiful housewife or pure daughter, the latter is often sexualised, though the division is far more about submission than it is about sex. For example, a subservient and docile junior employee, or a quietly attentive hostess might be seen in the former light due to behaving according to the rules of a 'pure', i.e. submissive, woman. Even if the interaction involves sex, it can be deemed traditionally acceptable if the woman accepts her allotted hierarchical status in the interaction. Meanwhile, an outspoken female co-worker or a sexually demanding woman might be seen as 'impure' or, as with the aforementioned Mr Mori, 'noisy' due to their failure to acquiesce to male dominance or established, patriarchal norms.

Though this mindset is far from all-pervasive, its influence can be seen in many areas of Japanese society, especially where sex might be seen as falling out of male control. One example would be the arrest, under obscenity laws, of artist Megumi Igarashi for producing artwork based on her genitalia (Abe, 2020). Meanwhile, sex toys based upon the genitalia of famous pornographic actresses are openly sold on major sites such as Amazon Japan.[2] In a similar vein, a 2003 book saw a collaboration between Tsunku, the producer of several wildly popular girl's idol groups, and Ganari Takahashi, the founder of one of Japan's major pornography labels (Takahashi & Tsunku, 2003). The book focused on something the two entrepreneurs had in common, namely the methods used to market and sell young girls, though one focused on images of purity and the other of impurity.

This dangerously unhealthy framework to try to confine women within is clear, and attempting to fit them into such limited moulds produces a warped and dehumanising view of women in general. This has frequently been highlighted using the way some of the afore-mentioned idol groups treat their young recruits,

---

[2]This can easily be verified by searching the site for the terms 女優 (actress) and 女ホール (the type of sex toy).

with those failing to abide by their rigid facade of purity receiving treatment verging on the abusive. This was perhaps most clearly seen in the cases of Maho Yamaguchi, who was forced to apologise to fans after she had been attacked by two of them (Tanaka, 2019), and Minami Minegishi, who shaved her own head as an act of contrition after daring to spend time with a boyfriend (St. Michel, 2013). Yet, this treatment of young women as marketable objects is just one negative element of an industry that feeds off a separate male emotional problem: a fixation upon non-threatening and submissive, juvenile females, something commonly known as 'Lolita Complex'.

## Lolita Complex

Japan has long had a cultural attraction to things that are delicate and ephemeral. The concept of *mono no aware* refers to the sadness of passing things, idealised in the annual cherry blossom viewings. From this came a fondness for things that are *kawaii*. Though translated to cute, it more broadly refers to things that are weak and in need of protection and can be applied to both inanimate and living things (Sato, 2009). The most notable element of this culture is perhaps the cartoon mascots that Japan embraces, cute characters like Rira Kuma, Hello Kitty and the various Sumiko Gurashi. The most notorious, though, is the fixation on young girls, whether of the animated or real kind.

According to Professor Kimio Ito, of Kyoto University, men's culture in Japan had lost its focus in the 1970s. For them, life was the simple commitment to work. In contrast, women were embracing new freedoms and being catered to by a wide variety of media in which their lives were represented with bright vivid colours and boundless opportunity. Young men began to fixate upon female characters as an alternative to relationships they were unable to develop in their own lives (Galbraith, 2017, p. 29). By the 1980s, this had developed into a wave of *seishun* or 'youth' entertainment; television shows and manga which focused on high school life as an idealised time of emotional growth and meaningful relationships. The first idol group, precursors to the wildly popular AKB-48 and similar groups, took form in O-Nyanko Kurabu (Kitten Club), 11 teenage girls who dressed in school uniforms and sang overly sexualised songs.[3]

At the same time, fictional female characters, 'magical girls' such as Sailor Moon, were becoming increasingly popular with male audiences. Both of these trends, the idols and the fictional characters were marketed on characteristics (purity, freedom, respect and a lack of threat) that would form the key appeal for men who embraced what came to be called *Lolicon* or Lolita Complex (Saito, 2013, p. 158). Mari Kotani, a Japanese pop culture critic, suggests that there is no difference between the idols and the cartoon characters as in either case the men are committing themselves to an idealised, utterly fictional creation (Galbraith, 2017, p. 35). The important factor in both cases, according to Yoshiko (1997, p. 183), is

---

[3]With titles like: *Don't make me take off my sailor uniform, Better be good, teacher* and *Uh-oh, a pervert!*

that inexperienced men's virginal fear of more mature women is alleviated by the imagery of undeveloped, unmotherly, innocent girls who represent no threat. Masahiro Morioka, a professor of ethics at the prestigious Tokyo University, freely admits to suffering from a Lolita Complex and links it specifically to having an emotional dependency on his mother, coupled with an inability to adjust to the sexual awakenings of puberty (Otake, 2017). For Morioka, his fixation on young girls was very much a rejection of his own masculinity.

This is something echoed by Maruta (2001, pp. 150–154), who claims that these adolescent girls represent an idealised form of kawaii as beauty. However, Maruta touches on the dark side of this attraction when he claims that sexual transactions between young girls and older men, what is known as *Enjo Kōsai* (literally 'social support' but more accurately 'compensated dating'), are not prostitution as it represents female equality with, or even dominance over, weaker men. This is certainly a problematic and superficial assessment, yet, it is not wrong in identifying the customers as men with serious emotional issues. In an analysis of compensated dating in Hong Kong, Chu (2018, p. 77) found that similar views were common among those who engaged in the activity. These were men between 18 and 44 years, whom the girls referred to as 'big brother', and who considered their activities as a form of relationship rather than prostitution. It is true that such activities often include non-sexual services, such as having dinner, watching movies or visiting amusement parks – and sex, where it does occur, usually happens after other activities (Wakabayashi, 2003). It is the age of the girls involved, however, rather than the specific activities, that make it exploitative and dangerous, even where no sexual activity occurs. Teenagers who engage in these activities very often come from families with internal dysfunctions, whether emotional absence, a lack of parental care or excessive control (Lee, 2016). In other words, they are children with a degree of emotional damage that leaves them vulnerable to manipulation.

At its height, in the late 1990s, an estimated 4% of both junior and senior high school girls were involved in such activities (Kadokura, 2007). The numbers have since declined due to government crackdowns and social pushback but it remains an ongoing problem that stretches into other areas, whether pornography, animated sexual cartoons or what is known as *chaku ero* (erotic clothing): a form of sexually targeted film which involves young girls (some of kindergarten age) being recorded in non-sexual but provocative poses and skimpy clothing. The films of younger girls are especially lucrative, making tens of thousands of dollars, and are nominally legal (Varley, 2017).

This is just one of the loopholes that continue to exist following the nominal outlawing of the possession of materials related to child sexual abuse in 2014.[4]

---

[4]The author agrees with the view that the term 'child pornography' is unsuitable in that it conflates something that is of arguable harm and of complete legality, with something that is inarguably harmful and rightfully illegal. The question of whether Chaku Ero, as a grossly exploitative abuse of young children in a blatantly sexual manner, should also be made illegal is not a question that currently seems to have a high priority for the Japanese government.

The problem is that for many with a more innocent/naive view of the world, such imagery (when not grossly indecent) is purely a representation of kawaii and any sexual elements are largely unnoticed. Keiji Goto, a lawyer campaigning for child rights, believes that many in Japan think the objectification of young girls falls into a grey area and is not inherently problematic (AFP, 2018), once again a nod to the deep-rooted gender norms which portray women as being either icons of purity or impurity. Hiroki Fukui, a psychiatrist who has treated paedophiles, says that there is a very low level of awareness in Japan of the dangers posed by child sexual predators and too many are not even aware that there is a problem (AFP, 2018). Morioka adds that a similar lack of awareness exists among the men themselves and that they display a deep 'lack of self-reflection on sexuality', and that, 'if more heterosexual men talk about their own sexuality, it could prevent or correct further "lolicon-ification" of Japanese society' (Otake, 2017). If, as Morioka claims, the underlying issue for many of these men is their inability to understand and come to terms with their own male sexuality, efforts to address such issues will almost certainly apply just as much to the aforementioned misogynistic individuals as to a group who have chosen to respond to problems of complex gender dynamics by retreating entirely from the playing field.

## Sōshoku Danshi

Birth rates in Japan have been declining for decades with each year bringing new record lows (Nikkei, 2020). At the same time, the average age of marriage, and the number of those who never marry, has been increasing. In 2019, the marriage rate was less than half of what it was in 1970, while the average age of marriage increased by 2.5 years and 2.8 years, for men and women respectively, over the past 20 years (SBJ, 2020).

Analysts have looked at a wide variety of factors that may have influenced these patterns and from 2009 a relatively new term suddenly became widely used in reference to the declining interest shown by young men in romantic relationships. *Sōshoku-kei danshi* (herbivore men or grass-eaters) was originally coined by the writer Maki Fukuzawa but took several years to gain widespread use. It referred to the unthreatening character of young men who are shy around girls, passive in their interactions and, importantly, happy to remain in the friend zone. Japan has a fondness for systems of classification and as the term grew in use similar expressions arose for other types of men: *nikushoku danshi* (meat eaters) for men who aggressively pursue women, *gyoshoku danshi* (fish eaters) for men who are attracted to women but more patient, *kurīmu danshi* (creamy) for men who are soft and gentle but still masculine (Nicolae, 2014, p. 71). Only the original, however, had a specific relation to changing patterns of masculinity that threatened to greatly exacerbate Japan's long demographic decline.

Social withdrawal is a particular aspect of Japanese culture that is most pronounced in the behaviour of the *hikikomori* (literally, those who pull inward), people who cut off all direct contact with others. Some think this may represent a distinct psychological disorder bound by elements of Japanese culture (Teo &

Gaw, 2010), and it may be that sōshoku danshi are exhibiting a similar response to social anxiety, albeit limited to the one area that gives them the most stress: sexual intimacy.

Authors such as Kitamura (2011) posited a variety of potential influences on this trend: pressure and stress surrounding the act of sex itself, the disparity between 'real women' and the idealised fantasies many young men had developed, a decline in communication skills due to modern lifestyles, and the burden of work leaving young people with little time or energy for romantic activity. One important factor, however, was not that all young men were shying away from sex but, rather, that there was a growing polarisation between those who engaged in sexual activity from a relatively young age and those who had no sexual experience at all. Surveys carried out by the Japan Association for Sex Education found a strong trend among young people, from teens to university students, to increasingly regard sex as something that was not pleasurable. The pattern was more pronounced among high school students and female college-age students and the authors contributed it largely to a breakdown in sexual communication. In other words, they noted an increasing difficulty, in part attributable to technology, for young people to have meaningful interchanges of opinions on emotion and interpersonal relations (NSK, 2019).[5]

Japan's Finance Minister, Taro Aso, rightly came under fire when he commented regarding Japan's declining population, 'The problem is those who don't have children' (Mainichi, 2019). There are many perfectly legitimate reasons why people might not have children. The problem is not that they do not have them, but rather that other factors may be preventing many people who might benefit greatly from romantic relationships – whether tied to childbirth or otherwise – from engaging in them.

A 2015 survey on Marriage and Family Formation by the Japanese Cabinet Office found that the most common reason for people not wanting a relationship was that, 'love is troublesome' (Sankei, 2015). Thousands of years of human experience would suggest otherwise – with love, and a desire to be accepted for who we are, whether by lovers, spouses or children – being one of the fundamental drivers of the human condition.

As Victor Hugo wrote in Les Misérables, 'The supreme happiness of life is the conviction that we are loved; loved for ourselves – say rather, loved in spite of ourselves'. Tolstoy, who was profoundly influenced by the earlier work of Hugo, said much the same in his opus War and Peace, 'Seize the moments of happiness, love and be loved! That is the only reality in the world, all else is folly. It is the one thing we are interested in here'.

In a similar vein, the Japanese author Arishima Takeo wrote, 'Where there is love, let there be family. Where there is none, let no family exist. Only by allowing this can men and women be freed from horrible lies'. Another well-known Japanese writer, Uchimura Kanzō, wrote of how 'Love is taken without reserve. It

---

[5]Kindle Edition, Chapter 1, Section 5.

has no fear, it is the highest morality. In love there is no doubt, for love is the greatest truth. Love has no bonds, it is true freedom'.

That so many people in Japan would now regard the pursuit of love as 'troublesome' suggests a growing divergence in understanding about what love and relationships mean to young people and the possibility that they are poorly educated about the benefits that such things can offer. Thankfully, there are aspects of Japanese male gender norms that have adopted a more healthy and engaged attitude towards the importance of relationships. One of these is the concept of *ikumen*.

## Ikumen

Ikumen is a portmanteau of *ikuji* (child-rearing) and *ikemen* (handsome) and refers to a type of man who is particularly attractive to women because they take an active role in raising children. The word was first used in 2010 and became part of an ongoing project by the Ministry of Health, Labour and Welfare to promote gender equality by having men take on more responsibility for childcare.[6] At the outset of the Ikumen project the idea of playing an active part in childcare was still rare with 26% of men agreeing with the statement that, 'a father's work-centred life is a key to family happiness', and the majority among those who did not explicitly agree still adhering to social expectations in this regard (Cabinet Office, 2012, p. 16). In the intervening years, views have shifted only slightly with 30% of men still believing that work should be prioritised over family and that women should carry out housework and child-rearing. These views are, however, higher for men in their 50s and 60s and notably lower for those in their 20s and 30s (Cabinet Office, 2021, p. 16).

The project has continued and the government's Gender Equality Bureau highlights the wide variety of programmes set up throughout the country to support men in becoming more involved in child-rearing, whether by learning to cut their children's hair, taking cooking lessons or practising first aid.[7] However, a 2019 survey by the Japanese Trade Union Confederation found that 45% of fathers said they spent only 5 hours or less with their children each week, with 13.5% saying they spent no time on child-rearing (Rengo, 2019, p. 6). When asked about which should be more important, childcare or work, 19.1% said work should come first, 14.1% said childcare should come first, while the majority (62.7%) said there should be a balance. Yet, when asked what came first in their actual lives, 56.5% said they prioritise work and only 6.8% said they prioritise childcare (Rengo, 2019, p. 9).

---

[6]Homepage of the Japanese Government's 'Ikumen' project at the Ministry of Health, Labour and Welfare, https://ikumen-project.mhlw.go.jp/.
[7]Examples of suggested measures to promote participation of men in housework, at the Japanese Government's Gender Equality Bureau, https://www.gender.go.jp/research/kenkyu/chiiki_h30.html.

There is clearly still significant progress to be made in encouraging men to take a more active and direct role in family affairs but the ikumen project faces some problems. One of these is that there has been a backlash against the male-centric focus of ikumen, with some viewing it as setting female household labour up as an expected inevitability, and male labour as something to be praised for its rarity (Asahi, 2019). Rather than helping erase rigid gender norms, some have argued that it may, in fact, reinforce them (Kayama, 2017), with one PR firm claiming that terms such as ikumen are outdated language in their gender specificity (Kamitaki, 2021).

An arguably more important criticism of the concept, however, is that it is very clearly focused on the issue of division of household labour, far more than it is the question of men's emotional roles within the family structure. The former is certainly something that needs to be addressed and a gender-neutral approach to household chores is a worthy but separate concern. The government's own Ikumen page explains its purpose as being that if men embrace ikumen, 'the way of life of women as wives will change. The potential of children and the nature of the family will change dramatically. Society as a whole will also grow more prosperous'.[8] It does not mention the emotional needs of the men themselves and the long pattern of distancing they have experienced from meaningful participation in family relationships. In a review of outstanding weaknesses in the ikumen policy, the Director of the government's Work Environment and Equality Bureau stated that 'It is very important for men to actively raise children from the perspective of enhancing the child-rearing environment and continuing employment for women'.[9] In short, the key flaws were identified as the failure of more men to take paternity leave from work and insufficient participation in childcare. Emotional health, in terms of helping men adjust their life priorities from career goals to relationship goals, was not significantly addressed. Part of this is likely to be that for the government, at least, ikumen is more an economic policy designed to encourage more women to join, or remain in, the workforce, rather than a sincere effort to adjust men's views on the importance of family bonds.

In his own assessment of the importance of sharing household chores, Sechiyama (2014) finishes by stating 'it is a blessing to be able to spend so much time with my children...the time I picked her up from nursery and she ran to me with her hands in the air and hugged me...I believe that we live for those priceless memories'. This is the reality of what men themselves need from ikumen. It should be not only a means of supporting their family but also a means of families providing emotional support and deeper meaning for men. There has to be a change in focus regarding men's roles in relation to their families, where they are viewed as more than simply a labourer, whether this is in terms of household chores or regarding a primary career. Just as burden-sharing is an important issue in terms of supporting the advancement of women, supporting the emotional

---

[8]From the 'About' section of the Ikumen Project site, https://ikumen-project.mhlw.go.jp/project/about/.

[9]Ikumen Project activity report for 2020, https://ikumen-project.mhlw.go.jp/project/activity/2020/.

stability and well-being of men, is something that will provide benefit not only for those men but also for their families and society as a whole.

## Conclusion

It is certainly true that the majority of men in Japan do not suffer from the issues (misogyny, lolita complexes, or rejection of relationships) that have been mentioned here. There are also a great number of Japanese men who do enjoy emotionally rewarding and meaningful familial bonds. However, it is the outlier cases and the aberrant behaviours that arise from them that highlight some deep problems within Japan's gender norms. Even men who do not exhibit extreme behaviour often suffer from emotional stress and distancing that affects how they view and interact with women. On an institutional and societal level, such attitudes can have a pervasive effect, influencing problems such as the commodification of sex and gender-based violence.

Schultz et al. (2010, p. 186) wrote that 'the liberalisation of gender beliefs will occur only insofar as the necessary social-institutional supports for the integration of women into the workforce are available and there is a demand on the part of women for a revolution in gender roles'. These changes cannot be restricted to how society views women: for deep change to occur and longstanding problems to be properly addressed, the way that men are viewed, and the way they in turn view women and families must also change.

The ikumen project was a positive move in this direction but it remains hampered by its excessive focus on men's family role being one of labour rather than one of love. There needs to be a greater focus on the importance of emotional communication, the development of more interactive and mutually respectful relationships between the genders, and frank and open discussion of sexual health. Ideally, this would occur from a young age so that both men and women in Japan can develop with a deeper and more positive understanding of, and attitude to, the opposite sex. In addressing the difficulties faced by women in society, it can be common to view men as being part of the problem. The reality is that such problems harm men as much as they do women and by addressing them, we can help society as a whole establish more equitable gender norms.

## References

Abe, S. (2020, June 4). ろくでなし子被告、3Dデータ提供で有罪維持の公算 [Megumi Igarashi is likely to remain guilty by providing 3D data]. *Asahi Shimbun*.

AFP. (2018, January 26). 'Male fans prefer primary school girls': How Japan walks a fine line when it comes to sexualising children. Agence-France Presse.

Alexy, A. (2010). The door my wife closed: Houses, families, and divorce in contemporary Japan. In R. Ronald & A. Alexy (Eds.), *Home and family in Japan: Continuity and transformation*. London: Routledge.

Allison, A. (2009). *Nightwork*. Chicago, IL: University of Chicago Press.

Asahi. (2019, October 19). イクメンどう思う？ [What do you think of Ikumen?]. *Asahi Shimbun*.

Asahi. (2020, December 7). 男らしさって？ [What is masculinity?]. *Asahi Shimbun*.

Asahi. (2021, February 3). 「女性がたくさん入っている会議は時間かかる」森喜朗氏 [Meetings with a lot of women "take too much time" Yoshiro Mori]. *Asahi Shimbun*.

Behrens, K., & Kondo-Ikemure, K. (2011). Japanese children's amae and mothers' attachment status as assessed by the adult attachment interview. *International Journal of Psychology*, *46*(5), 368–376.

Benedict, R. (1989). *The Chrysanthemum and the Sword: Patterns of Japanese culture*. Boston, MA: Houghton Mifflin.

Cabinet Office. (2011). 「男性にとっての男女共同参画」に関する意識調査報告書 - 第2章 調査結果の概要 [*Gender equality for men: Awareness survey report – chapter 2, summary of survey results*]. Japan Cabinet Office, Gender Equality Bureau.

Cabinet Office. (2021). 「令和3年度　性別による無意識の思い込み（アンコンシャス・バイアス）に関する調査研究調査結果」 [*Survey research on unconscious beliefs (unconscious bias) by gender survey results*]. Japan Cabinet Office, Gender Equality Bureau.

Cherry, K. (2016). *Womansword what Japanese words say about women*. Berkeley: Stonebridge.

Chu, C. S. K. (2018). *Compensated dating: Buying and selling sex in cyberspace*. London: Palgrave MacMillan.

Dentsu. (2021, February 5). ジェンダーに関する意識調査 [Gender awareness survey]. Dentsu Communication Institute Compass.

Doi, T. (1973). *The anatomy of dependence*. Tokyo: Kodansha International.

Galbraith, P. W. (2017). *The Moe Manifesto: An insider's look at the worlds of manga, anime, and gaming*. Clarendon, VT: Tuttle Publishing.

Hashimoto, N., Ushitora, K., Morioka, M., Terunori, M., Tanaka, K., Tashiro, M., ... Sawamura, F. (2017). School education and development of gender perspectives and sexuality in Japan. *Sex Education*, *17*(4), 386–398.

Iwao, S. (1993). *The Japanese woman: Traditional image and changing reality*. New York, NY: Free Press.

Johnston, E. (2020, March 6). Women in Japanese politics: Why so few after so very long? *Japan Times*.

Jolivet, M. (1997). *Japan: The childless society? The crisis of motherhood*. London: Routledge.

Joyce, L., Paulson, J., & Powers, E. (1976). *Women in changing Japan*. Boulder, CO: Westview Press.

Kadokura, T. (2007). Total value of boryukudan activities and the enjo-kosai market. *Japanese Economy*, *34*, 62–87.

Kamitaki, K. (2021, March 25). PRに求められるジェンダーのアップデート、イクメンは誉め言葉でなく死語 [Gender update required for PR, Ikumen is a dead language, not a compliment]. Kyodo PR.

Kayama, R. (2017, August 7). クメンという言葉こそジェンダーギャップの象徴？ [Is the word Ikumen a symbol of the gender gap?]. *FQ Magazine*.

Kinouchi, T. (2021, March 6). Japan adds female executives but they take only 8% of board seats. *Nikkei Asia*.

Kitamura, K. (2011). セックス嫌いな若者たち [Young people who do not like to have sex]. Tokyo: Media Factory.

Kitayama, S., Mesquito, B., & Karasawa, M. (2006). Cultural affordances and emotional experience: Socially engaging and disengaging emotions in Japan and the United States. *Journal of Personality and Social Psychology*, *91*, 890–903.

Komatsu, K. (2011). *Attachment and amae: A comparative study of mother-child close relationships in Japan and Britain*. Edinburgh: University of Edinburgh.

Koyama, S. (2013). *The educational ideal of 'good wife, wise mother' in modern Japan*. Leiden: Brill.

Kuwahara, R. (2019, October 31). Children deprived of the right to learn about sex. Retrieved from Nippon.com.

Lee, T. Y. (2016). A longitudinal study of compensated dating and juvenile prostitution behaviors among adolescents in Hong Kong. *Journal of Pediatric and Adolescent Gynecology*, *29*(1), S31–S37.

Mainichi. (2019, February 5). Politicians show ignorance in attacks on women for not having children. *Mainichi Japan*.

Manne, K. (2019). *Down girl: The logic of misogyny*. Youngstown, OH: Penguin.

Maruta, K. (2001). 誰が誰に何を売るのか?–援助交際にみる性・愛・コミュニケーション [*Who sells what to whom?–Sex, love, and communication seen in Enkou Dating*]. Nishinomiya: Kwansei Gakuin University Press.

Miyamoto, M. (1994). *Straight jacket society: An insider's irreverent view of Bureaucratic Japan*. Tokyo: Kodansha.

Nicolae, R. (2014). Sōshoku(kei) danshi: The (un)gendered questions on contemporary Japan. *Romanian Economic and Business Review*, *9*(3), 66.

Nikkei. (2020, February 23). Number of births in Japan falls to record low in 2020. *Nikkei Asia*.

NSK. (2019). 第8回「若者の性」白書 [*8th white paper on youth sexuality*]. Shougakukan: Nihon Seikyouiku Kyoukai.

Ochiai, E. (1997). The Japanese family system in transition: A sociological analysis of family change in postwar Japan. LCTB International Library Association.

Otake, T. (2017, May 5). Professor examines Lolita complex by first looking at his own experience. *Japan Times*.

Rengo. (2019, October 8). 男性の家事・育児参加に関する実態調査 [Survey on men's participation in housework and childcare]. Japan Trade Union Confederation Rengo.

Salamon, S. (1974). Male chauvinism as an expression of love in Japanese marriages. In T. S. Lebra (Ed.), *Japanese culture and behaviour selected readings* (pp. 130–141). Honolulu, HI: University of Honolulu Press.

Saeki, E., Watanabe, Y., & Kido, M. (2015). Developmental and gender trends in emotional and interpersonal competence among Japanese children. *The International Journal of Emotional Education*, *7*(2), 15–35.

Saito, K. (2013). Magic, Shojo, and Metamorphosis: Magical girl anime and the challenges of changing gender identities in Japanese society. *Journal of Asian Studies*, *73*(1), 143–164.

Sankei, S. (2015, July 30). 草食どころか絶食に？！ 恋愛しない若者が急増中 [Fasting instead of herbivorous? Young people who are not in love increasing rapidly]. *Sankei Shinbun*.

Sato, K. (2009). From Hello Kitty to Cod Roe Kewpie: A postwar cultural history of cuteness in Japan. *Education About Asia*, *14*(2), 38–42.

SBJ. (2020). *Statistical handbook of Japan 2020*. Tokyo: Statistics Bureau of Japan.

Schultz, L. K., Tufis, P., & Alwin, D. (2010). Separate spheres or increasing equality? Changing gender beliefs in Postwar Japan. *Journal of Family and Marriage, 72*(1), 184–201.

Sechiyama, K. (2014, March 14). 東大ジェンダー学者の戦略的イクメン化計画: 育児で男にできないことなんて、何ひとつない [The University of Tokyo Gender Scholar's Strategic Ikumenization Plan: There is nothing a man can't do when raising a child]. Tokyo Keizai.

Silva-Grodin, M. (2010). Women in ancient Japan: From matriarchal antiquity to acquiescent confinement. *Inquiries Journal, 2*(9).

St Michel, P. (2013, February 8). A pop star shouldn't shave her head in shame for having a boyfriend. *The Atlantic*.

Takahashi, G., & Tsunku. (2003). てっぺん (Top). Bijenesu-sha.

Tanaka, C. (2019, January 11). Outrage erupts online in Japan after assaulted NGT48 pop idol apologises for 'causing trouble'. *Japan Times*.

Teo, A. R., & Gaw, A. C. (2010). Hikikomori, a Japanese culture-bound syndrome of social withdrawal? *The Journal of Nervous and Mental Disease, 198*(6), 444–449.

Tocco, M. C. (2003). Norms and texts for women's education in Tokugawa Japan. In D. Ko, J. K. Haboush, & J. R. Piggott (Eds.), *Women and confucian cultures in Premodern China, Korea, and Japan* (pp. 193–218). Berkeley, CA: University of California Press.

Ueno, C. (2019). ミソジニーとは何か？ 上野 [What is misogyny?]. 立教大学ジェンダーフォーラム年報 [*Rikkyo University gender forum annual report*], *21*, 1–20.

Uno, K. (1993). The death of "good wife, wise mother". In A. Gordon (Ed.), *Postwar Japan as history*. Berkeley, CA: University of California Press.

Varley, C. (2017, March 7). Is Japan turning a blind eye to paedophilia? BBC.

Wakabayashi, T. (2003). Enjokosai in Japan: Rethinking the dual image of prostitutes in Japanese and American law. *UCLA Women's Journal, 13*, 143–184.

Yano, C. (2009). Wink on pink: Interpreting Japanese cute as it grabs the global headlines. *The Journal of Asian Studies, 68*(3), 681–688.

Yoshiko, M. (1997). Excerpts from 'sexuality'. In S. Buckley (Ed.), *Broken silence: Voices of Japanese feminism* (pp. 170–183). Berkeley, CA: University of California Press.

# Chapter 9

# Intersectional Influences of Sexual Orientation Microaggressions in South Africa

*Deepesh Nirmaldas Dayal*

## Abstract

Following South Africa's democracy, a new constitution was adopted that allowed for freedom of all citizens. This legal protection has, however, not fully translated into a change in attitudes of members of society. Raising the topic of gender being on a spectrum in an African context is bound to result in controversy. Many African countries continue to criminalise same-sex relationships. Therefore it can be understood that the notion of a same-sex desire is seen to be un-African. A common view is that the spectrum of gender identities is a Western import. This chapter focuses on how cultural nuances hinder South African Indian gay men from fully expressing themselves within the South African Indian community. Non-acceptance of South African gay men by the South African Indian community is often based on factors such as religion, patriarchy, hetero-normativity and the idea of same-sex relationships being un-African. Theoretically, intersectionality is used to make sense of discrimination. Intersectionality also serves as a lens because it considers an individual has multiple identities based on race, culture, gender, social class, age and sexual orientation, which are derived from power, history and social relations. Within this chapter, accounts from research studies as well as e-zine articles will be used to demonstrate aspects of the intersectionality theory.

*Keywords*: South African Indian; LGBTQ+; microaggressions; inter-sectionality; religion; homosexuality

Gender Violence, the Law, and Society, 161–174
doi:10.1108/978-1-80117-127-420221013

The self has many different identities. Usually, people are categorised by their core identities, such as race and sex, and often these identities intersect. Within the realm of my research interests, which investigates the identity development and microaggression experiences of South African Indian gay men, I explore the intersectional influences that contribute to their experiences. Born in South Africa, South African gay Indian men hold multiple identities: that of being South African, being of Indian descent and self-identifying as gay. Research on intersectionality informs us that due to our multiple identities, our life experiences diverge, where 'the simultaneous experiences of all the (different) identities result in different meanings and experiences than what could be captured by consideration (of a single category alone)' (Stirrat et al., 2008, p. 91).

This chapter will attempt to integrate some aspects of the multiple identities that South African Indian gay men hold, and how that leads to the microaggressions experienced by them. There will be a focus on the un-Africanness of identifying as LGBTQ+ in South Africa, patriarchy, collectivism and religion. These provide a unique examination of the lives of South African Indian people who identify as LGBTQ+. It must be remembered that the political climate that South African LGBTQ+ people live in, which was discussed in Chapter 6, is as much an intersectional influence as the other categories discussed in this chapter. The chapter will end with a discussion, which attempts to integrate the various intersectional categories. This discussion will involve a snapshot of the theme from a research study by the author of this chapter, Dayal (2021), focusing on 'Honour and Shame', which will be used to practically demonstrate intersectional discrimination.

## What Are the Types of Intersectionalities and How Do We Make Sense of Them Using an Intersectionality Framework

Through an intersectionality lens, identities such as race, class and gender are seen to intersect with each other 'together or simultaneously to get some sense of the ways these spheres of inequality support each other to maintain the status quo' (Zerai, 2000, p. 185). People's identities are therefore pluralistic and layered, with linkages to history, social categorisation, social interactions and power relations. Through this interplay, people can be advantaged in one category, while simultaneously being disadvantaged in another. Despite these definitions and attempts to simplify the definition of intersectionality, we need to remember that intersectionality has definitional fluidity, as the intersections of our identities and the definition of our being are constantly evolving.

Crenshaw (1991), who provided a foundational framework for intersectionality, presents a threefold typology of intersectionality, namely structural, political and representational intersectionality. Structural intersectionality covers those oppressions based on race, gender, class and other identities which come from state structures. An example of this is a police force which may not be suitably trained to assist LGBTQ+ people with their reports of hate crimes or discrimination and end up perpetuating the same experience that victims ask them to address. Political intersectionality occurs when political movements seek justice for certain groups of people – such as LGBTQ+ people or people from a certain race group – thus reinforcing inequality by excluding the needs of certain other groups. The final type, representational intersectionality, is visible when images of a group distort the complexities of the group.

The four main benefits of intersectionality are simultaneity, complexity, irreducibility and inclusivity (Carathathis, 2014). Many models exist that aim to add categories of influence on a list, ranked from most important to least important and these categories usually allow us to understand the various influences on one's identity. However, often these models are additive and simply add to each other, where some categories are privileged and some are disadvantaged. Categories are individually explained; however, their combined impact often is not. Within the intersectionality framework, a monistic approach is taken where multiple identities are seen to have unitary influences, where the different influences on identity are seen as all-encompassing, thus protecting against heteronormativity, elitism and power dynamics (Carastathis, 2014). In this way, intersectionality aims to be anti-categorical, emphasising that 'social life is considered too irreducibly complex, overflowing with multiple and fluid determinations of both subjects and structures, to make fixed categories anything but simplifying social fictions that produce inequalities in the process of producing differences' (p. 1173). Identities are seen to be more fluid, and the intersectionality approach aims to remedy the challenges faced by the monistic approaches which fail to capture simultaneous oppressions. This is of great value within all identity creation, and in South Africa, the categories of race, class and gender intersect on a historical and current basis.

Despite the theoretical victories of intersectionality theory, there are also some departures. Intersectionality theory has been criticised for being too vague, as the mechanism behind determining the multiple influences of identity is not clearly explained. For Ludvig (2006, p. 247), definitions of intersectionality are open to subjective bias. He asks: '[w]ho defines when, where, which and why particular differences are given recognition while others are not?'. It is also seen as too flexible, and to contain an inherent focus on categories, even as it claims a departure from them (Crenshaw, 2015). Despite claiming a desire to be anti-categorical, some researchers who use the intersectionality theory believe that there is merit in having categories, as it helps us to determine occurrences of sociocultural power and privilege present in interlocking identities (Shields, 2008). These challenges make intersectionality theory difficult to use in research studies. The outcomes of research studies using intersectionality as a framework, then, are often seen to be more descriptive than practical (Verloo, 2013).

## Intersectionality of South African Indian LGBTQ+ Experiences in South Africa

LGBTQ+ people of all races face challenges in South Africa – though historically, White LGBTQ+ people tended to enjoy greater freedoms and protections (Gevisser, 1994). Especially South African Indian LGBTQ+ people have historically experienced intersectional challenges due to their race. These challenges were tied to politics, access to resources, infrastructure, education and other disadvantages. Today, despite Constitutional freedoms, aspects of these oppressions still exist. They are often attributed to the multifaceted influences of culture, race, class, gender, patriarchy and socioeconomic status. Some of the intersectional influences on the lives of South African Indian LGBTQ+ people will be discussed. Despite my reliance on identity categories, however, an effort will be made to integrate categorical influences, in keeping to the suggestions derived from the critiques of the intersectionality theory.

### Un-Africanness of Identifying as LGBTQ+ in South Africa

The lived experiences of LGBTQ+ people of Indian descent in South Africa appear within the context of a racially and culturally pluralistic South Africa. Raising the topics of gender identity and sexual orientation diversity in South Africa continues to be contentious within some communities. Within the African context, same-sex desires are seen to be un-African, and these desires are labelled as a Western import (Msibi, 2011). It has been argued by some community leaders that same-sex desires have never existed within the African context and that these undesirable phenomena have been brought to the African continent through the movement of Western people, who brought their own cultures and identities (Msibi, 2011). Often, community leaders, who are mostly male, enforce dogmatic and patriarchal stances against LGBTQ+ people, promoting discrimination of same-sex relationships (Bennett & Reddy, 2015). This reminds us of the impact that patriarchy and the influence of hegemonic masculinity may have in encouraging the discrimination of LGBTQ+ people. The notion that LGBTQ+ identities are un-African creates an unsafe and challenging environment for LGBTQ+ people to navigate, as they find difficulties in openly expressing their gender identities and sexual orientation (Msibi, 2011). South African LGBTQ+ people of Indian descent are seen to navigate an identity within an African context, and therefore the rhetoric surrounding the un-Africanness of same-sex relationships creates an unsafe environment for them to develop this part of their identity in. The expressions of gender identity and sexual orientation are seen to intersect with a stifling community culture and a structural unsafeness related to same-sex identity views.

### Hegemonic Masculinity and Patriarchy Within the South African Indian Community

Within different communities and in different cultures, there are different understandings of and associations with the concept of masculinity. Within the study of masculinities, there exist the understanding that there's a variety of types of masculinities, which can be dominant in a specific context to varying degrees (Connell, 2005). The type of masculinity which is called 'hegemonic' is the dominant type in most contexts and is seen to subjugate both women and diverging forms of masculinity. Often, gay men are perceived to be inferior by men who take on hegemonic masculine traits. Gay men are perceived in stereotypical ways which are often linked to effeminate traits. A gay man in Dave's (2011) study reveals:

> You know I don't like this very stereotypical gay scene. The negative aspects if you say you're gay is that you're immediately placed in a box and that box is often you know very feminine guys and you know you see these guys everywhere... they carry little handbags around, um they have this squeaky voice and things like that. I just feel if you say you're gay then you get put into that box, which I don't see it as something that's positive because if I think you gay you can still be yourself, you don't need to feel gay and feel feminine.
>
> (Dave, 2011, p. 23)

Men who subscribe to the ideal of hegemonic masculinity often embrace 'social dominance orientations', meaning they attempt to dominate other people. Gay men are particularly vulnerable to this domination (Ratele & Suffla, 2010). Within the South African Indian community, the perpetrators of gender identity and sexual orientation-based microaggressions are usually male (Bonthuys & Erlank, 2012; Coopoosamy, 2018; Martin & Govender, 2013; Moonsammy, 2009; Sheldon, 2016). Within the South African Indian communities, men have historically been the financial providers for their families and due to the power associated with money, the communities have been largely patriarchal (Carrim, 2015; Patel, Govender, Paruk, & Ramgoon, 2006). This has made people who are dependent on these men for financial resources vulnerable, and these people are often made to follow certain rules set out by the patriarchal societies, which may disadvantage them.

Due to the patriarchal nature of the South African Indian community, positions of power held by men can be used to subjugate other men who they do not seem to approve of – often gay men. Connell summarises this as the subjection of gay men to 'political and cultural exclusions, cultural abuse, legal violence, street violence, economic discrimination and personal boycotts' (2005, p. 78). Traditional masculine values are believed to be learned in early childhood development, where attitudes such as status-seeking, antifemininity, heteronormativity, a focus on athleticism and the lack of emotional displays are taught as accepted behaviours for Indian boys and men (Martin & Govender, 2013). There is also debate that the portrayal of men as being muscular and physically strong may emanate from the representation of Indian men in Bollywood movies, which often display strong and dominant heroes and villains with muscular bodies and physically dominant traits (Kaur, 2017; Martin & Govender, 2013). Younger boys and men who behave in ways that are in opposition to these traditional ways of being are discriminated against (Dayal, 2021). South African Indian gay men are marginalised by the intersections of culture, patriarchy and traditional gender norms. These South African gay Indian men feel threatened to express their masculinity in a way different than expected, as they fear being labelled and 'othered' in a negative way.

## Collectivism

Collectivism is a focus on the importance of the group over the individual and serves as an important identity marker of Indian communities (Triandas, 1995). Indian people often construct their identities based on familial and communal markers of belonging. Aspects such as community beliefs, community relationships and community daily norms and practices are a regular part of the lives of Indian people. These practices are inherited and seen as a respectable part of community life. Interactions with family members and members of the community are seen as being of utmost importance and a key foundation to building a strong identity. In South Africa, the nuclearisation of Indian families was believed to be a product of Apartheid, under which systems Indian people in South Africa were moved to areas that involved high-density living (Khan, 2012). These areas produced unique living circumstances for South African Indian people, as they often lived in small homes, within close proximity, and shared communal resources. This made community interactions easy, as neighbours would know about each other's comings and goings due to the proximity in which people lived. A result was the collective responsibility that community members often took in terms of shared households and resources.

Some Indian people responded positively to collective living: many Indian people have found merit in living in communities where they feel supported (see e.g. Pillay, 2015). However, LGBTQ+ people who live within close proximity to relatives believe that collective living makes it difficult for them to fully express their sexual orientations (Bonthuys & Erlank, 2012; Moonsammy, 2009). This is due to the fact that many LGBTQ+ people feel that they have to constantly live up to traditional norms and values, such as getting married, starting a family and, for men, being breadwinners. This made living a life that was different from the traditional norm difficult (Moonsammy, 2009). The end of Apartheid signalled an opportunity for Indian people to move away from these restricted areas. South African Indian people are now free to live in areas all across the country. However, the culture of collectivism remains. Some people find great joy in these living arrangements, whilst other people find limitations and challenges to creating a true identity amidst a collective lifestyle. The impacts of politics, culture and sexuality are seen to co-exist during the process of creating an identity that is not always accepted and celebrated. Collective living may result in the policing of conservative and community practices that are often unsupportive of same-sex relationships.

### Religious Practice

An important part of collectivism within Indian communities is the practice of praying together. Within South Africa, religion and prayer form an important part of the national identity. People find great comfort in praying and as a result, South Africa is rich in religions, places of prayer and community support systems that emerge from religious organisations. There is often a certain cultural identity that emerges from each religious organisation, which comes with its own community practices, ways of life and beliefs about the world.

Whilst conflicts between religion and same-sex attractions have been well documented (Bonthuys & Erlank, 2012), some parents of children who identify as gay are known to seek solace in religion when making sense of their children's sexual orientation (Livingston & Fourie, 2016). Despite the benefits that emerge from religious affiliations, studies in South Africa have shown that some people with strong religious beliefs were seen to discriminate against LGBTQ+ people at a higher rate than the national average (Mavhandu-Mudzusi & Ganga-Limando, 2014; Mukwevho & Fhumulani, 2018). There are also some instances of reparative sexual orientation therapy in South Africa, in which gay men are subjected to therapeutic practices aimed to change their sexual orientations (Van Zyl, Nel, & Govender, 2018). These men are made to believe that identifying as gay is a sin.

The incompatibility of religion and LGBTQ+ identities within the Indian community has been written about in many studies in both South Africa and other countries (Bhugra, 1997a, 1997b; Bonthuys & Erlank, 2012; Dave, 2011; Jaspal, 2012; Jaspal & Cinnirella, 2010; Minwalla, Rosser, Feldman, & Varga, 2005). Religious practices within the South African Indian community mainly emphasise the importance of religion as a vehicle of living a life that involves family, marriage and procreation (Bonthuys & Erlank, 2012; Hassim, 2013). Marriage is commonly understood as being between a man and a woman, and LGBTQ+ people who have different thoughts about what signifies a marriage are seen as unnatural. The close ties of community to religion in South Africa make it difficult for South African LGBTQ+ people of Indian descent to openly express their sexual orientation out of fear of being discriminated against on the grounds of religion. South African Indian gay men often believe that religion is used as a way to instil fear in them and that, often, religious texts are interpreted in ways that disadvantage them. Religious dogmas that stigmatise LGBTQ+ people are often expressed by conservative religious community leaders who display hegemonic masculine traits. However, some religious leaders openly accept same-sex relationships. Some researchers have reported instances where the 'community has been accepting of same-sex marriage, there is no fuss about it. Society does not frown on it either' (Coopoosamy, 2018). These religious leaders provide a safe place for LGBTQ+ people to practice their religion in a non-threatening way. Despite challenges faced within religious communities, in a recent study, Dayal (2021) showed that South African Indian gay men still hold a strong connection to religion, and they find benefits in prayer and religious practice. Coopoosamy (2018) recorded a similar sentiment in his study when quoting from an interview with an openly gay man in South Africa. This interviewee told him that religion is a powerful vehicle for him to make sense of the world and that:

> All these contradicting things confused me because even at that time I knew I did not choose to be gay and why would such compassionate and a merciful God send me to hell for something that I did not choose?
>
> (Coopoosamy, 2018)

Therefore, he firmly sees the good in religion and finds the interpretations of religion that oppress gay men as being unfair and confusing. Another South African Indian gay man in Dave's (2011) study shared these sentiments: 'I don't believe in a God that is um twisted or vengeful and I don't think he'd make people this way and want them to be another way for some unknown point' (Dave, 2011, p. 25).

The release that religion provides gay men was further revealed in a study on the coming-out experiences of South African gay men and lesbian women (Nair, 2020). In this study, a gay man expressed:

> I do hold my religion very dear to me it's not something that I want to let go of. I was able to sit on my prayer mat again and I'll never forget the very first conversation I had with God after many many years was, 'I'm so sorry but I'm gay' that was the first thing that I said and 'you're going to kill me and strike me dead now's your time just strike me dead because I've had it I cannot keep this lie going on I need to talk to you I need you'. You know I broke down in tears and from that point on I was like ok that felt good I actually need to do more of these conversations and I started praying more often […].
>
> (Nair, 2020, p. 55)

What is evident is that many South African gay Indian men believe that identifying as gay is a part of one's being and one's sexual orientation should be lived out and not changed based on societal expectations. Some gay men are made to feel ashamed about their sexual orientation due to societal views about the incompatibility of identifying as LGBTQ+ and community values. This balance between honour and shame is discussed next.

## Honour and Shame

This section of the chapter focuses on a theme from the aforementioned study by Dayal (2021), which focused on the microaggression experiences of South African Indian gay men. One of the themes accounted for the major focus on honour within the South African Indian community and the emphasis on the shame that emerges from supposed non-conforming behaviours from members of the community.

### *'What Will People Say?'*

Honour and respect are strong notions that form the foundations of self-worth and status within Indian communities (Bhugra, 1997a, 1997b; Dave, 2011; Dayal, 2021). Members of the family are often reminded that they need to be responsible for their actions as their actions are firmly tied to the honour of their families. There is a clear association with other collectivist cultures where members of the Indian community are expected to sacrifice aspects of individuality to please group beliefs (Dayal, 2021; Triandas, 1995). Within Dayal's (2021) study, a participant mentioned that when he openly expressed his sexual orientation, his mother was more concerned about community messages than his feelings. He reveals: 'I am very close with my mother and it was particularly hard on her, you know, and one of her biggest concerns was, "What were people going to say?"' (Dayal, 2021, p. 69). Families often discount the feelings and experiences of individuals, giving importance to the views of the community. There is often an embarrassment attached to men identifying as gay within the Indian community (Dave, 2011; Dayal, 2021). These messages are direct microinsults as they openly express condemnation of gay men. However, there are also microinvalidations, where the lived experiences of gay men are being ignored, and their sense of vulnerability is not supported.

Another participant in Dayal's (2021) study revealed an experience of telling his mother about being in an open same-sex relationship. She expressed condemnation:

> I told my mother that I want to bring my boyfriend to a family function. Only she knew that we were dating. She said that he [Participant's boyfriend] was too effeminate. She was more worried about other people's opinions. I was so fed up of always living in this dark cloud of the community. It was always, 'What would people say, what would people think. You are supposed to have a girlfriend, not this! This is not normal'. So silly! It really hurt.
>
> (Dayal, 2021, p. 70)

These microinvalidations are linked to assumptions that identifying as gay is unnatural and being in a same-sex relationship is not normal. The participant in

Dayal's (2021) study is made to believe that what he is doing is not right and is against the natural order of society.

Many South African Indian gay men and lesbian women have experienced negative responses upon openly expressing their sexual orientation (Bonthuys & Erlank, 2012; Dave, 2011; Moonsammy, 2009). Studies in India and the United Kingdom have also confirmed these experiences of gay men being discriminated against when expressing their sexual orientation (Bhugra, 1997a; Jaspal, 2012; Medora, 2007; Mimiaga et al., 2013; Træen, Martinussen, Vittersø, & Saini, 2009). Studies in South Africa by Dave (2011) and Moonsammy (2009) revealed that the message of non-acceptance of gay men and lesbian women within the South African Indian community is due to the idea that they are sexually deviant, and the open expression of sexual orientation will bring shame to the family name. The underlying rejection is often tied to the religious beliefs and the collective culture that values marriage and procreation, which, according to members of the community, can only be achieved through heterosexual marriage and a heteronormative way of life.

The fixation on what people will say is also rooted in the practice of gossip. The free flow of information between community members is said to be common practice within the South African Indian community (Dayal, 2021). Therefore there is always a high degree of vigilance around what is being shared with community members – out of fear that the messages will be perceived in a negative way, or the messages will be used to spread gossip about something that will potentially bring shame to the family. Due to this, many gay men and lesbian women of Indian descent compartmentalise their identities out of fear of being ridiculed or discriminated against. Gay men and lesbian women 'tend to be narrowly portrayed [... they] are hidden groups within our small community that have remained largely invisible' (Pillay, 2017).

The narrow focus on community over the lived experiences of LGBTQ+ people within the South African Indian community results from intersections of culture, religion, heteronormativity and societal expectations. What is evident is that the community views and opinions are prioritised over the well-being of LGBTQ+ people. These priorities are especially visible in the question most frequently asked of gay Indian individuals: 'When are you getting married?'

### *'When Are You Getting Married?'*

Marriage is a very important part of life within the Indian community. Fatima Meer noted that 'inwardly family ties and religion keep them [the Indian community] firmly together' (1999, p. 103), and marriages are a way to accomplish this. Despite changes in the forms of relationships and the different concepts of intimacy that are becoming increasingly common, Indian communities continue to place great importance on the traditional heteronormative institution of marriage (Hassim, 2013).

The pressures to engage in heterosexual marriages were reported by many participants in Dayal's (2021) study. Participants who are openly gay frequently expressed variations on this remark of one participant: 'During my twenties, they [family members] forever went on about when am I going to get married' (Dayal, 2021, p. 73). It must be noted that these participants confirmed that the questions they received focused on the heterosexual idea of marriage. Heterosexual marriages are seen to be influential in ensuring the continuation of cultural practices (Jaspal, 2014). Marriage is understood as a means to bring families together and gay men often experience great pressure from their families to marry women – in order for the family to keep family honour and maintain a certain image and status in society (Jaspal, 2012). There are also instances of people believing that if a gay man marries a woman he will be 'cured' and that his sexual orientation will revert to heterosexuality (Bonthuys & Erlank, 2012). There is a stigma associated with waiting too long to get married. Families who do not openly allow their gay sons to reveal their sexual orientation to the community fear that their 'secret' will be revealed if their sons do not get married before a certain age.

According to a participant in Dayal's study, some family members would curiously say: 'It's time you get married or else people are going to start wondering, they're going to think something is wrong with you' (Dayal, 2021, p. 74). This microinsult from a family member made the participant feel inferior. There may be cultural norms that dictate when one should get married; hence, the influence of cultural norms, traditional beliefs, gender roles and norms and societal expectations are at interplay in adding pressure on gay men to getting married.

The preoccupation of family members with heteronormative marriages leads gay men to conceal their same-sex relationships, out of fear of discrimination. One participant from Dayal's (2021) study said:

> Every time I had to hear my family go on about my brother's beautiful wife, and how 'you should get one too', I wish I could tell my family about my beautiful boyfriend, they know he exists, but I can't even talk about him. He had to remain hidden. I had to live this alternate reality, hiding important parts of my identity, just to not rock the boat.
>
> (Dayal, 2021, p. 84)

The participant, who is an openly gay man, is in a comfortable relationship with another man. However, he feels hesitant to reveal this relationship to his family. This is due to his family inadvertently rejecting his relationship without him. His family is focused on him getting married to a woman. As they are aware that he is gay, the insinuation that he should get married to a woman is seen as a microinsult, as his sexual orientation is not treated with respect. Consequently, conversations about his sexual orientation lead to insensitive responses from his family members.

## Conclusion

The identity creation of LGBTQ+ people is marked by many intersectional influences. These influences have been shown to have the potential to simultaneously disadvantage and advantage an individual. South African gay Indian men are believed to experience intersections of different parts of their identities, which make their individual and collective experiences unique. These intersections often lead to accounts of microaggression which negatively impact the lives of these South African gay Indian men and other people with diverging gender or sexual orientations within the South African Indian community. Despite these challenges, several research studies highlight how many LGBTQ+ people reflect on their experiences and attempt to make sense of the intersectional influences that are present in their lives, in an attempt to gain freedoms within these structures. South African gay Indian men are seen to attempt to transcend societal shame, working towards a more whole sense of self.

# References

Bennett, J., & Reddy, V. (2015). African positionings: South African relationships with continental questions of LGBTI justice and rights. *Agenda*, *29*(1), 37–41. doi: 10.1080/10130950.2015.1015829

Bhugra, D. (1997a). Experiences of being a gay man in urban India: A descriptive study. *Sexual & Marital Therapy*, *12*(4), 371–375. doi:10.1080/02674659708408180

Bhugra, D. (1997b). Coming out by South Asian gay men in the United Kingdom. *Archives of Sexual Behavior*, *26*(5), 547–557. doi:10.1023/A:1024512023379

Bonthuys, E., & Erlank, N. (2012). Modes of (in)tolerance: South African Muslims and same sex relationships. *Culture, Health and Sexuality*, *14*(3), 269–282. doi:10. 1080/13691058.2011.621450

Carasthathis, A. (2014). The concept of intersectionality in feminist theory. *Philosophy Compass*, *9*(5), 304–314. doi:10.1111/phc3.12129

Carrim, N. M. H. (2015). Stepping out of the fish tank: Ethnic identity work of Indian parents. *Journal of Family Issues*, *37*(16), 2368–2392. doi:10.1177/0192513X14561521

Connell, R. W. (2005). *Masculinities*. Cambridge: Polity Press.

Coopoosamy, D. (2018, March 4). Same sex marriage in the SA Indian community. *Indian Spice*. Retrieved from https://www.indianspice.co.za/2018/03/04/same-sex-marriage-in-the-sa-indian-community-religious-leaders-speak-out/

Crenshaw, K. (1991). Mapping the margins: Intersectionality, identity politics, and violence against women of color. *Stanford Law Review*, *43*(6), 1241–1299. doi:10. 2307/1229039

Crenshaw, K. (2015, September 24). Why intersectionality can't wait. *Washington Post*. Retrieved from https://www.washingtonpost.com/news/in-theory/wp/2015/09/24/why-intersectionality-cant-wait/

Dave, P. (2011). *Experiences of Indian gay and lesbian individuals*. Honours thesis, University of Cape Town, Cape Town, South Africa. Retrieved from http://www.psychology.uct.ac.za/sites/default/files/image_tool/images/117/Punam.Dave.pdf

Dayal, D. N. (2021). *Microaggressions against South African gay Indian men*. Master's thesis, University of Johannesburg, Johannesburg, South Africa. Retrieved from https://ujcontent.uj.ac.za/vital/%20access/manager/Repository/uj:43235?view=null&f0=sm_creator%3A%22Dayal%2C+Deepesh+Nirmaldas%22&sort=sort_ss_title%2F

Gevisser, M. (1994). A different fight for freedom: A history of South African lesbian and gay organisation from the 1950's to 1990's. In M. Gevisser & E. Cameron (Eds.), *Defiant desire* (pp. 14–88). Johannesburg: Raven Press.

Hassim, R. (2013). *An exploratory study into the perceptions of young Muslim South African adults regarding marriage.* Master's thesis, University of the Witwatersrand, Johannesburg, South Africa. Retrieved from http://wiredspace.wits.ac.za/

Jaspal, R. (2012). I never faced up to being gay: Sexual, religious and ethnic identities among British South Asian gay men. *Culture, Health and Sexuality, 14*(7), 767–780. doi:10.1080/13691058.2012.693626

Jaspal, R. (2014). Arranged marriage, identity, and well-being among British Asian gay men. *Journal of GLBT Family Studies, 10*(5), 425–448. doi:10.1080/1550428X.2013.846105

Jaspal, R., & Cinnirella, M. (2010). Coping with potentially incompatible identities: Accounts of religious, ethnic, and sexual identities from British Pakistani men who identify as Muslim and gay. *British Journal of Social Psychology, 49*(4), 849–870. doi:10.1348/014466609X485025

Kaur, P. (2017). Gender, sexuality and (be) longing: The Representation of queer (LGBT) in Hindi cinema. *Amity Journal of Media and Communication Studies, 7*(1), 22–30. Retrieved from https://ajmcs.blogspot.com/

Khan, S. (2012). Changing family forms, patterns and emerging challenges within the South African Indian diaspora. *Journal of Comparative Family Studies, 43*(1), 133–150. Retrieved from http://www.jstor.org/stable/41585384

Livingston, J. & Fourie, E. (2016). The experiences and meanings that shape heterosexual fathers' relationships with their gay sons in South Africa. *Journal of Homosexuality, 63*(12), 1630–1659. doi:10.1080/00918369.2016.1158009

Ludvig, A. (2006). Differences between women? Intersecting voices in a female narrative. *European Journal of Women's Studies, 13*(3), 245–258. doi:10.1177/1350506806065755

Martin, J., & Govender, K. (2013). "Indenturing the body": Traditional masculine role norms, body image discrepancy, and muscularity in a sample of South African Indian boys. *Culture, Society and Masculinities, 5*(1), 21–45. doi:10.3149/CSM.0501.21

Mavhandu-Mudzusi, A., & Ganga-Limando, M. (2014). Being lesbian, gay, bisexual, transgender and Intersex (LGBTI) students at a South African rural university: Implications for HIV prevention. *Africa Journal of Nursing and Midwifery, 16*(2), 125–138. doi:10.25159/2520-5293/38

Medora, N. (2007). Strengths and challenges in the Indian family. *Marriage & Family Review, 41*(1), 165–193. doi:10.1300/J002v41n01_09

Mimiaga, M., Biello, K., Sivasubramanian, M., Mayer, K., Anand, V., & Safren, S. (2013). Psychosocial risk factors for HIV sexual risk among Indian men who have sex with men. *AIDS Care, 25*(9), 1109–1113. doi:10.1080/09540121.2012.749340

Minwalla, O., Rosser, B., Feldman, J., & Varga, C. (2005). Identity experience among progressive gay Muslims in North America: A qualitative study within Al-Fatiha. *Culture, Health and Sexuality, 7*(2), 113–128. doi:10.1080/13691050412331321294

Moonsammy, D. (2009). *What will people say? Three stories of Indian women loving women in Jozi.* Master's thesis, University of the Witwatersrand, Johannesburg, South Africa. Retrieved from http://wiredspace.wits.ac.za/handle/10539/45/browse?value=Moonsammy%2C+Davina&type=author

Msibi, T. (2011). The lies we have been told: On (homo) sexuality in Africa. *Africa Today, 58*(1), 54–77. doi:10.1353/at.2011.0030

Mukwevho, M. H., & Fhumulani, T. (2018). Perceptions, knowledge and observation of rights by campus students on the LGBTQ community in a rural-based university in South Africa. *Gender and Behaviour, 16*(2), 11377–11392. doi:10.4314/gab.v16i2

Nair, V. (2020). *Negotiating the coming out process within the South African Indian community*. Master's thesis, University of the Witwatersrand, Johannesburg, South Africa). Retrieved from https://wiredspace.wits.ac.za/handle/10539/30590

Patel, C. J., Govender, V., Paruk, Z., & Ramgoon, S. (2006). Working mothers: Family-work conflict, job performance and family/work variables. *SA Journal of Industrial Psychology, 32*(2), 39–45. doi:10.4102/sajip.v32i2.238

Pillay, K. (2015). South African families of Indian descent: Transmission of racial identity. *Journal of Comparative Family Studies, 46*(1), 121–135. Retrieved from https://www.jstor.org/journal/jcompfamistud

Pillay, S. (2017, September 13). Exhibition brings to light LGBT Indians in SA. *Post*. Retrieved from https://www.pressreader.com/south-africa/post-southafrica/20170913/28205050 7228253

Ratele, K., & Suffla, S. (2010). Men, masculinity and cultures of violence and peace in South Africa. In C. Blazina & D. S. Shen-Miller (Eds.), *An international psychology of men: Theoretical advances, case studies, and clinical innovations* (pp. 27–55). New York, NY: Routledge.

Sheldon, R. (2016, October 31). Inside Cape Town's gay mosque. *Independent Online*. Retrieved from https://www.iol.co.za/news/south-africa/western-cape/inside-cape-towns-gay-mosque-2085211

Shields, S. A. (2008). Gender: An intersectionality perspective. *Sex Roles, 59*(5–6), 301–311. doi:10.1007/s11199-008-9501-8

Stirratt, M. J., Meyer, I. H., Ouellette, S. C., & Gara, M. A. (2008). Measuring identity multiplicity and intersectionality: Hierarchical classes analysis (HICLAS) of sexual, racial, and gender identities. *Self and Identity, 7*(1), 89–111. doi:10.1080/15298860701252203

Træen, B., Martinussen, M., Vittersø, & Saini, S. (2009). Sexual orientation and quality of life among university students from Cuba, Norway, India, and South Africa. *Journal of Homosexuality, 56*(5), 655–669. doi:10.1080/00918360903005311

Triandas, H. C. (1995). *New directions in social psychology, individualism & collectivism*. Boulder, CO: Westview Press.

Van Zyl, J., Nel, K., & Govender, S. (2018). Gender identity issues in pastoral reparative therapy in the Nederduitse Gereformeerde Kerk (NGK), South Africa. *Gender and Behaviour, 16*(1), 10668–10676. Retrieved from https://www.ajol.info/index.php/gab

Verloo, M. (2013). Intersectional and cross-movement politics and policies: Reflections on current practices and debates. *Signs, 38*(4), 893–915. doi:10.1086/669572

Zerai, A. (2000). Agents of knowledge and action: Selected Africana scholars and their contributions to the understanding of race, class and gender intersectionality. *Cultural Dynamics, 12*(2), 182–222. doi:10.1177/092137400001200205

# Postscript

*M. Susanne Schotanus*

Like the introduction, this conclusion will come in a different shape than you're used to. Though in every conclusion there is the urge to tie everything together with a neat little bow, I am reminded here of the recent awareness in trauma and conflict studies that sometimes what is needed is to 'stay with the conflict' (see, e.g. Mayer, 2009). As the authors have shown time and again, all types of gender-based violence are embedded in a complex web of influences. Consequently, it won't be possible for one book to resolve all the factors that lead people to commit violence against others because of their gender identities and expectations. To realise the utopia that so many think we've already achieved – a world where violence is on the decline, where everyone has the freedom to develop their own identities and where people live in collective harmony – will require us to untangle these webs, make the taboo a topic of conversation and stay sensitive and respectful to cultural, subcultural and individual differences. Let's face it: that's quite a challenge.

Still, it's easy to become complacent. It is fantastic that we get to celebrate 'gay pride' and 'women's day'. It's amazing that we're at a point where the equal rights of women and people with LGBTQ+ identities are secured in so many countries' constitutions. These are no small victories. But what the three authors in this volume have shown is that even though laws can be changed in relatively short time spans, they do not automatically result in or even reflect cultural shifts. Constitutional protection is no guarantee of an absence of violence. Just because there might be laws against hate crimes and sexual assault does not mean that the legal system is designed to protect victim-survivors of these crimes. Even if sex work is seen by many as a necessary element for a healthy and harmonious society, as it is in Japan, people who engage in this work can still experience institutional discrimination and economic and symbolic violence. And though patriarchal societies have been shown to assign men certain privileges that are denied women, the associated gender norms can be as violent and damaging to men's mental well-being as they are to those of people of other genders.

Instances of gender-based violence take place every day. And though the concrete milestones that we get to celebrate might be important steps forwards, they are only steps on the very long road to the utopia I described previously. We need to keep reaching for these milestones. But simultaneously it is necessary to look at these issues in the larger web they're embedded in. It's necessary to start untangling the plethora of factors that have contributed to environments in which the types of gendered violence can multiply, mutate and find new hosts and targets.

It is with this aim in mind that the chapters in this book have explored those types of gender-based violence that are often excluded from the conversation. This book, therefore, combines often-silenced narratives into a nuanced snapshot of violence itself. Though the use of the term 'snapshot' might seem odd here, especially considering the historical narratives presented in some of the chapters, it's rather deliberate. As I said: types of violence can mutate, they change. In the words of Judith Butler: violence 'renews itself in directions that exceed both deliberate intention and instrumental schemes' (Butler, 2020, p. 23). And as violence changes, so do our understandings of the concept of violence itself. In this book, violence has been shown to be dynamic and adaptable. It has the uncanny ability to identify cracks in the systems we've thrown up to keep it out and worm its way through – weakening the systems themselves. Whenever a new communication medium pops up, ways are found to enact violence through it. Violence is changeable, and if we actually want a violence-free society, we need to change our understanding of it as soon as it changes its face. This requires vigilance, study and publications such as these: books that identify the different ways in which violence takes place in our societies and the factors that contribute to its prevalence and specific natures. We need to look for violence beyond the obvious places. To properly understand it, we need to study it in its diversity – by studying it within the different (national) contexts it exists in and in all the different shapes it can take.

Though the authors have made a fantastic start with this project, by bringing cases from India, Japan and South Africa to the attention of the international research community; by bridging disciplinary boundaries and by expanding the definition of gender based violence as its often researched – there is only so much that can be done in any one book. In the introduction I briefly touched on the limited definition of gender that has been employed in this book. In future studies I hope this gap can be redressed, by doing for *gendered* violence what this book has aimed to do for gendered *violence*. The geographical scope of this book comes with similar caveats: in our desire to produce a comparative, cohesive work on the different forms gendered violence can assume in different parts of the world – in addition to the obvious focus on only three of the world's countries – most cases analysed have also focused on experiences from only the largest urban centres of each country. In future studies the scope can be broadened by not only actively seeking contributions on countries that are largely absent from the international interdisciplinary debates but also by paying attention to similarities and differences between urban, suburban, rural and other geographical contexts. By expanding the conversation of gendered violence, through new interdisciplinary work, it is my hope that we might come to a better under-standing of the project ahead, to address the issues on all relevant levels and in all relevant arenas and, consequently, to make the world a safe place where people of all genders can express themselves authentically without fear of violent retribution.

## References

Butler, J. (2020). *The force of non-violence: An ethico-political bind.* London: Verso.
Mayer, B. S. (2009). *Staying with conflict: A strategic approach to ongoing disputes.* Hoboken, NJ: Wiley.

# Index